# How to Start a Home-Based
## Pet Care
### Business

## Help Us Keep This Guide Up to Date

Every effort has been made by the author and editors to make this guide as accurate and useful as possible. However, many things can change after a guide is published—establishments close, phone numbers change, facilities come under new management, etc.

We would love to hear from you concerning your experiences with this guide and how you feel it could be improved and kept up to date. While we may not be able to respond to all comments and suggestions, we'll take them to heart and we'll also make certain to share them with the author. Please send your comments and suggestions to the following address:

The Globe Pequot Press
Reader Response/Editorial Department
P.O. Box 480
Guilford, CT  06437

Or you may e-mail us at:
      editorial@globe-pequot.com

Thanks for your input, and good luck!

HOME-BASED BUSINESS SERIES

# How to Start a Home-Based
# **Pet Care**
# Business

by Kathy Salzberg

The
Globe
Pequot
Press

Guilford, Connecticut

Text design: Mary Ballachino

**Library of Congress Cataloging-in-Publication Data**
Salzberg, Kathy.
    How to start a home-based pet care business. / by Kathy Salzberg.
        p. cm. —(Home-based business series)
    Includes  bibliographical references (p. ).
    ISBN 0-7627-1022-5
        1. Pet industry—Management. 2. New business enterprises—Management.
3. Home-based businesses—Management. I. Title. II. Series.

SF414.7 .S26 2002
636.088'7'0681—dc21                                              2001033958

Manufactured in the United States of America
First Edition/First Printing

*To David, my beloved husband, teacher,
mentor, and business partner, whose loving spirit
continues to guide me in all things.*

# Contents

# Acknowledgments

I'd like to thank the following individuals for providing guidance, inspiration, and information, gratefully acknowledging the ripple effect of their presence in my life: My daughter and business partner, Missi Salzberg, whose talent in business, communication, and loving support have been invaluable to me in preparing this book.

My sons David Jr. and Peter, my daughters-in-law Aline and Julie, and my granddaughters Allison and Cara for their constant love and encouragement.

My dear friend Dennis Smith, for his assistance with computer matters and his unwavering belief in my ability to complete this project.

My wonderful staff at The Village Groomer, for adding to my knowledge and inspiration on a daily basis.

All my friends in the pet care industry who so generously offered their expertise: groomers Susan Viveiros, Diane Betelak, Carrie Prest, Elaine Belrose, Toni Coppola; pet sitters extraordinaire Catherine Flynn and Ken Clark; obedience trainers Nancy Bradley, Caryl Crouse, Donna Laconti, and Steve Appelbaum; *Off Lead* Editor Therese Backowski, Intergroom Show Organizer Christine DeFilippo; mobile grooming pioneer Dina Perry, and all the other colleagues who allowed me to pick their brains during the research process.

Shirlee Kalstone and Dorothy Walin, the godmothers of the grooming industry who have paved the way for us all.

Laura Strom, Mary Luders, and Shelley Wolf of The Globe Pequot Press, my editorial midwives who guided this "baby" through the delivery process.

Three generations of four-legged customers and their devoted owners who have blessed my life.

# Introduction

When I joined my husband, David, at The Village Groomer twenty-five years ago, I had no intention of making pet grooming a lifelong career. My plan was to learn a new skill and help him out at the business he had founded in 1970. I really didn't have a commitment to being a self-employed business owner, but life stepped in and did the planning for me.

Although David dearly loved our grooming business, he also loved working with people in the health care field. In order to combine both occupations, David decided to return to school to earn a nursing degree. He was an eclectic person with omnivorous curiosity who succeeded at several occupations over the course of his life. The fact that our marriage survived his teaching me how to groom was a miracle in itself.

I left my job as a newspaper correspondent to master the art of grooming, trading in my pen and notebook for a pair of scissors and a clipper. Interestingly enough, I found I could make more money by grooming pets than I did covering local government and politics. My new job soon became much more than an interesting sideline. I found I had a passion for grooming and experienced a genuine connection to the dogs and cats that came to our shop. Like falling in love, it came as a surprise. Thirty years later, that little shop David opened on Main Street has grown and blossomed into a much larger facility.

As the business grew, my husband was drawn back into it, taking pride in its growth and relishing the friendships he forged with our clients and fellow pet care professionals. Our grooming and pet supply business had a hold on his heart; he could never leave it behind.

When David became seriously ill in 1994, our daughter Missi came into the business to help out for a while. Lo and behold, the same thing happened to her. Her heart was captured and her mind intrigued by this profession. She left the world of corporate sales and never looked back, taking over the day-to-day management of The Village Groomer as if she had been born for the job. She modernized our salon and ushered our business into the twenty-first century.

Just like me, many of my fellow colleagues in pet care just happened into this line of work as well. You may have picked up this book because you are bored or unhappy in your present job and looking for an alternative way to make a living.

You may be waiting for the answer to present itself, for something new to catch your fancy.

Although some folks still don't consider pet care a "real" job, doing it successfully can be challenging. The best groomers are always developing their skills and talents. The best trainers embark upon a lifelong quest of learning about animal behavior. The best pet sitters gain a knack for business and often expand to offer many other services as they grow. You don't need an Ivy League degree, you don't have to look like a supermodel, and you don't need the talent of a Michelangelo to succeed here. With love and dedication, you can build a career and a life.

If you wish to pursue a career in this field, it will be up to you to discover your own path to success. No matter which pet care career you choose, I sincerely hope this book will serve as a guide for you, explaining the current market for your services, outlining the talents and skills required for each career, and describing the methods of training. I have tried to instruct you on various aspects of setting up your business, including the legal and financial information you need to make it a reality.

You will need plenty of drive and determination to thrive in pet care. You will also need a special love and appreciation for our companions in this trip through life, our pets. Even though it really is fun to work with animals, a career in pet care is a serious business. You may be your own boss working from your home, but you will need discipline to succeed. Study the checklists carefully and follow the steps to make sure you have sufficient resources before you launch your home-based business. Seek the best legal and financial advice you can afford.

Reading this book is a first step toward starting your pet care career. I congratulate you and sincerely hope you will find success beyond your wildest dreams, discovering an unusual and rewarding way of life in the process.

If one advances confidently in the direction of his dreams, and endeavors to live the life which he had imagined, he will meet with a success unexpected in common hours.

—HENRY DAVID THOREAU

# Chapter One
# Why Pet Care?

Are you an animal person? Does a backyard romp with your golden retriever refresh your soul? Is the sound of a cat purring your favorite lullaby? Do you find yourself telling your troubles to your poodle? Do you snuggle up to your pet in bed each night? There's no need for you to feel embarrassed. You can come out of the closet now. You have plenty of company.

We are rapidly becoming a nation of pet-crazy people. U.S. consumers are spending more on their pets today than ever before. In 1994, we spent $17 billion on our furry, finned, and feathered friends. In 2001, that figure grew to $28.5 billion. Most of us only wish we could track the same kind of growth in our investment portfolios!

We tend to put our money where our hearts are. According to the latest survey by the American Animal Hospital Association, 75 percent of pet owners would willingly go into debt for their pet's well-being; 93 percent lavish their pets with gifts—for birthdays, holidays, and for no occasion at all. Some 66 percent happily prepare special foods for their animals, and 44 percent pick up souvenirs for Fido and Fluffy when they go on vacation. Chalk it up to love, guilt, or insanity, but 37 percent take it even further: They phone home to talk to their cherished critters when they are away.

The results of a 1999 study conducted by the Pfizer Animal Health and the Gallup Organization revealed that the majority of Americans consider their dogs to be better companions than some family members. Current research on stress reduction seems to underline their point. Just a few minutes spent stroking a pet significantly reduces our stress level and lowers our blood pressure. Owning a dog may be every bit as beneficial as visiting a therapist. In fact, dogs are becoming increasingly popular in therapy work, used in hospitals and nursing homes to lift the spirits and awaken the communication skills of the elderly and ill.

A recent study by the HomeCare Council revealed that up to 66 percent of pet owners think of their pets as surrogate children. An amazing 88 percent would gladly risk their lives to save their pets, while 22 percent told pollsters they felt closer to their pets than they do to their spouses.

These survey results make interesting reading, but they don't surprise me in the least. After almost three decades in the pet care field, I know firsthand how precious pets can be to their people. Believe me, pet owners dropping off their furry babies for a day of beauty at the groomer's can be every bit as anxiety-ridden as parents leaving their human offspring at the day care center. I learned long ago that many members of my clientele look upon their animals as child substitutes. I've even heard it remarked that a child is a good dog substitute! I know that statement sounds outrageous and may even ruffle some feathers, but that's the thing about pet ownership: It makes us lighthearted. It gives us permission to be silly. It charges up our capacity for play.

Since I entered the field in 1976, the pet care industry has come of age. When I left my job as a newspaper correspondent to groom dogs with my schoolteacher husband, I heard a lot of jokes about "going to the dogs" or "playing with the pooches" as opposed to having a *real* job. In twenty-plus years of working together, David and I raised and educated three children, one of whom is now my business partner. Until my husband's death in 1996, we enjoyed running a successful small business, gaining the friendship of countless four-legged friends and their human owners. We were rather unlikely entrepreneurs, "flower children" of the sixties who came full circle, becoming respected burghers in the small-town business community and savoring many unexpected rewards in the process.

Since we opened that first little mom-and-pop shop three decades ago, the grooming industry has been transformed. We now use state-of-the art equipment, most of which was nonexistent when I was apprenticing to learn my grooming skills. Electric tables, force dryers that sweep moisture from the coat, labor- and water-saving bathing systems, improved clippers, superb scissors, computers, automatic vacuum systems for clippers, attractive hair-proof uniforms, plus a plethora of products to make pets look and feel beautiful—all these have transformed what was once considered a hobby into an increasingly respected profession.

This ever growing passion for pet ownership has not gone unnoticed by corporate America. Although the pet care industry is still dominated by small businesses, many groomers now face increased competition from the pet superstore chains, which now offer obedience classes and grooming services in addition to food and supplies. Popping up all over the country to compete with pet sitters and kennel operators are aggressively marketed corporate boarding facilities that are as streamlined and luxurious as posh hotels for humans. Despite this trend, independent pet care providers continue to thrive. There's room for us all in this animal-worshipping lovefest.

Compare it to making your travel plans; you could book reservations at a Holiday Inn or choose instead to bunk at a quaint bed-and-breakfast. It's a simple matter of preference. Pet ownership occupies a special place in the innermost sanctuary of our hearts. Pet owners treasure a supremely personal connection when it comes to the people to whom they entrust their precious animals. Pets are, after all, family members, and the importance of that familiar caring bond in delivering quality pet care can never be overstated.

# Pet Services in Demand Today

The pet parade marches on. During the past decade, the number of pet-owning households in the United States has continued to surge. According to the American Pet Products Manufacturers Association (APPMA), that figure now stands at 61 percent, up from 56 percent in 1988.

Economists tell us this trend will continue no matter how the economy dips and surges. Pet ownership appears to be recession-proof. Even when we refrain from travel, gourmet dining or buying a new car, our joy in owning pets hits us where we live. Their reassuring presence adds to our enjoyment of the comforts of home. As the number of pets increases, so does the need for pet care services.

## Pet Grooming

With a dog and cat population of 127 million, the grooming industry is undoubtedly on the move. At last count, there were 25,000 pet groomers in the United States, averaging out at approximately 5,100 pets per grooming establishment. Those are interesting statistics, but in reality, only half of all this country's dogs and cats regularly visit a groomer. As the public becomes increasingly aware of the benefits of grooming to dog and owner alike, the business will continue to mushroom. The truth about cats and dogs is this: They need groomers.

All dogs and cats benefit from professional grooming. Yesteryear's amusing stereotype of the froufrou "poodle parlor" is fading as owners realize that a clean, well-groomed pet is much more enjoyable to live with and love than the smelly, matted "backyard dogs" we might have known when we were growing up. Even shorthaired dogs shed and need periodic brushing, bathing, nail trimming, and ear cleaning. Longhaired and double-coated breeds need frequent brushing to reduce shedding and keep their coats from turning into tangled tumbleweeds. Longhaired cats require frequent grooming to keep them looking gorgeous, and their short-haired counterparts benefit from an occasional bath and brushout as well.

Like human haberdashery, canine coats come in all types and sizes. Their different grooming needs determine the amount of money owners will have to spend to care for them properly. Every breed of dog should visit a professional groomer at least four times a year. Most dogs shed heavily in the spring and fall, but many drop coat year-round. This is largely due to the fact that today's dogs are true members of the family. They live with us indoors, sharing our heated homes under artificial lighting, their coats no longer taking seasonal cues from Mother Nature.

The professional groomer learns to execute the proper trim on all breeds and to groom mixed breeds to look like the type of dog they most resemble. A monthly trip to the groomer is highly recommended for those breeds requiring the most up-keep: the Lhasa apso, shih tzu, standard poodle, Maltese, Afghan hound, soft-coated wheaten terrier, bichon frise, Old English sheepdog, bearded collie, and American cocker spaniel. These are the high-maintenance beauties of the dog world.

Requiring grooming every six weeks or so are the mini and toy poodle, miniature schnauzer, Pekingese, West Highland white and Yorkshire terriers, springer spaniel, and Portuguese water dog. An eight-week grooming schedule is advisable for the golden retriever, Irish and English setters, and such terriers as the wire-haired fox, Scottish, cairn and Airedale.

Dogs that require no haircut but need to see the groomer every eight to twelve weeks for coat upkeep include the German shepherd, collie, Samoyed, husky, malamute, keeshond, Akita, Shetland sheepdog, and Newfoundland. Smooth-coated dogs like the basset hound, bulldog, pug, beagle, Labrador retriever, dalmatian, and rottweiler are kept clean and odor-free by visits to the groomer at least four times a year. The amount of grooming an individual dog will need also depends on the amount of upkeep the owner is willing to provide between grooming appointments.

The remarkable array of dog breeds in all its beautiful variety and the vast amount of knowledge to be learned about their care are part of the lure that draws people to a career in grooming.

## Pet Sitting/Dog Walking

When I was growing up back in the fifties, there was no such thing as a professional pet sitter. Sure, people had lots of pets, but their role as surrogate children was mainly an idiosyncrasy of the very wealthy classes whose retinue of servants probably fulfilled the caretaking function.

When the rest of us went on vacation, we put the dogs in a kennel, or maybe a kindly neighbor or relative took care of Fido and Fluffy and fed the fish. To be sure, such informal arrangements still exist today, but many of us recognize the importance of pets as family members and are willing to pay to have them pampered right at home. They need and deserve their own baby-sitters—or rather, pet sitters.

Back then, the family vacation was an annual two-week event. In those simpler times, not many people logged hundreds of thousands of frequent flyer miles in the ordinary course of doing business. Women tended to follow the Donna Reed model: They got married right out of school, then they had babies. Stay-at-home moms were the norm.

In the decades since then, society has undergone a sea of change. Life has become much more fast-paced and everyone, including Mom, is working outside the home. Young couples often postpone having children while they establish their careers. They may be upwardly mobile and always on the go, but deep inside they still feel the need to nurture. Pets have become their babies, and doting owners love to pamper them, spending billions on veterinary care, supplies, toys, treats, grooming, and training.

At the other end of the spectrum, empty-nesters find great joy in lavishing their pets with unconditional love. Pets and senior citizens have a mutually therapeutic effect on each other. In addition to the measurable physiological changes that come from interacting with a pet—lower blood pressure and stress levels, faster recovery from surgery and illness—caring for a pet gives purpose to our lives and staves off loneliness. Beyond providing good company, a pet's presence gives an owner a sense of security. No matter how big or small, a dog's bark to warn of an intruder can be a strong deterrent to crime. With more and more single people of all ages in our society and an increasing number of senior citizens, the role of the pet as a treasured companion is assured. The need for the pet sitter goes hand in hand with this trend.

Our burgeoning pet population is not limited to felines and canines. Pet sitters also count birds, fish, and reptiles in their clienteles. According to the 1999–2000 APPMA pet ownership survey, there are now 100 million fresh- and saltwater fish swimming around inside 11 million homes, while 15 million birds brighten the days of their owners in 6 million households. Four million homes shelter another 12 million small animals—bunnies, hamsters, gerbils, guinea pigs, mice, domestic rats, chinchillas, and pot-bellied pigs—while 7 million reptiles—turtles, tortoises, iguanas, snakes, lizards, frogs, and toads—are a source of fun and fascination in 3 million homes. When their owners are away, all these cherished creatures need to be fed and cared for.

Dog walking is also increasingly in demand as hard-working owners are realizing that most dogs were not bred to be couch potatoes. Tossing Rover a tennis ball on the weekend simply does not provide enough exercise and stimulation. Keeping a working or hunting breed cooped up all day is often a recipe for disaster. A bored dog will find things to do, most of them destructive. They don't do this out of spite. Just like human children, dogs suffer from separation anxiety. Digging, chewing, and even self-mutilation are some of the ways they relieve such stress.

Some dogs lapse into depression and lose their spirit from extended isolation. Dogs like these are getting a whole new lease on life from their much anticipated midday outing with the dog walker or through regular visits to a doggie day care center. Most pet sitters also provide midday walks as well as frequent daytime visits to help crate-train puppies. It's impossible to housebreak a pup when you are away at work all day long.

Other offshoots of a pet sitting operation include meal service and pet food delivery, administering medications, plant care, yard cleanup, pet taxi service to and from the groomer or vet, and puppy play group. Just like humans, dogs form friendships with each other. They love to romp and play with their pals. Of course, they should be tested for temperament before they join such a play group; not all dogs are compatible. Those showing signs of aggression, fear, or shyness would benefit most from a one-on-one midday outing.

When I was young, my mother cleaned the house and cooked the meals while my father mowed the lawn and washed the car. Hiring a cleaning service, having meals cooked elsewhere and delivered, paying a lawn care professional, or having the car detailed were alien concepts to them. Today, many of us depend on service professionals to handle such tasks, freeing us up to take care of business or simply enhancing our quality of life.

The old concept of the neighborhood has fallen by the wayside as well. In today's hectic world, we relocate more often. Most of us barely know our neighbors. The idea of asking them to take care of our pets would seem like an imposition. We are also more security-minded. Now more than ever, the news of the day on TV or in the newspaper could more accurately be called the bad news of the day. Crime and violence are usually the leadoff stories. No matter where we live, we are not immune. Our homes and automobiles are equipped with alarm systems, and it's hard to imagine a time when we didn't look over our shoulders and lock our doors.

The idea of a trustworthy, bonded pet sitter coming and going in and out of our home while we are away is reassuring. Pet sitters make the house look lived in, taking in the mail, opening and closing the blinds, switching lights on and off as they go about their business. Their presence increases our sense of security, another reason why the demand for this service is on the rise.

Pet sitters also enhance the lives of our pets as they deliver personal attention, food, exercise, play, and loving care in familiar surroundings. Owners need not transport them to boarding facilities or worry about leaving them in a strange place. I do not intend to denigrate kennels here. They play a huge role in the pet care industry. Many are clean and modern boarding facilities owned by people dedicated to providing excellent care, but although some pets eagerly anticipate their "vacation" away from home, not all pets adjust well to their stay at the kennel. If pets could talk, many would echo Dorothy's sentiments in *The Wizard of Oz:* There's no place like home.

A 1995 survey by Pet Sitters International showed that pet sitters served less than 1 percent of the pet-owning public. As far as potential goes, pet sitting is still just a baby. Its future is being created as this career comes of age.

## Obedience Training

Dogs are always learning, even when you're not trying to teach them. That old adage "You can't teach an old dog new tricks" is simply not true. Canines continue to learn throughout their lives. It's part of the reason they have survived and thrived since they came in from the cold to join us at the campfire 13,000 years ago.

When I was growing up, dogs roamed the neighborhood and more or less did what they pleased. One of our dogs was a canine bigamist. He had two homes and two families who fed him and enjoyed his company, the best of both worlds. Those were the days before leash laws, before litigation at the drop of a hat, when no one ever heard of a pooper-scooper law.

Dogs have not changed in the intervening years, but times have. It is no longer safe or acceptable for dogs to roam at large. Unsupervised dogs can be destructive. They defecate on public and private property, fight with other dogs, frighten and injure adults and children. From the dog's own standpoint, the situation is even worse. Loose dogs can be hit by cars, stolen, poisoned, or shot.

Every dog needs obedience training. It's not about learning to roll over and play dead or sit up and beg. It's all about happily coexisting with man in an age-old partnership. It is no longer acceptable to have a dog that interferes with anyone else's lifestyle. Besides, training your dog is fun! Most dogs cherish this special one-on-one activity. It gives them a challenge and a purpose, and they get to spend quality time with you. A dog with a job is a happy dog. For the dog owner, it increases the joy of dog ownership a hundredfold.

Training cements the bond between dog and master. Just like us, dogs communicate, but they speak in a language of barks, whimpers, grunts, and growls punctuated by an amazing array of behavioral displays. As a professional trainer, you will gain access to this whole new lexicon and learn to transmit your wishes as well. Training opens up the lines of communication between *Homo sapiens* and *Canis familiaris*—man and his longtime best friend. As a professional trainer, you will serve as an intermediary between these two worlds.

From the owner's standpoint, the key to a mutually rewarding relationship with a dog begins with teaching the pet good manners both at home and in public. The ultimate goal is a dog you can take anywhere. In a basic obedience course, the pet learns to come when called, sit, heel on and off leash, stay, and drop to a down position on command. In some situations, mastering these commands could save the pet's life. The dog should also learn to wait when a door is opened, to walk on a leash without pulling its owner's arm out of the socket, and to refrain from jumping up on people or chewing on the furniture. Rowdy behavior may be amusing in a puppy, but dogs grow very fast and there is nothing cute about being bowled over by a 100-pound adult animal or getting dragged into traffic when your furry friend heeds the call of the wild.

Beyond basic obedience lies a whole university of postgraduate courses, including competition obedience, agility, tracking, herding, search and rescue, protection training, hunting, field trials, sledding, racing, lure coursing, carting, weight pulling, water sports, therapy, and service dog training. As a professional dog trainer, you could spend your whole life studying and never run out of new areas to explore.

Many owners feel that they can train their pets themselves. If they are willing to put in the time and effort on a consistent basis, they probably can. In the course of sharing the same living space, everyone who has owned a dog has participated in its training in some way, and today we have a whole library full of training books and videos with which to supplement our knowledge. However, there is a lot to be said for the structure that goes along with regular participation in a course with a skilled instructor. Not all owners have the innate ability or self-discipline to do it on their own.

"Fifty percent of the population has a natural ability for this work. The other 50 percent are clueless," observes Caryl Crouse, a veteran trainer from Franklin, Massachusetts, known locally as Miss Canine Manners. "They don't understand about tone of voice, body language, or other signals we give. It's a different form of communication."

"A big part of our job is teaching the owners that dogs are not people," says trainer Nancy Bradley of Norton, Massachusetts. "A lot of people anthropomorphize dogs, but they don't think like people, they don't act like people, and you can't teach them like people."

Dogs are intelligent, thinking beings, but they are driven by instinct. They are also pack animals that feel most secure in a well-ordained hierarchy. The facility to master "dogspeak" is a prerequisite for a professional trainer. It goes hand-in-hand with the love and respect for dogs that drives a person to excel in this line of work.

The first thing you need as a professional trainer is a well-trained dog of your own. "If you can't train your own dog, don't try to train someone else's," Crouse advises. She also feels it's imperative for a trainer to be involved in some form of canine competition. In her view, such participation sharpens the trainer's skills. "If you can't problem-solve in the competitive behavioral area, you can't expect to do it for the public." All of the instructors on Crouse's growing staff are successful and active with their own dogs in some form of competition.

Myriad personality types exist within the canine family. The trainer must learn to deal with dogs that are submissive, fearful, dominant, or aggressive. "Every dog responds differently," Crouse observes. "A trainer needs to learn from multiple sources. If you learn only one method, you are locking yourself out of other methods that might be more effective in a particular situation with a particular dog. Every dog is different. Even within a litter, each one has an individual personality."

Bradley shares her house with three large male dogs, two German shepherds and a Labrador retriever. All three came with a litany of health and behavioral issues, but her home is a peaceable kingdom. "I tell them when to do everything, when to pee, eat, and sleep," she says with a smile. "I teach the client how to lead the dog. Once the dog realizes you are the leader, it won't try to lead you."

A well-trained dog does not interfere with anyone else's lifestyle. It becomes an asset, not a liability. As our population—both human and canine—grows and our open spaces shrink, the need will grow for professional trainers who can impart their skills so that our pets fit into our lives and our communities as true family members.

In the United States today, the service sector looms larger than ever. It has accounted for 22 million of the 25 million new jobs created in the past thirty years. Careers in pet care are connected to this trend, and the best part of all is that you can begin your own career right where you live, working from your home.

## Is This the Field for You?

You may have picked up this book because you are toying with the idea of making a career switch into the pet care field yourself. You may be fed up with your job in the corporate world, arising each morning to dress for success as your enthusiasm for running in place on the fast-track treadmill continues to wane. You may be a stay-at-home parent toying with the notion of combining your workplace with the comfort and convenience of being at home, or maybe you're a harried commuter who spends far too many hours of your precious time on the freeway. I know bankers, lawyers, secretaries, teachers, real estate brokers, military retirees, and downsized dot-commers who now make their living caring for pets. So your dream may not be so farfetched after all; in a 1999 Petgroomer.com survey of people seeking a career in this field, 67 percent of those who responded had never worked with pets before.

Then there is the lure of being your own boss. Recent surveys reveal that one in three Americans would prefer to earn their pay right where they live. In 1997, 7.7 million workers were home-based, according to the Bureau of Labor Statistics. With today's mind-boggling advances in technology, this figure will increase every year. Sure, you'll work longer hours and probably take a hefty pay cut for the privilege of building your own business, but there is no denying the heady feeling of pride and self-esteem that comes from declaring your financial independence.

You have the desire to become an independent businessperson and the dream of working from your own home. But how do you know if pet care is the right choice for you?

# The First Ingredient Is Love

Unlike the Beatles hit of long ago, love is not all you need. To succeed in this field, however, it is undoubtedly the first ingredient. Pet care professionals must project their love for animals. If you are cranky or indifferent to an animal in front of its owner, believe me, you have just lost a customer. Pets themselves know who their friends are. They tune in to your emotions of love and kindness with an almost mystical ability. When it comes to your feelings for the animals in your care, you just can't fake it.

On a day when every dog you groom is either trying to leap off your table, take a bite out of the brush and/or your hand, or bark so long and loud that your head is throbbing, you will need a truckload of patience and a mountain of maturity. When that sparkling white bichon frise you just scissored to perfection has an "accident" in its crate and must go back in the tub for another bath while its owner taps her foot waiting for you to finish, you'd better have a strong stomach and nerves of steel.

When your first session of basic obedience class could pass for a canine wrestling match or when you drive fifteen minutes over icy roads to care for a puppy and find its owners home ahead of schedule, happily watching TV in their jammies, your people skills will be sorely tested.

When the little pup is spinning like a top as you try to brush it and trim its nails, or the canine senior citizen needs to be groomed lying down instead of standing because her hindquarters are weakening, you will need unlimited patience and understanding. But if you are a dyed-in-the-wool animal person, such situations will probably not dissuade you. You know who you are.

Still not sure you've got the animal person gene? The following scenarios might help. Which of these ring true?

- When visitors to your home object to a little pet hair, you suggest they meet you elsewhere—or bring their own lint brush.
- When your puppy needed leg surgery, you gave up that beach house vacation rental in a heartbeat to pay the vet bill.
- When your neighbor's dog was hit by a car, no one but you could function to drive it to the vet.
- The stray cat population has designated your house a favorite stop on its mysterious underground trade route.

- Your backyard has recently become the unofficial headquarters for the neighborhood puppy play group.

Any one of these examples might be the sign you've been searching for. Your future may lie in working with animals.

This is not to infer that true "animal people" are confined to the pet care industry, but the best pet care providers I know do happen to fall into this category. They share a reverence and respect for all living creatures. They seem to possess an uncanny ability to communicate with pets via a look, a touch, or a word. Call it telepathy or ESP, but sometimes it seems a mutual trans-species mind reading occurs. Being open to this human-animal energy flow is a gift, but I believe it can also be learned. Our Native American predecessors had this ability and used it well. You may suspect that I'm becoming a bit too earthy-crunchy here, but working with animals is unlike working with computers, flow charts or other inanimate objects. You will need to indulge me here. Attempting to explain it is like trying to use words to describe a piece of music.

As part of your research into entering this field, may I suggest some field trips? Ask if you can spend a day at a grooming salon. While observing this occupation up close and personal, you can help out by sweeping the floor or volunteering to be the gofer at coffee time. Befriend a pet sitter (one who's far enough away so that you would not be considered potential competition) and ask if you can tag along on some home visits. To watch a professional trainer in action, take your dog to obedience school. You can take it a step further by offering your services at a local shelter. There are never enough compassionate souls to care for all the homeless animals that are still a heartbreaking reality in our affluent society. You may learn that you don't have the stomach to scoop the poop, that pet hair makes you sneeze, or that the sound of all that barking makes you want to bang your head against the wall. Chalk it up to research and move on.

If you're convinced you have the animal-loving gene, good for you! You're on the right road, but you've only just begun. There are some other qualities you will need. I've seen many people who could scissor and clip a poodle so exquisitely that it looked ready to take its place in the show ring, and I've known some whose business savvy left me in the dust, but they lacked the temperament needed for this kind of work. Many of the most talented groomers I know are dyed-in-the-wool animal lovers; unfortunately, not all of them have acquired the business skills needed to to turn their talents into profitable careers. For such humanely oriented individuals, it's all too easy to work for insufficient financial compensation. After all, in their minds, they are performing a labor of love. Some would do it whether they got paid or not! Others have not learned that until their prices reflect that they themselves value their services, no one else will.

Although there is nothing wrong with gaining satisfaction and experiencing joy in working with pets, there is also nothing wrong with making a profit. You can feed your soul and enjoy your four-legged patrons, but you also deserve to make a living, take care of your family, and plan for a comfortable retirement. Mastering the management of your home grooming business is every bit as vital to success in this career as perfecting the art of styling the various breeds.

Many pet care providers fail as business owners because they do not have enough capital behind them to keep the business going until it turns a profit. Starting your own business in any field is a risky endeavor. As many as 75 percent of all new businesses fail within five years due to undercapitalization. To make it in your own pet care business, you will need to wear two hats: that of the knowledgeable animal lover and that of the astute businessperson.

My husband used to say that groomers are artists who work on the most difficult canvas of all, a living creature. With love and skill, they transform a sometimes dirty, smelly, matted dog into an attractively coiffed canine. I'm not saying you will need to be a Picasso or Michelangelo to succeed at this vocation, but you will need a measure of manual dexterity.

The next ingredient in this stew is the dedication to work hard and learn every day. For instance, there were 158 dog breeds represented at the Westminster Kennel Club Dog Show last February. A professional groomer should know the breed standard for each and every one. And despite the arrival of labor-saving tools to make the job easier, it still requires a strong and energetic person to do this type of work day in and day out.

Strength and energy are needed by dog trainers as well. Realistically speaking, your goal will be to turn dog owners into dog trainers. Your job will be that of a coach. It's serious work but you need a sense of play too. Shared fun between humans and canines enriches the bonds for both species!

For the pet sitter, dependability and energy are a must. Like the postman, neither rain nor snow nor dark of night may deter you from your appointed rounds. You'll be at your busiest when most people are enjoying their holidays. Burnout is an occupational hazard here. No matter how much you love those furry customers, your job will lose its appeal if you become exhausted.

# More Than Playing with the Puppies

Although pet grooming has come a long way, there are still many people who consider it a rather amusing way to make a living. They simply can't resist hurling those clever little barbs: "What? You want to be a doggie hairdresser?" "You want to primp poodles for a living?" Being taken seriously can be a challenge in pet care occupations. To the uninitiated, the pet sitter's job is seen as a cute little hobby, not a responsible and needed professional service. The obedience trainer has often been characterized as a rigid authoritarian, not a skilled animal behaviorist who helps integrate our canine companions into our lives. Some people take a more starry-eyed view: "I bet that job is lots of fun. I wish I could play with the puppies all day and get paid for it!"

Well, yes, working with animals is a great way to make a living and you can have fun with your four-legged customers, but pet care occupations can be extremely demanding.

Groomers are prone to back problems from lifting heavy dogs, and carpal tunnel syndrome from the repetitive motion of scissoring, brushing, and hand stripping. Learning to groom sitting down on a stool is a great idea. As is the case with human hairstylists, a groomer's legs can suffer from standing all day over a long period of time. Circulation problems, varicose veins, overstressed tendons and ligaments—these are also common ailments in the grooming profession. So here's another qualification to consider: You need to be in shape as much as you need to love and respect animals.

In addition, pet care workers tend to get caught up in their work, sometimes to the detriment of their personal lives. You will need to balance your life so that it does not sap all your attention and energy. When I got into this profession, I was such a workaholic that I missed out on some important moments with my children: prom pictures, Little League games, school Christmas pageants. I can't have those opportunities back, but you might be able to profit from my experience. If you start off strong and healthy and work smart, these occupational hazards can be avoided.

People come into this career for myriad reasons, not all of them well founded. I can't recall how many times I have heard this statement: "I want to work with animals because I can't stand working with people." Well, you've got yourself a problem here. Every single one of those four-legged patrons of yours is brought in by an owner, sometimes a whole carload full of them!

People skills are a necessity. You will need them to explain why these sometimes obsessive owners should trust you to groom little Fluffy. You will need them to educate your clients about caring for their pet's coat between visits so that it doesn't resemble a bramble bush each time it comes in. You will need them to tactfully inform these folks that little Benji is sorely in need of an obedience trainer, or that he needs to be neutered so he will stop trying to leave his personal marker on every square inch of the world, including those plush new pet beds in your retail section. You will need them to explain to the harried mom that her children cannot dismantle your cookie bins and play catch with the kitty toys while she agonizes over which credit card to use.

In other words, when it comes to people skills, it's a job like any other. When you are dealing with the public—or with employees as your business grows—you will run across an amazing cross section of humans with all their stellar attributes and maddening foibles. Pet care is a service industry and all service industries require the ability to interact favorably with people.

You will also need the burning desire to get the proper training. Mastering the necessary skills takes patience and perseverance. A third of professional groomers still learn to groom on the job, but there are now many grooming schools throughout the country that offer professional training. Starting out with an entry-level position like groomer's assistant or bather-brusher is a great way to familiarize yourself with the world of pet grooming before you commit your time and money to professional training.

The doors to a career in obedience training are opened to many men and women when they discover the joy of training their own pets. Yet obedience trainers must commit to lifelong learning. Many pet sitters begin as animal lovers who do a favor for a friend or neighbor, taking care of canines and kitties in their friend's absence. The light bulb goes on when these amateur pet sitters realize that for precious little in the way of startup costs, they could be making a living in this flexible career. However, even pet sitters need training in operating and promoting their businesses.

Last but not least, you will need a thick skin. To grow and learn in this profession, you must be open to constructive criticism, from your teachers, from fellow pet care professionals, and even from your clients. Sure, you are bound to hear some unfounded criticism along the way, but try not to take it personally. Discard those defense mechanisms and be open to learning something new, or at least looking at your work in a new light.

# Honestly Assessing Your Capabilities

Let's reexamine our list of the qualities needed to succeed in pet care: love for animals, good business skills, sufficient capital to get started and stay in business, physical health, the drive to work hard, people skills, the desire and commitment to master the proper skills, the dedication to keep learning and improving, a thick skin, an open mind and, of course, a sense of humor. Pet ownership is all about joy! You will also need lots of patience and understanding for pets and owners alike in pet-related occupations.

Those considering a career in grooming will also need a good eye to be able to visualize the result you are trying to create, as well as the motor skills to produce it with clippers and scissors. Developing such skills takes time and talent, but some artistic ability and creativity are also needed for this job.

As an obedience trainer, in place of artistic ability you will need self-confidence and leadership skills. Can you see yourself taking charge of a whole roomful of people and their dogs? As a professional instructor, you will be educating owners every bit as much as you are instructing their pets. The most effective trainers are assertive and decisive. They exude confidence without appearing to be know-it-alls.

A good trainer never stops learning. In fact, it becomes a lifelong mission. You will need the dedication to stay abreast of changes in your field by attending conferences and workshops as often as you can. Most trainers I know live and work with dogs in an almost primitive connection. Their calling is a ruling passion in their lives.

For a pet sitting career, you can learn the ropes through reading and researching on your own. The key ingredient needed here is dependability. To run this type of business well, you need excellent organizational skills; they become ever more important as your business grows. You also need the willingness to leave the comforts of home to care for your furry charges early in the morning and late at night, on weekends and holidays, regardless of the weather. This is no small commitment; in this job, your willingness to care for these dependent creatures must override all personal concerns.

Wow! That's quite a shopping list, isn't it? How did you stack up? If you think you have the right stuff, read on—and advance confidently in the direction of your dreams!

# What It Takes to Succeed Checklist

COMPLETED

1. **Prepare a business plan, including:**

   Your goals . . . . . . . . . . . . . . . . . . . . . . . . . . . . . . . . . . . . . . . . . ☐

   Marketing plan . . . . . . . . . . . . . . . . . . . . . . . . . . . . . . . . . . . . . . ☐

   Competition research . . . . . . . . . . . . . . . . . . . . . . . . . . . . . . . . . ☐

   Financial plan . . . . . . . . . . . . . . . . . . . . . . . . . . . . . . . . . . . . . . . ☐

   Office and grooming shop plans . . . . . . . . . . . . . . . . . . . . . . . . . ☐

   List of equipment needed . . . . . . . . . . . . . . . . . . . . . . . . . . . . . . ☐

   Shipping and delivery schedule for equipment . . . . . . . . . . . . . ☐

   Cash flow projections . . . . . . . . . . . . . . . . . . . . . . . . . . . . . . . . . ☐

   Growth plan . . . . . . . . . . . . . . . . . . . . . . . . . . . . . . . . . . . . . . . . ☐

2. **Announce your plans to open a business to family and friends.**
   (Stress confidentiality at this point in time.)

   Enlist their aid in helping you set up your business. . . . . . . . . . . . ☐

3. **Purchase a daily planner book or electronic device to track
   personal and professional tasks.** . . . . . . . . . . . . . . . . . . . . . . . . . ☐

4. **Strengthen your winning attitude.**

   Listen to motivational tapes. . . . . . . . . . . . . . . . . . . . . . . . . . . . . ☐

   Read everything you can about pet care. . . . . . . . . . . . . . . . . . . . ☐

   Join business groups. . . . . . . . . . . . . . . . . . . . . . . . . . . . . . . . . . ☐

5. **Create a better personal reputation.**

   Request and edit your credit profiles. . . . . . . . . . . . . . . . . . . . . . ☐

   Pay bills on time and make sure you keep your word. . . . . . . . . . ☐

   Treat everyone you meet with respect and courtesy—
   they are all potential customers! . . . . . . . . . . . . . . . . . . . . . . . . . ☐

# Chapter Two
# Before You Begin

Before you embark upon any journey, you need to chart your course. In the pet care field, there seem to be as many roads to success as there are professionals. Happily for those who aspire to this work, you can begin your training while working at another job, planning your strategy as you move toward your goal. One of the blessings of this field is that if you are serious about making a living by working with animals, doors will open as you proceed.

## Training Needed

There are many training options available to those who want to get started in each of the pet care professions. Here are just a few of the training opportunities that you can take advantage of.

### Grooming: Apprenticeship vs. Formal Training

When I began my career as a groomer, most of us learned through the apprenticeship method, but there are certain limitations involved in learning how to groom on the job. The first constraint is time. In today's salon environment, it is difficult for the busy groomer to instruct a trainee. Because of the safety issues involved and the responsibility of turning out quality grooming for the paying customer, close supervision is required. This tends to cut down on shop productivity. In the grooming world, time is definitely money!

Another drawback to the apprenticeship method is that you learn only your employer's methods of grooming. If your teacher is one of the great ones, you will be fortunate; if not, you may find that you wish to grow beyond his or her level of competency.

The grooming industry offers a wealth of opportunities for improvement through in-service training, certification programs, workshops, national and international seminars, and grooming competitions. Catch the magic as you watch the world's best groomers compete at Intergroom, an international conference held annually in April in Somerset, New Jersey, or GroomExpo, a huge event held each September in Hershey, Pennsylvania. Both events are showcases for the latest trends in grooming products and great places to shop for your salon. In addition, there are state and regional conferences that draw the big guns of the grooming world to your locale to share their expertise. Join your state grooming association and attend these conferences to open your eyes to a wonderful world that few outside our industry are aware of.

The money you invest in yourself and your career will be worth every penny. For me, it was an eye-opener to see the leading lights of the grooming industry—superstars who regularly win trophies, ribbons, and cash prizes—attending these seminars and polishing their skills. They keep growing in this arena because they are always open to learning more. Read every book and magazine article you can get your hands on. Profit from the experience of pet care pioneers like Dorothy Walin, Shirlee Kalstone, and Ben and Pearl Stone.

The decision to enroll in a grooming school should not be made lightly. Check out the schools close to you and do some surfing on the Internet to investigate other institutions, beginning with their Web sites.

You will need to check each school's accreditation and licensing. Most states require schools to furnish contact information for the state agencies in charge of licensing vocational schools. Make sure the information is current and the school is on firm financial footing. A few years back, some unfortunate grooming students in my home state were left high and dry when the institution of their choice closed its doors due to financial problems before their courses of study had been completed. Look for a reference list of graduates you can call on for feedback.

There are many questions to ask when investigating a grooming school. These schools usually operate in conjunction with a grooming salon; find out if the number of dogs provided is sufficient for plenty of hands-on training. Will you be taught to groom all the major dog breeds, mixed breeds, and cats?

How much business training is provided? Because your likely goal is to start your own business, courses in business management, including the use of computer programs developed specifically for the pet industry, would be highly important to the grooming entrepreneur.

What is the ratio of students to teachers? Is it small enough to provide adequate individual attention? What about the background of the instructors? Are they experienced professionals who have achieved success in the grooming field?

If a school under your consideration is not within commuting distance, check out the availability and cost of student housing. Ask about tuition costs and whether a full kit of grooming equipment is included in this fee. Find out if financial aid, including student loans and Pell Grants, is available and if job placement is provided. Because of today's increasing shortage of trained groomers, most students should have a job waiting for them upon graduation.

Gathering such information should not be a struggle for the prospective student. The school should freely and enthusiastically provide it.

With established groomers competing for the pool of available talent, some busy shop owners are now sending their promising homegrown prospects to grooming school, footing the bill for an agreement to work in their employ for a specific period of time. PETsMART, one of the "big box" pet superstores, now offers training as part of its job recruitment program. Applicants must first be employed full-time for a minimum of thirty days and the store in which they work must have the need for a pet stylist. The training lasts six months, after which they would be under contract to work for PETsMART for a minimum of three years. Participants are trained at one of three grooming schools: the Nash Academy in Kentucky or New Jersey, or the Paragon School of Pet Grooming in Michigan.

Petco, another pet industry giant, also grows its own groomers at four of its training centers. (This number will grow to six by 2002.) Trainees are paid while they learn to groom. The number of hours varies between 600 and 800, depending on individual progress. Once their training is completed, groomers must work a full-time flexible schedule and must sign an agreement to work for the superstore chain for a year.

You should be aware that it's common within the grooming industry for an employee to be asked to sign an agreement prohibiting him or her from opening a business within a certain distance from the employer. Even with this restriction, the experience of working for someone else could be very beneficial to the budding groomer-entrepreneur. Whether such a contract would hold up in court might vary from state to state. However, I strongly recommend that you be fully aware of your contractual obligations and that you live up to them. Burning your bridges—and those who have nurtured you along the way—is always a bad idea. Friendships are important and beneficial in this industry. Furthermore, as long as you honor your obligations to your employers and mentors, your intent to be your own boss should be perfectly understandable. True friends will celebrate your success.

Contact the schools that interest you most and request a catalog. After careful review, follow up with a visit to the school to tour the facilities and to schedule a preliminary interview with the administrators. Look for clean, modern, well-lighted instruction areas and state-of-the-art equipment. Make sure students are well supervised and animals are treated with kindness and respect. The atmosphere should come as close to that of a professional salon as possible. Your training in this career will constitute the foundation of your success, so choose your school carefully. It is a very important step in your journey to become a pet care professional.

Most grooming schools offer courses at different levels for prospective groomers, bather-brushers, or grooming assistants. Most also offer full-time, part-time, evening, and weekend training. By and large, a course of study to become a full-finish groomer would involve a minimum of 600 hours, although my search through many school Web sites indicated that such courses vary in length from 350 to 1,000 hours. Average tuition for a full course of study ranges from $4,000 to $6,000.

## Pet Sitting: What It Takes to Make It a Business

Beyond a passion for pets, a desire to work from your home, and superb organizational skills, there is not a lot of formal training offered out there for those wishing to transition into this career. Among the best how-to books on the subject are *Pet Sitting for Profit* by Patti J. Moran and *The Professional Pet Sitter* by Lori and Scott Mangold.

Moran is recognized as the unofficial godmother of this growing industry. When she entered the field in 1983 after being downsized from a corporate management position, there were few resources available for budding pet sitters. She ran her "Crazy 'Bout Critters" pet sitting company for ten years, a one-woman operation that eventually grew to employ forty-one sitters. Her experiences led to a book and a products company, Patti Moran's, in King, North Carolina, from which she markets pet sitters' supplies, business forms, videos for training and public relations, and even a line of pet sitting attire. Such items are available online at www.petsitproducts.com. Ms. Moran also founded the two leading industry organizations, Pet Sitters International (PSI) and The National Association of Professional Pet Sitters (NAPPS), between them boasting some 5,000 members.

Lori and Scott Mangold also evolved into pet sitting from successful careers in the airline industry. Operating their business, Paws for Awhile, out of Portland,

Oregon, their book provides a blueprint for those who wish to follow in their footsteps. Industry magazines such as *The World of Professional Pet Sitting* are also informative for budding pet sitters.

Business know-how in general is available on-line through the United States Small Business Administration (SBA) at www.sba.gov. With offices nationwide, the SBA provides a wealth of information on planning and launching a business, as well as numerous publications on all aspects of business management, some of which are free of charge. Attending adult education courses in your local school system or enrolling at a community college or university for some business-related courses would also sharpen your savvy before you take the leap into your new occupation.

In many communities, business courses dealing with record keeping, taxes, and pertinent federal and state laws are offered through SCORE, the Small Business Development Center. Your local chamber of commerce also provides seminars, workshops and mentoring programs for its members, a good reason to join. Some chapters of the Better Business Bureau also provide similar services and information for the budding entrepreneur.

The most important factor in making a success out of your pet sitting business is having a professional attitude and becoming proactive about promoting your services. To be taken seriously as a professional pet care provider, you must first take yourself and your ambitions seriously.

## Obedience Training: Who Trains the Trainer?

Obedience trainers come to their calling via their passionate involvement in the world of dogs. Chances are their interest was initially sparked when they trained their own dog, igniting that special bond of communication between dog and owner. There are many prerequisites to making a serious commitment to this occupation. The best dog trainers continue to learn throughout their lives; this profession is all about the journey, not the destination.

Ideally, you will have achieved some success in training your own dogs, preferably achieving some obedience titles along the way. If you are serious about training, your participation in classes with your dogs will likely lead you to the next step, membership in an obedience club. Here you will learn more and make new friends and connections in the training world. Before you join, make sure the club's training philosophy meshes with your own. Training should always be a humane and positive endeavor—and it should be fun!

You should familiarize yourself with the various breed groups and the instinctual drives that govern their behavior: the hound's zeal for trailing and tracking, the herding dog's drive to contain and control its charges, the sporting dog's hunting and retrieving abilities, the working dog's need to serve and protect. You should be well versed in "dogspeak," knowing how to read a dog's body language and evaluate its behavior. As you enter this arena, having the dream is not enough. It also helps to have a history.

Set your feet on the path to your goal by attending conferences, workshops, and seminars on all aspects of training. They will introduce you to such diverse canine activities as obedience competition, puppy training, housebreaking and crate training, handling techniques, dog sports (Agility, Flyball, Frisbee and Freestyle), protection work (including Schutzhund training), canine anatomy and health issues, therapy training, search and rescue, service dog training, and police and military work with dogs.

There are also annual conferences offered by such training organizations as the Association of Pet Dog Trainers (800–PET–DOGS), the National Association of Dog Obedience Instructors (www.nadoi.org), and the American Dog Trainers Network (www.inch.com/~dogs).

At the college level, animal behavior programs of study are offered at institutions that have veterinary programs such as Cornell University in Ithaca, New York, or Tufts University in Boston, Massachusetts, and Mercy College in New York, New York. Also in New York City, the American Society for the Prevention of Cruelty to Animals offers its own animal behavior course.

In addition to consumer publications such as *Dog World, Dog Fancy,* and the American Kennel Club's *AKC Gazette,* which regularly cover obedience topics, there are magazines aimed specifically at trainers and training enthusiasts such as *Off Lead, Front and Finish, Fetch the Paper,* and *Dog Sports Magazine.* There are countless books on training aimed at a wide audience, from the first-time puppy owner to the experienced trainer. Dig in and devour as many as you can.

The American Dog Trainer's Network recommends many training schools and apprenticeship programs; the full listing is available on its Web site. Courses for budding instructors run anywhere from eight weeks to six months, with some offering apprenticeships and internships upon completion. Again, such programs do not pretend to be all-inclusive. A dedicated trainer keeps learning and growing throughout his or her career. Expect to put in three to five years of your own training and studying before you consider yourself a qualified novice obedience instructor.

Before enrolling in any training school, make sure harsh and abusive methods are not used. Ask for references and check with graduates to determine whether the information offered covers a broad scope and has a sound scientific basis with an up-to-date knowledge of canine behavior. Look into the accomplishments of the instructors. Are they reputable and proven in this highly competitive field?

As dog ownership becomes more and more tightly controlled in our communities, the need for qualified obedience trainers is on the rise. This particular calling is not for the timid, but it offers the satisfaction of knowing you are improving the quality of life for pets and responsible owners who want to enjoy their dogs and live in harmony with their neighbors.

## Your Support System: Family and Friends

Starting your own business is a life-changing decision. These days, few of us stay on the same career track for our entire working lives, retiring with a gold watch and a pension after thirty or more years of service, so you are probably approaching this decision with a job history as well as family connections and obligations. How you handle combining your personal and professional lives can play a huge role in whether you will be successful in achieving your goals.

Establishing a new career is a gigantic leap. Sometimes you feel like you've jumped out of the plane but you're still waiting for the parachute to open. Enlisting the aid and goodwill of those nearest and dearest to you can be a crucial factor in your success. Look upon it as your first public relations challenge. You need to make your significant others part of your team.

In the planning stages of a new business, commercial loans may not be available to you. If your own savings and other sources are insufficient for your goals, financial assistance from relatives and friends may be a great blessing to you as you get started. It is imperative, however, to keep such agreements on a strictly business basis. If you borrow money, put your loan agreement in writing and spell out how and when it will be repaid once you are in a position to draw an income. Relationships with family and friends can be permanently damaged if all such arrangements are not drawn up legally to make sure everyone's position is completely understood.

Family members will want to be included in the birth process of your new creation. Recruit their support in the planning stages by holding family meetings at which everyone gets a chance to talk—and to listen. Starting any business necessarily involves some sacrifice and inconvenience, especially if family members are accustomed to being your top priority, but embarking on a home-based business brings its own set of challenges to the table. Your spouse or children may be apprehensive about possible disruptions and invasions of their privacy in that most precious of all sanctuaries, their home.

Friends will also react to the changes that starting a new business will bring. Some will cheer you on, rolling up their sleeves to help and offering support. If you let them in on the planning process, you may be amazed at their enthusiasm and their creative input. Until you pick their brains, you may have no idea of their particular areas of expertise or the connections they may have to others who can assist you.

Other friends may resent your passionate new involvement. Like any life-changing event, this can be a true test of friendship. It's always a good idea to listen to friends' concerns with an open mind, but the negative nonbelievers and doubting Thomases can be a drain on the motivation and confidence you need right now. It just might be time for a weeding-out process. It takes courage to start a business and it takes strength to leave nonnurturing relationships behind.

The best way to gain the support of those closest to you is to include them in your vision. Listen to their concerns and fears and also let them know they will be needed and included in your plans. There will be days when your attention is focused on designing and constructing your home office or shop, working on marketing strategy or an advertising campaign, or meeting with accountants, attorneys or local officials. These hectic days may lead to nights when takeout meals are eaten off paper plates. If your family shares your spirit of adventure, such inconveniences can be treated with a lighthearted and loving attitude. Down the road, the success of your home-based business will become a source of family pride. It will also keep you closer to your loved ones as you work from your home.

It will not, however, be all sweetness and light. If family members will be working with you, there can be some rough spots. The potential pitfalls can be illustrated by comparing it to an office romance. There are valid reasons that management frowns upon on-the-job romantic entanglements. Combining business and personal concerns can be like playing with fire. As you forge ahead with your family business, what happens when your mate becomes involved in its ups and downs as you focus on it over breakfast, lunch, and dinner?

As a business partner first with my husband and currently with my daughter, I have found that viewing the business as a process rather than an entity unto itself helps make things flow more smoothly. As a business ebbs and flows, struggles and grows, everything should be negotiable; our roles should not be carved in stone.

Can you and your mate share home-front responsibilities as you face the demands of building the business? Can you be open to discussions on why one design would work better than another without turning it into a power struggle? So-called "control issues" can rock the boat when it comes to family members interacting on the job. In my own experience, what worked best for my family was a division of labor and responsibilities according to our individual strong points.

My husband, David, was a superb salesperson. Luckily for me, my daughter inherited his talent. Their outgoing personalities fueled our retail business and drew people to our shop like a magnet. My place to shine was the grooming room, where I kept our standards high and transmitted motherly love and concern to the pets in our care, always stressing kindness and compassion as I worked with our staff to make our four-footed customers look and feel beautiful.

As the business grew and changed over the years, I discovered my daughter was a far better staff manager than I was. She is able to walk that fine line between being the boss and being friendly with our groomers. I had always been too much of a people-pleaser in that role, getting so close to some employees that the lines of the personal and professional became blurred.

I was also more threatened by new technology than my husband or daughter, but came to realize along the way that change is not only inevitable, it can be exciting. Updated equipment and computerization lightened our workload and made us money. Taking advantage of new technology boosted morale and made us feel proud. In a successful family business, we can learn to focus on each other's strong points and encourage each other's growth. When it works the way it should, all of our special gifts and strengths can be woven together into a beautiful tapestry.

If your husband is the handyman type, his talents can be invaluable in designing and building your workspace. If your wife is a computer buff, enlisting her to set up your computer system can be a great financial boon. Your son may be a budding artist. Call on him to design your logo, your business cards, your brochure. Even the youngest family members can stuff envelopes, distribute flyers, or stock shelves. (A cautionary note to home groomers: If your relatives or friends are carpenters, plumbers, or electricians, by all means solicit their services to save on startup costs—but make sure the work they perform is in compliance with local building codes.)

In many family businesses, husbands and wives clock as many as seventy to eighty hours a week on the job, working to provide a better future for themselves and their children. How do they do it without getting on each other's nerves? Sometimes it helps to have a few ground rules, such as keeping business problems out of the bedroom or not tackling tough issues over dinner. My husband declared business matters off-limits when we took a weekend drive to our summer camp. Because I've always been the type of person who chews over every problem like a terrier working on a bone, this was an not easy policy for me, but that little weekly break became part of our routine, helping us reconnect as husband and wife, rather than as business partners.

Your home-based business can create family wealth for current and future generations. It can become an expression of your family values as you work together to make it grow. More than 75 percent of all U.S. companies are family owned; the largest percentage of these falls into the small-business category. They account for more than 40 percent of the gross national product and play a significant role in the health of our economy. The challenges of working with family can be daunting, but the rewards are great. As you set sail upon your dream, make sure to invite the ones you love onboard!

## Attitude Is Everything

Your dream is taking shape! You wake up one morning and you know deep inside it's time to be the boss, to take your future into your own hands. You feel six feet tall and bulletproof, ready to take the plunge. Wouldn't it be great if you had this positive, confident feeling all the time? Unfortunately, those moments of worry and indecision will probably come back, creeping up to nibble at your optimism like gypsy moths on the leaves of your maple tree. How do you get those pesky parasites to fold their tents and stop feeding on your confidence? You need to make a decision to have a winning attitude every day.

Some fortunate folks are born with that upbeat quality. They have relentless determination to succeed, twenty-four hours a day, seven days a week. The rest of us have to work at it. We all know people stuck in the "ain't it awful" mode. The weather is always too hot or too cold. The traffic is horrible. They may look like the picture of health but they will soon fill you in on their litany of health problems.

These folks always view the glass as half empty; unfortunately, their pessimism is contagious.

Work on developing an optimistic attitude. Focus on the positive aspect of every situation. At first, you may need to switch your new attitude on every morning, but eventually it will become a habit. Every problem you encounter presents an opportunity to think creatively and come up with a possible solution. Every negative individual you encounter gives you a chance to practice being positive. As Eleanor Roosevelt said, "No one can make you feel inferior without your consent."

Here are some hints to help you stay positive as you proceed:

- Get some motivational tapes and listen to them whenever you can: driving the car, exercising, folding laundry, emptying the litter box. Wayne Dyer and Tony Robbins are my personal favorites, but there is a whole industry of such inspired and inspiring speakers to bring on board as your personal coaches. Empower yourself!
- Join business groups. Find out which ones will help you to gain clients and allow you to network with fellow businessmen and -women. Attend a few meetings to familiarize yourself with the group's overall mission. Your mother was right: Hanging out with the wrong crowd will bring you down to their level. Cultivate some new associates who have a winning attitude.
- Read books by successful entrepreneurs. There are many Horatio Alger stories on the bookshelves. Learning how others have overcome adversity and triumphed in business and in life will help you to follow their example.

## Your Word Is Your Bond: Building a Golden Reputation

Decide from Day One that you will build a superb reputation. Your word really is your bond. Get in the habit of keeping your promises and meeting your financial obligations. Return phone calls and show up on time for your appointments. Your reputation precedes you in business and will last long after you have sold it or passed it on to a family member. When you decide to retire, it will have a direct bearing on what your business will be worth.

Most of us have dealt with a friend or relative who borrows money then conveniently forgets to repay it. People like this put us in an awkward position when we have to chase them and remind them of their obligations. In business, it's the same scenario. Your creditors will not respect you if they have to hound you to pay your bills.

The pet care industry has come of age, but in its formative days it saw its share of shady characters who proved to be bad credit risks. It's up to us to put this impression to rest and gain the respect we deserve. Viewed from a more concrete perspective, if you don't pay your bills, you will soon be out of business.

Your accountant will be your right hand when it comes to financial planning. This valuable team member will advise you on managing the costs of setup and operation in the planning stages. He or she will provide you with a monthly profit and loss statement so you manage according to your cash flow, gauge your progress, and plan future expenditures.

Don't be an ostrich. If you have trouble paying a bill, hiding your head in the sand only makes things worse. Facing up to your obligations like a responsible adult will preserve your reputation and lessen your stress level. Contact the company or utility to make arrangements for a payment schedule. It goes without saying that you cannot take a salary before your business pays its bills.

These suggestions will help you to make sure your reputation is one of your greatest assets:

- Request your credit profiles from TRW/Experian, (800) 397–3742 or www.experian.com; Equifax, (800) 997–2493 or www.equifax.com; or Trans-Union (800) 888–4213 or www.transunion.com. It may not be possible to erase a negative credit history, but you can review it for discrepancies and find out what information is being furnished to banks and other potential creditors. Obtain this information before you apply for a loan or request credit from your distributors.
- Take a good look at how you manage your personal finances. Do you pay your bills on time? If you regularly lose track of due dates, you must learn to live by your daily planner, whether it's a book or a pocket-size electronic device. From now on, it's your bible. Enter the due dates and get those checks in the mail five days before they're due.
- Treat everyone like a potential client. Refrain from denigrating your competitors. It's disrespectful and unprofessional. Besides, someday they may send business your way, come to your aid in an emergency, or work with you on a common problem. To preserve your golden reputation, practice living by the Golden Rule.

# The Pet Population in Your Area

You need to do your homework to determine if there is a need for the pet care services you wish to provide in your locale. The first step is to find out how many pets live in your town and the surrounding towns from which you will draw your customer base. To determine the number of dogs in any community, contact the town clerk's office to request the number of licensed dogs. For a small fee, you can also get a printout of the names and addresses of their owners, pertinent data when it's time to publicize your services.

The numbers and types of other pet care services in your area are also a good indication of potential opportunity for your business. If there are several grooming salons as well as pet supply chains that offer grooming services, you will know that the market is being served, but that does not necessarily mean that there would not be room for one more. When you market yourself as a home-based groomer, you would need to stress what makes your services unique and desirable. It may be the homelike atmosphere without the hustle and bustle of a large salon, or the individual attention pets would receive, especially important to owners of senior pets with special needs. Although I have sometimes questioned whether leaving a pampered pet for grooming was more traumatic for its owner than it was for the pet, I know that some dogs don't do well in a setting with several other dogs. There are other pets with health issues who must get in and out as soon as possible. You can create your own niche.

If pet sitting is your goal, do some research in your community to determine if such services are already being offered. The first place to look is the yellow pages. (One indication that pet sitting has come into its own is that it now has its own listing instead of being lumped under Kennels.) Next, call or visit veterinarians, groomers, and pet stores to ask if they know of any pet sitters and if they think there is a need for more. In my hometown, for example, there is already one pet sitting business, but it is so busy and booked up that its owners are taking new clients only by referral. Therefore, the demand for pet sitters in this particular town exceeds the supply.

In some areas, pet sitters have started their own networking groups, with members meeting on a regular basis. Sitting in with the sitters could provide you with a look at how their businesses work. With pet sitting coming of age as a career, there may even be veterans to mentor you or serve as consultants.

The type of community you live in also dictates the potential need for pet sitting in your area. If it's a bustling urban area or an affluent growing suburb, you can be sure there is room for one more. If you live in a rural area, the need may be there but it may be different. You may need to include livestock in your list of animals to be cared for when their owners get a chance to travel. You may need to offer a menu of other services as well.

If obedience training lights your fire, see what is offered in your area and how close it is to potential clients in your town. Ask veterinarians and groomers whom they recommend when clients request training information. Because this particular occupation requires lots of hands-on experience, by all means get involved by training your own pet. You might end up assisting an experienced trainer as another step in preparing for your own career.

When studying the demand for your potential business, your local chamber of commerce can be a valuable source of demographic information. It usually conducts periodic surveys on per capita income, population growth, and the number of service businesses the community supports. It pays to be a member. It will give you a great opportunity to network and become part of the fabric of the local business community.

As indicated by the unprecedented growth of pet ownership nationwide, where there are people, there are pets. If you live in a populated area that supports many growing businesses of all types, chances are excellent that there is a place for the service you wish to provide. If you have the love of animals, the business skills, and the burning desire to make your living doing something close to your heart, I am convinced that there will be room for you in the ever growing world of pet care.

## What's in a Name?

What will you name your baby? As a prospective parent, this was one of the most delightful decisions I ever had to mull over. In retrospect, it seemed a lot easier than picking a name for a new business!

Your business name will be one of your most important assets. In christening this new venture, you will want to pick something that reflects what you do and who you are. I have to add my two cents here! In my opinion, the pet care industry suffers from an overabundance of "cutesy" names. It probably has to do with the way people baby their pets. I'll admit it: I often lapse into baby talk myself when communicating with my own animals or beloved canine and feline customers, but if I were you, I would shy away from picking a name that is too cute for your new venture. "Pepi's Poodle Palace" or "Connie's Cuddly Critters" may work for you, but I prefer something that conveys a more professional image.

Another point to ponder: Humorous references can be fun, but in naming a grooming business, I would avoid the words "Dirty" or "Hairy." The picture these words call to mind is not the image you wish to convey to potential clients. For any pet care venture, something that relates to warmth, safety, caring, and kindness is reassuring to the pet owner searching for your services. A little snob appeal doesn't hurt either. People like to think that they are providing only the best services for their beloved pets.

The name you choose should be easy to remember and should make a personal statement. It should not be difficult to spell or pronounce and it should not resemble another company's name except in the common denominator of "Grooming," "Pet Sitting," or "Training." Because there is such a proliferation of pet care businesses today, it's a good idea to have a few names under consideration. Mull them over before you commit yourself. Run them by family and friends to solicit their opinions.

Once you have settled on a couple of favorites, check the local registry of deeds to see if anyone else in your area is using the names. You can also check your local city or town hall, the library, and the yellow pages. Your next stop is the secretary of state's office, where you can find out if your prospective names are already in use within your state.

There are actually three types of business name categories. The one you choose will play a part in how you register or officially file your name. *Trade names* identify a specific company, like Reebok, Pepsi Cola, or Microsoft. (Any type of business can call itself a company.) *Corporate names* identify corporations. You can tell they are incorporated by the word "Incorporated," "Corporation," or "Limited" (usually abbreviated Inc., Corp., or Ltd.) after their name. You cannot legally use these terms in your name unless you are actually incorporated. If you have decided on a name for your corporation but are still in the planning stages, you can contact the corporations division in your state and reserve the name for thirty days. This will protect the name you have chosen from infringement by others while you are preparing to incorporate. In my state, this must be done in writing, and a small fee is charged for the service.

If someone else is already using the name you would like, you would, of course, be prohibited from using it. In some cases, an exemption can be made if you are able to obtain a letter of consent from the other corporation, giving you permission to use a similar name, but to avoid confusion or legal ramifications, having a name that is uniquely your own would be your best bet.

*Trademarks* are words, symbols, or a combination of the two that identify a business and distinguish its products and services from others. The purpose of registering your name as a trademark is to protect your exclusivity. It gives you the right to bring an action against anyone who uses the same or a similar name or product. Often the name of the first producer of a product or service becomes a generic term for that item, such as Kleenex for a facial tissue or Rollerblade for in-line skates. In the early stages, when you have no competition, it may not matter if your name becomes synonymous with your product or service, but when competitors spring up and use your name as a generic term for their product or service, you are faced with a major problem.

Product names fall into generic use with the public anyway, but the battle wages on. To keep it from generic use, the Kimberly-Clark Corporation refers to its product as "Kleenex brand facial tissues," to make sure that Kleenex is the brand or trademark. Rollerblade, Inc., officially terms its product "Rollerblade in-line skates." These big companies retain a team of lawyers just to police the publishing world and protect their trademarks.

On a far smaller playing field, when my husband called our grooming shop "The Village Groomer" back in 1969, we did not take the time to register or trademark our name. With our industry's growth, there are now at least a dozen "Village Groomers" scattered around the country. I have met some of my fellow Village Groomers at industry conventions, and sometimes we get each other's e-mail by mistake. Although I have no grounds to complain about sharing the name with these colleagues, I wish we had planned ahead and taken the time to protect the name we gave "our baby" all those years ago.

You can determine if there is a federal trademark on a name you are considering by contacting the United States Patent and Trademark Office (PTO) in Washington, D.C. You can do trademark research yourself or you can hire an attorney specializing in patents and trademarks. The search option is available to you at any federal depository library, with branches in all fifty states. Call (800) PTO–9199 or (703) 308–4357 for the nearest location, or log on to the PTO Web site at www.uspto. gov/web/menu/tm.html. In some cities, there are trademark search services available for a fee. Some public libraries will perform a computerized search for you, also usually involving a small fee.

Once you receive your forms from the PTO, review them thoroughly and request help from the PTO staff if you need it. The paid services of an attorney well versed in the process would make this job a lot easier. The PTO's current application fee is $325. Get the wheels in motion early; approval can take up to two years.

You are probably thinking all this research is overkill for a small fish like you, but it really is worth it. After you have gone to all the trouble and expense of launching your own little labor of love and establishing its name, it would be a major setback to get a cease-and-desist letter in the mail ordering you to stop using that name because it is already federally trademarked by someone else. It would be upsetting and costly to change all your business forms, stationery, literature, and advertising, as well as having to explain it to your clients. Do your homework before you christen your "new baby." In the long run, it will be well worth it.

Once a name has been chosen, you need to check to determine where you are required to file it to comply with state and local laws. Your accountant and your attorney can advise you on how you should proceed so you will be in full compliance.

In most communities, a person doing business under a name different from his or her own must file a business certificate or "dba" at the city hall or town clerk's office. The only exception to this rule is if you are doing business under your own complete name, such as "The Kathy Salzberg Company." The fee varies from town to town; in my home state, it's around $25 and it's good for four years. Unlike a corporation filing or a trademark, this local registration does not protect your company name. It primarily allows consumers and creditors to identify who you are. The public has a right to know who owns your business. When you open your business account, your bank will also require proof that you have filed your business name with the local authorities.

If you are incorporating your business, you need to file with the secretary of state's office, under the corporations division. In my state, this requires a $200 filing fee. You do not need to file with the city or town hall if you file with this state office.

Certain partnerships are also required to file at this state level, so it's best to check with your attorney to make sure that you comply. A general partnership, by far the most common type of this setup, would need to file locally, following the same course of action as a sole proprietorship.

The quality of your products and services and the goodwill symbolized by your mark can be valuable commodities and are worthy of protection from infringement by others. A central file listing all trademarks is available in your

*Bedlington and Burrows, Attorneys at Law*
1000 Lake Front Avenue
Chicago, IL 60604

July 1, 2002

Mary Ann Smith
Pink Poodle Emporium
200 Garden Grove Road
Wentworth, CA 90970

Dear Ms. Smith:

Your company name (Pink Poodle Emporium) is in violation of trademark infringement against our client, who has legal claim as the sole bearer of this name under the laws of the U.S. Department of Commerce, Patent and Trademark Office.

You are advised to immediately cease and desist using the name Pink Poodle Emporium, striking it from all stationery, literature, and materials in your possession. We expect confirmation of the termination by mail within thirty days of receipt of this letter. Failing to comply with this request will result in costly legal consequences.

Please call us at (312) 555–3456 if you have any questions. Thank you for your cooperation in this matter.

Sincerely,

Edgar T. Bedlington, Esq.

**Sample cease-and-desist letter**

# Business Registration Form

State of _____

County/municipality _____

The undersigned hereby certifies that _____ is conducting

business under the name _____ which operates

as a ____(sole proprietorship, partnership, corporation)____ under the laws of the

above-named state.

The business is located at _____(complete street address)_____ ,

_____(suite/room/apt.)_____ , _____(city/state)_____ , ___(zip code)___ .

The nature of this _____(product or service)_____ business is

_____(explain fully)_____

_____

The names and addresses of all owners of the above-named business are as follows:

Name

Address (if post office box,
also list street address)

_____        _____

_____        _____

_____        _____


The representative of this business declares that the above information is true and
correct.

_____
Signature

_____        _____
(print name)                                              Date

Signed in the presence of:

_____        Witnessed this _____ day of
Signature of witness
                                                              _____ , 20 _____

_____
(print name)

**Sample business registration form**

state's trademarks division office. Once you have started using your trademark, you must register it in your state. This usually costs around $50 and the mark will be registered for ten years, after which it can and should be renewed.

If you are going into business for the long haul, researching your business name and obtaining your own trademark are important steps in protecting the name you seek to establish.

# Chapter Three

# Getting Down to Business

A passion for pet care and a head for business don't always go hand in hand. For example, although most people are drawn to grooming because of their love for animals, a 1999 PetGroomer.com survey disclosed the fact that 90 percent of those entering the profession eventually seek to open a grooming business of their own. Interestingly, 90 percent of these business owner wanna-bes said they had no previous experience as a business owner of any kind.

If you are operating a home-based service business, you might think it is inconceivable that you would need to comply with all the local, state, and federal regulations that apply to commercially located businesses, but unfortunately, this is not the case. The temptation is always there to ignore some rules and regulations, but in the long run, you could be causing yourself problems and stress. Take the time to research the laws that apply to you. Structure your business so that it will be in compliance from Day One and you will be in a favorable position to succeed and grow.

## Your Mission Statement

Every business needs a mission statement to identify its purpose and its goals. A pet care business is no different. It spells out why you chose this business and what you hope to provide for your clientele. It tells people who you are and what you're about.

This statement of your purpose can serve as a source of inspiration for you and your staff. Our mission statement begins with a brief reference to our founder, my late husband, and how his love for pets led him to found this business. It goes on to state:

"At the Village Groomer and Pet Supply, our philosophy is to respect that connection between our clients and their humans and to treat every pet in our care as if it were our own. In moments when we are challenged by a nervous pet or a behavioral problem, we try to sense the source of the fear and work with the animal to calm them and make them feel safe. It is our belief that if we always do what is best for the pet, we can't go wrong.

"We strive every day to create a fun, loving, unique experience for pets and their humans. Just come by and see for yourself. The Village Groomer and Pet Supply, celebrating thirty years of caring for pets . . . and the people they own."

This heartfelt message tells people that first and foremost we are in this business because of our love for animals. It lets them know that we provide a safe place, we have a long history, and we have high standards for the quality of our work. Tap into your own creativity and passion for pet care when you compose your mission statement.

If you went into the business because of your love for animals, let your mission statement announce it to the world. If you say you want to be an active part of the animal community, do it. Volunteer to groom shelter pets looking for a new home, help organize and sponsor a pet walk for the humane society, host school field trips to your shop. If you say that your business means more to you than simply a way to make money, then you should show it in your actions as well.

## Creating a Business Plan

Having a business plan is essential whether you are seeking financial assistance or not. Think of this plan as a road map to help you get where you want to go with your business. Sure, you could still get there without a map, but you would probably take a few wrong turns along the way. A comprehensive business plan outlines the services you plan to provide, your projected cash flow, and your marketing strategy. As conditions change in the economy in general and the pet industry in particular, your plan will need periodic updating to keep you on track with regard to your services, pricing, and products as well as how and when you will need to add employees to your staff. It will measure your milestones and track your progress as you become a seasoned veteran in the pet care field.

For help on compiling a business plan, you may also turn to that marvelous resource, the SBA. With approximately 750 of its Small Business Development Centers scattered throughout the country, this agency offers assistance free of charge whether you are seeking an SBA loan or going through a bank. To locate an office near you, check out its official Web site, www.sba.gov. Another great source of help and advice can be found online at www.BizPlanit.com.

# BUSINESS PLAN FOR
# FUR MAGNOLIAS GROOMING

402 Maple Lane

Plainfield, MA 02011

(508) 555-8770

Prepared by Jane Smith, Owner

January 1, 2001

**Sample business plan, cover**

# TABLE OF CONTENTS

## REASONS TO START THIS BUSINESS

I find that I am happiest and most fulfilled when working with animals. I have become adept at grooming my own pets, and for the past two years I have worked on Saturdays and vacations at a nearby grooming shop, helping out and learning the ropes of this business. I started as a bather-brusher and progressed to performing basic clipper trims on various breeds. My employer and her customers have praised my work as I have steadily improved my skills. I now feel I am ready to be on my own and open my own grooming business in my home. The idea of setting my own hours and being my own boss is very appealing to me.

I know I have enough artistic ability to bring out the beauty of each breed entrusted to my care. I have the natural aptitude and I believe I also have the positive attitude needed to succeed. I am very responsible, dependable, and able to work well with people. I am in good health and have a high energy level, so I know I can handle the physical aspects of this profession. Most of all, I have a deep love of animals and the desire to work with them, making pet ownership more enjoyable for my clients by keeping their pets healthy and beautiful while earning my living in the process.

## CREDENTIALS

I am now completing a course in pet grooming, which I have been attending on a part-time basis for the past year. Upon graduation, I will receive a diploma stating that I have passed the course and now have the skills needed to groom most breeds of dogs and cats. I will display this formal recognition of my achievement to let my clients know that I am a trained professional.

In my current office job, I have mastered the use of the computer. I have experience in solving customers' problems and explaining complicated information. I will need further training in business management to gain a better understanding of record keeping, taxes, and federal and state laws governing my business. These resources are provided through SCORE, the local Small Business Development Center, and small-business and tax workshops offered periodically by the state and through my local chamber of commerce. Evening courses in business management are also offered at a nearby community college. Plans to strengthen my credentials in this area are listed on the attached Action Plan.

## MARKETING PLAN

I have studied the demographics of my town and the general region and observed that new home construction is on the increase. On average, new homes in this area are selling in the range of $300,000 to $400,000 and are being purchased mainly by upwardly mobile young families drawn to this area because of the growing high-tech industry and our highly rated schools. Most of these newcomers fit the picture of typical suburban family life. Their children are involved in sports and youth groups; the parents own two cars, one of which is often a sport-utility vehicle. The ownership of pets fits right in with this family picture.

The area has also seen an upswing in condo construction, with residents almost evenly split between older empty nesters and younger professionals, both single and married. Many empty nesters find joy in nurturing pets, mainly dogs and cats. They treat their animals as beloved family members and will spend money to keep them healthy and nice to be near. In general, the young marrieds are on the career track, postponing children until they are established. For them, pets serve the role of surrogate children, playing a big part in their enjoyment of leisure time. Many of the condo dwellers do not own dogs but have cats, an easier pet to keep when one works very long hours and travels frequently.

My town has a population of 18,000, with more than one hundred service-related businesses. The town clerk's office informed me that there are just under 2,000 licensed dogs in town. Because cats do not require licensing, I was not able to get a figure on how many residents own cats. However, the population supports one other groomer, four veterinarians, two professional dog trainers, three boarding kennels, one cattery, and two pet sitting and dog walking businesses. I plan to introduce myself to these fellow animal care professionals and give them my business cards as well as requesting their cards to hand out to my clients.

## Pet Population Statistics for Potential Customers

I have contacted the town clerks in my hometown and in two neighboring towns and received a list of all licensed dogs and their owners in these communities. The figures will provide me with a database for a mailer announcing the opening of my grooming business.

## Promotions

I have volunteered to visit the local high school as part of its career day presentations. With the principal's permission, I will bring my own dog and cat to demonstrate basic grooming techniques. I will also hand out pet grooming pamphlets, featuring my business name and phone number, for students to bring home to their parents. I produced these on my computer using bright-colored paper and clip art of dogs and cats as a border.

I have visited two area animal shelters and volunteered to professionally groom pets that they are seeking to place for adoption, as long as they are current on their vaccinations. The shelter personnel were extremely appreciative, agreeing to hand out my cards to people who adopt pets. Each shelter has its own newsletter and both plan to highlight my services in upcoming issues.

## Advertising

I will inquire about the cost of advertising in the newspapers, one local weekly and one regional weekly as well as two metropolitan dailies. I will also explore advertising in the yellow pages under the "Pets–Grooming" heading, and look into advertising in the smaller community phone book, published by a private firm. Radio and television advertisements do not fit into my budget at this time.

My computer software gives me many options to create my own stationery and business cards on quality paper purchased from a local office supply store. My color printer will help make the stationery look more professional. I have already printed sample flyers on my computer to mail directly to potential clients. Business cards will be handed out when I visit area vets, kennels, dog trainers, pet sitters, and shelters. I will investigate the cost of magnetic billboards for my van as well as looking into any potential liability I might incur if I am involved in an accident.

## Web Site

I plan to create a Web site for my business, initially for promotional purposes but later to feature interactive capabilities. My site will have biographical information and photographs of myself, my pets, and my family. Eventually I will also feature pets from my clientele. I will offer seasonal information on pet safety and links to information on pet bereavement, pet adoption, and various breed rescue organizations, as well as to the Web site of the American Kennel Club (AKC).

Preliminary research shows that the name "furmagnoliasgrooming.com" is available, and I will register through Buydomain.com, a domain name registry. I wish to protect my Web name, so I will also register under furmagnoliasgrooming.net and furmagnoliasgrooming.org, so no one else has access to these variations. At present, the cost of each registration is $40 per year. My Internet service provider has Web-hosting rates comparable to several other providers, but to conserve my finances, I will look into setting up my Internet site through a free hosting service. My final decision will depend on how my domain name can be displayed and how many other similar businesses are on the server. (I do not want to be at the bottom of a listing of 5,000 sites that takes an unduly long time for the user to load.) Hosting fees start at $20 per month.

I need to investigate the pros and cons of Web site design as well. According to my preliminary inquiries, Web site design packages start at $100 for a one-page site. This would have no e-mail or ordering capabilities, but it would secure my site and put my name out on the Internet. I need to look into software packages for Web site design and the possibility of taking a course in design instruction at the local community college. I know I must weigh the cost factor as well as the demands on my own time as I focus on starting my business. Establishing my Web site will be irrelevant if no one can find me, so I need to determine how to register it with the most popular search engines, such as

Yahoo, AltaVista, Go, and Google. With the explosion of sites on the Web, one way to do this would be to register it with SubmitIt!com. For $59 per year, this company will submit my site to up to 400 search engines and directories.

### Customer Follow-up

After I have groomed a pet, I will suggest rebooking it for the next appointment. I may offer a 10 percent discount if one automatically rebooks, at least for the first year or two while I am building my clientele. I could offer special membership cards, entitling these "Preferred Pets" to the discount. This would make the owner feel special, providing a sense of belonging to an exclusive club. I will also call clients a few days ahead to remind them of upcoming appointments.

## COMPETITION

Pet grooming is offered at two other locations in town: a downtown pet grooming salon and a veterinary hospital. Within 25 miles there are four more grooming shops plus one obedience training facility with a groomer on staff, one veterinary clinic with a groomer on staff, and one pet supply superstore that offers grooming.

### Competitors' Strengths and Weaknesses

Pet grooming salons have the advantage of high visibility and both pedestrian and automobile traffic. On my visits to these groomers, however, I have discovered a few individual weaknesses.

One shop did not look or smell clean and the owner was equally unkempt and unprofessional in her appearance. Another groomer was abrupt when I visited and introduced myself, possibly viewing me as unwanted competition. She declined to answer any questions about her experience or her pricing. At this establishment, I heard her coworker angrily yelling at a dog in the background, audible in spite of the loud rock and roll music playing on the radio.

The groomers at the pet superstore were friendly and all were novices to the industry. I liked the open setup that allowed pet owners and shoppers to observe the grooming operation through windows.

At the obedience training school, I was warmly welcomed by the owner. She offered me advice and assistance as well as a tour of her facilities. This was not the case at the vet clinic, where the receptionist told me it was impossible for me to talk to the groomer because he was too busy that day.

These visits showed me that the groomers were busy, highlighting the demand for my service. The varying degrees of courtesy and professionalism with which I was received gave me added incentive to put my best foot forward and make my clients feel welcomed and appreciated. It also brought home the importance of maintaining a bright, clean environment and a warm, friendly manner to make clients feel comfortable about leaving their pets in my care.

## FINANCIAL PLAN

My current salary is $36,000 a year, with a savings of $5,000 for emergencies and an untouchable 401K plan. Listed here are my monthly salary and approximate expenses to show any monies left over to use for financing my proposed business.

### Monthly Income and Expenses

#### Income

| | |
|---|---|
| Salary (after taxes and health insurance): | $3,000 |

#### Expenses

| | |
|---|---|
| Mortgage payment: | $750 |
| Food (including takeout): | $300 |
| Car payment: | $300 |
| Gas for car: | $50 |
| Car insurance: | $140 |
| Lunch: | $35 |
| Utilities: | $100 |
| Telephone: | $50 |
| Cable TV: | $45 |
| Cellular phone: | $30 |
| Credit Cards: | $150 |
| Laundry and dry cleaning: | $20 |
| Miscellaneous (clothing, toiletries, hairdresser, gifts, pet care): | $100 |
| Recreation (movies, clubs, theater): | $50 |
| Internet fee: | $20 |
| Newspaper and magazines: | $15 |
| **Total:** | **$2,155** |
| **Remainder/(deficit):** | **$845** |

I will open business checking and savings accounts immediately. I am determined to put at least $500 a month in the savings account to help finance my grooming business.

I will request credit history data from three major credit reporting firms and review the data for discrepancies and repair.

## Alternative Money Sources

### Bank

My current bank is friendly. Officers and tellers know me well and I have a long history with this institution. This will make it easier for me to inquire about building reputable credentials to apply for a future loan.

### Credit Cards

Two credit cards will be designated for business use only. Charging no more than $300 on each card per month is an affordable limit for me to repay without incurring additional interest charges.

### Other Banking Needs

Because clients will expect payment options other than cash or checks, I will inquire about a Visa/MasterCard/Discover merchant account and processing ATM debit. If my bank does not offer merchant accounts, I will need to move my business account to another bank. I will also call American Express to request a merchant application, as this company requires applicants to contact them directly. At the same time, I will request a corporate card for my own use.

### Equipment

I already own some grooming equipment (one standard size portable table and one standing floor dryer as well as basic grooming tools purchased through my grooming school). The following list encompasses what would be needed for a home-based grooming salon. Even though I will initially work alone, it makes sense to have space for two grooming stations, as I expect my operation to grow.

For a shop with two grooming stations, I will need the following equipment:

2 hydraulic grooming tables

2 adjustable grooming posts

1 grooming stool (a bar stool would work)

2 standing floor dryers

1 cage dryer

1 high-velocity dryer

1 conventional bath tub

Cages or crates, 6 small and 6 large

2 clippers plus a complete assortment of blades (two in each size) and a set of snap-on comb attachments

Clipper supplies: blade wash solution, lubricating spray, grease and oil for clipper maintenance

Scissors, 2 straight, 2 curved for finish work, 1 small straight for feet and ears, 1 blunt tipped for use around eyes, 1 heavy-duty stainless steel for prep work, 1 pair of thinning shears

2 universal slicker brushes with curved metal bristles

2 stainless steel double-sided combs with both wide and narrow teeth

2 mat combs

2 dog nail trimmers, 1 large and 1 small, pliers type

1 cat nail trimmer

Nailfiles
2 pairs of forceps, 1 straight,

1 curved, stainless steel

Ear powder

1 nylon muzzle in each size

1 plastic "basket" muzzle in each size

1 pair of heavy-duty suede animal handler's gloves

1 heavy plastic bather's apron

---

**I wil need to purchase the following products:**

Shampoos, one case (4 gallons) of each of the following types:

Hypoallergenic, conditioning, medicated (oatmeal and tea tree oil), flea and tick, bluing for white coats, protein-enriched, and all-purpose

Conditioner, 4 gallons

Eye drops

Ear cleaning solution

Pet cologne, 2 different fragrances

Cotton balls or a box of rolled cotton

First-aid supplies: elasticized gauze bandage rolls, bandages, adhesive tape, instant hot and cold packs, hydrogen peroxide,

antibiotic first-aid cream

Medicated spray to treat "clipper burn"

Styptic powder

Wide-spectrum disinfectant to clean grooming tools, tables, crates, and floor

Flea and tick spray: One type for use on pets who come in with fleas, another to prevent flea infestation in the shop

2 groomer's uniforms

Conditioning sprays: One type to "set" styles, another to combat static electricity in the pet's coat

1 box of latex gloves

---

**Cleaning Supplies**

Vacuum cleaner (a commercial "shop vac" will work best)

1 broom and dustpan

1 extra-large trash barrel

Heavy-duty extra-large trash bags

Fire extinguisher

## Purchasing Plan

I am relying on my contacts in the grooming business to advise me on equipment selection. I know that for this type of business, the least expensive piece of equipment may not be the wisest choice because it must stand up under constant usage. I am researching and reading every book I can find on this subject. Grooming trade shows are held annually in several regions of the country; I plan to attend one of these prior to setting up my shop.

For installation of built-in crates, the bathtub, walls, flooring, electrical outlets, lighting, and a partition between my work area and reception desk, I will need the services of a carpenter, electrician, and plumber. I have friends and family members who work in these trades, so that will help keep the costs of constructing my home grooming shop as low as possible.

## HOW TO START THE BUSINESS WHILE I'M WORKING

My employer has asked if I can continue to work two days a week, and I plan to do so while I am building my clientele. The income will help to support me and increase my capital for the new venture. I will have my answering machine take requests for appointments and I will return those calls when I return home in the evening.

## OFFICE SETUP AND STRUCTURE

I plan to house my home grooming shop in the "family room" addition off the kitchen that has its own entry. Within this large room, I will partition off a space for use as my office. I have a large closet in which I will install lighting and shelving for storage of supplies.

### Business Registration

After researching the federal trademark records to see if the name I have chosen for my business is already in use, I will register my name with state and federal officials. Next, I will request the necessary paperwork from the town clerk and state tax department, fill out the forms and have them notarized, then deliver them for processing.

### Mail

Although I have looked into having a separate post office box, for the sake of convenience, I will have my business mail delivered to my home location.

### Insurance

General liability insurance for my business must be obtained. According to my current insurance agent, property and liability coverages are extremely limited or excluded in most cases involving home-based businesses.

Other possible sources for insurance coverage may be offered through membership in my local chamber of commerce or the National Dog Groomers Association of America, Inc. I will need coverage for the building, personal property, and liability—extremely important for all persons involved in animal care.

### Office Needs

I will use my home computer in my business operation. It includes a word processing program and an inkjet printer. I have a printing program that I can use to make signs and stationery. Initially, I will record clients' names and grooming records on large index cards, but I will look into software programs tailored specifically for the grooming industry.

I will call the telephone company and have another phone line installed for my business. I will also need an answering machine for business use only. Eventually, I may add another line for a fax machine.

I will need a file case for my index cards, and legal pads to record scheduling and grooming instructions for each pet being groomed on a specific day. I will record the date and note the type of grooming I have done on the back of the card. I will also need a daily appointment book and a supply of pens and whiteout tape or liquid to make corrections and changes in my appointment book.

My reception area where I will receive and release customers will be partitioned off from the grooming room. I plan to have a counter installed where my cash register and computer will be kept. Having a separate area will look more clean and professional and keep clients out of my work area.

I will also need a "sandwich board" style sign listing prices and services.

### EXPANSION

Within one year I anticipate that my business will be generating sufficient revenue for me to hire a bather-brusher. This will make it possible for me to use more of my time in actual grooming, thus increasing my productivity and profit. As with most new businesses, I do not expect to make a profit the first year. The cost of starting up, including training, equipment, remodeling, advertising, and professional services will take a while to pay off, but I expect to be turning a profit in my second year. I do not think I could expand my staff further at this location because of traffic and parking as well as neighborhood relations.

## ACTION PLAN WITH COMPLETION DATES

### Credentials
1. I will graduate from grooming school in January 2002. I will have completed one year's training, which will sharpen the skills I learned while helping out at my former employer's grooming shop and making me more knowledgeable about the proper breed standard for each dog. My diploma posted on the wall will give clients reassurance that I have received professional training.
2. I will further my education by attending trade shows and grooming seminars. (Intergroom in New Jersey in April 2002 and GroomExpo in Pennsylvania, September 2002). If I cannot afford to attend both, I will choose one this year, the other next year.
3. I will immediately request training materials from SCORE, the local Small Business Development Center, and also sign up for any business and tax workshops sponsored by the state. (At this time, my schedule will not allow me to enroll in a course at the community college, but I will have that option when I have left my current job and am working out of my home-based business exclusively.)

### Marketing
1. Send mailing to all residents who have licensed dogs in my town announcing the opening of my business (March 2002).
2. Advertise my "Grand Opening" in local and regional weekly newspapers (April 2002).
3. Call the telephone company to place my ad in the yellow pages (January 2002).
4. Call my attorney regarding the use of magnetic signs on my van. If he approves, order the sign (January 2002).
5. Compare Web hosting services and select one to support my Internet site. Also contact Web site designer and research software to see which course to take in constructing my site (January 2002).

### Financial Plan
1. Request personal credit reports from three agencies (immediately).
2. Open business checking and savings account at my current bank or other local bank if mine doesn't offer merchant credit card processing (February 2002).
3. Deposit $500 per month into savings account for business capital (ongoing).
4. Consult with loan officer regarding borrowing options and credential updating (January 2002).
5. Call American Express to request merchant account application (January 2002).

**Purchasing Plan**

1. Contact distributors in my area to set up credit account and price grooming equipment (January 2002).
2. Contact manufacturers to compare prices and order from the one with the best prices and credit terms. I can also use one of my business credit cards to finance these purchases (January 2002).
3. Buy grooming equipment and supplies after conducting thorough research and planning purchases on a buying chart (first quarter 2002).
4. When products arrive, inspect for damage before installing at shop.

**Shop Setup**

1. Go to library to check federal records for business name duplication (fourth quarter 2001).
2. Get business registration papers from county and state officials. Complete and return promptly.
3. After inquiring among family and friends, select carpenter, electrician and plumber to convert family room into grooming shop (first quarter 2002).
4. Contact insurance agent to find out coverage needed to take care of my business (first quarter 2002).
5. Purchase telephone with answering machine for business use (February 2002).
6. Contact phone company to make appointment for installation of additional line for business phone (February 2002).
7. Make appointment with health inspector to visit my business (March 2002).

**Expansion**

1. Review plans regarding hiring an assistant after six months.

# Why You Need an Attorney

It's time for you to seek professional help. No, I'm not questioning your sanity for seeking to enter the crazy world of pet care. I just need to point out that a good working relationship with professional advisers—first an attorney, then later an accountant and an insurance agent—will help you organize your business from Day One.

An attorney can make sure you comply with all legal and licensing regulations with your business. You probably don't have time to stay up-to-date on the ever changing laws relating to small businesses. You might need help in trademarking your business name. You might need advice on hiring employees, applying for business loans, and entering into contracts. Don't wait until you slip and fall into a legal pothole. Find a lawyer while your business is still in the planning stages.

If you don't know an attorney in your community who specializes in small businesses, ask around. Your friends or other small-business owners may know just the one for you. You could also contact your state bar association, asking for a small-business attorney referral. You may need to meet with a few before you "click" with the right one for you, someone who seems interested and engaged in your plans, an enthusiastic individual who is easy to talk to and knowledgeable about issues concerning your business.

Consider your attorney as a valuable resource, an important member of your team. Be honest and up front about your financial limitations and ask him or her to keep you up to speed on fees as you proceed. It will give you an added sense of security to know that when in doubt, you can pick up the phone and talk to your lawyer. Your attorney will be on your side. He or she wants you to succeed.

When working with animals, there is always a risk involved. Two dogs can get into a knock-down drag-out fight in a training class. A canine escape artist can make its getaway on a midday walk with the pet sitter. A grooming shop employee can slip in a sudsy puddle by the tub. A dog that is severely matted can emerge from your shop with raw, irritated skin that needs veterinary attention. A pet whose health is compromised by illness or old age can depart this world when it comes to you for a grooming. Scenarios like this are not pleasant to contemplate, but we all face them occasionally.

Your attorney can advise you on liabilities related specifically to your pet care business. He or she should review any release forms having to do with dogs at risk that are left in your care. As pet care businesses become more mainstream, they have also come to the attention of federal regulators, notably the Occupational Safety and Health Administration (OSHA). Your lawyer can advise you on safety regulations, record keeping, and training required for employees to make sure you are in compliance with OSHA regulations. (To find out more, log on to OSHA's Web site at www.osha.gov.)

Because laws regulating businesses vary widely from state to state, your attorney should be consulted to help you meet all of your legal requirements. These will depend on your business structure, but may include employment laws, partnership agreements, licenses, reviewing and negotiating contracts, changes in laws and regulations affecting your business, product liability, and protection of your name and trademark.

# Business Structure Options

One of the most important areas in this shopping list concerns the legal structure your business will take. That structure will outline control of the business, your legal and financial liability, continuity and transferability of the business, and your tax obligations. The legal structure is the foundation upon which you will build your own little empire, so your attorney's advice is essential in this area.

Once you have chosen a name for your business, the way you proceed next will be determined by the type of business structure you plan to set up. The legal structures most small businesses use are the sole proprietorship, the partnership, and the corporation.

## Sole Proprietorship

If you intend to be the head honcho, the one in charge of all decisions, you will probably choose the sole proprietorship, whether or not you eventually plan to hire employees. Most home-based businesses are set up under this category. Within the grooming industry, 88 percent of those starting out are sole proprietors. As the name implies, you will be the only owner. For all intents and purposes, you *are* the business. (The one exception to this rule occurs in community property states, where the sole proprietor's spouse is deemed to have a half interest in the business.)

Under a sole proprietorship, the business itself does not pay taxes. Its profits and losses pass over to your personal income tax returns. With you as the sole owner, the business will be set up and funded through your own personal assets and credit sources. Most sole proprietors work alone, but some employ family members or hire help during busy times. This type of business cannot be transferred to another person or handed down to another. If you die, it would cease operation and pass to your estate.

One of the reasons most entrepreneurs choose this form is that it is the easiest way to set up a business. There will be some fees involved in obtaining your business licenses from your local authorities and for your business name registration. Attorney's fees will be less than for other types of business because there is less preparation involved. You do not need to file any applications with government agencies. If you have no employees, you won't even need to apply for a federal tax identification number.

The main disadvantage of a sole proprietorship is that the responsibility for everything that happens within the business belongs to you and you alone. As the sole owner, you have unlimited liability in the event of damages, lawsuits, or other financial losses. All of your personal assets (home, car, bank accounts, etc.) are subject to seizure if the business fails. In assessing the risk factors, you need to consider the type of services you plan to provide, the losses that could be incurred, and the extent of your personal assets. It sounds pretty scary, as if you're stepping out on a tightrope without a net, but if you have sufficient capital to see you through the early days, enough insurance to protect you from losses, and sound legal advice, you will probably see it as a risk worth taking. After all, that risk-taker component is part and parcel of the entrepreneurial spirit!

If you plan to hire employees right out of the gate, you will need that all-important federal tax identification number. The same is true if you choose to set up under the partnership structure or as a corporation.

## Partnership

A partnership is like a sole proprietorship that has two or more owners. There are several variations of this form. The two most common are general and limited partnerships. A general partnership can be formed by a simple oral agreement between two or more persons, but a legal partnership, drawn up with the help of an attorney, is a far better way to go. The drafting of this formal agreement is the major difference in setting up a partnership as opposed to a sole proprietorship. True, it does involve another expenditure for legal services, and you may be asking yourself if that step is really necessary. You and your prospective partner have a trusting relationship and similar goals—what could possibly go wrong? (Happy honeymooners think this way too.)

The partnership agreement is a tool for handling problems when they crop up. Like what? you ask. Call me a wet blanket if you will, but let me count the ways. The agreement should cover *(a)* the type of business you are setting up, *(b)* the amount invested by each partner, *(c)* how the profits or losses will be divided, *(d)* each partner's compensation, *(e)* the distribution of assets in case the business dissolves, *(f)* the time limit or duration of the partnership, *(g)* a dispute settlement clause, *(i)* restrictions of authority and expenditures, and *(j)* settlement in case of the death or incapacitation of a partner.

Be smart and get it in writing. Think of it as a prenuptial agreement if you like! With the agreement in place, there will be a reduced risk of misunderstandings about authority, responsibility, control, and the share each party will have regarding profits and losses, depending on what they put in and take out of the business. Each partner is legally considered an "agent" of the business and is legally liable for the actions and liabilities of the other partner, so this is not a matter to be taken casually. In some instances, you can be held liable for your partner's activities even if they occur outside the partnership.

If any partners are added in the future, a new agreement must be drawn up. Like the sole proprietorship, the partnership normally requires no government applications, just business licenses.

A partnership really is like a marriage. In fact, many married couples own their businesses as equal legal partners. As in a marriage, before you recite those vows or sign your name on the dotted line, ask yourself if you can work with this person in harmony day in and day out. Do you have unlimited trust in each other's honesty and good judgment? Are you willing to stake your personal assets on his or her actions?

Like a marriage, a partnership offers some advantages. It allows you to start out with more resources and offers more man-hours to devote to the new venture. You feel as if you have more of a support system in place. In a seven-day-a-week business like pet sitting, this is no small consideration. Unlike a one-person show, you always have a backup. In setting up a partnership, personal trust and a shared commitment to the success of your new venture are key considerations. It's like a bicycle built for two. It only works well if both riders do the pedaling.

## Corporation

A corporation is a legal entity, separate and distinct from its owners. It is the most complex of the business structures we are dealing with and the most costly to organize. It must be chartered to do business by the state in which it is located. Its owners are the stockholders who contribute capital by buying shares in the corporation. They are compensated by dividends, a portion of the corporation's profits. Those with the most shares control the corporation. With control of 51 percent of the stock, a person or group is able to make policy decisions. A corporation's owner can also be an employee and draw a taxable salary.

The stockholders elect a board of directors to run the corporation and act in their interests. In this way, the business owners delegate responsibility and control for day-to-day business operations. Control is exercised through regular meetings of the board of directors as well as annual stockholders' meetings. Strict records and minutes of every meeting must be kept to document all decisions by the board of directors.

The corporation's life is unlimited. If you die, it is easily transferred to another person with no effect on the business (except, perhaps, closing down for the day to give you a proper sendoff!).

The major difference between a corporation and a sole proprietorship or partnership is that as a separate entity, the corporation is liable for its debts. While officers and members of the board of directors are responsible for their actions and can be fired or voted out, with few exceptions their responsibility does not extend to risking their personal assets. The stockholders are liable only to the extent of their investment. This limitation on liability is the major reason most businesses become incorporated.

For small businesses, the main disadvantages to incorporating boil down to time, expense, and red tape. To become incorporated, you must draft bylaws, submit articles of incorporation for approval by the state agency that charters corporations, issue capital stock and record its ownership, and pay fees for incorporating that can amount to several hundred dollars.

Once you become incorporated, you must adhere strictly to legal requirements, such as making all decisions through your board of directors, conducting regular meetings of the board as well as annual stockholders' meetings, and filing annual reports with the state. In addition, your tax requirements become more complicated. The corporation itself must pay corporate income taxes on its profits, and the stockholders must pay income taxes on the remaining profits, which are distributed to them in the form of dividends.

One type of corporation, the "S" corporation, is gaining in popularity. It presents less of a hassle to the small-business owner. In terms of legal requirements, it is similar to any other corporation, but its profits pass through to stockholders in direct proportion to their number of shares. In this way, it operates more like a partnership. It does not need to pay corporate income taxes. It files tax returns, but they are for informational purposes only. For the small operation, this form offers tax advantages plus the protection of liability not available to the sole proprietor or the partnership. If you are seriously considering incorporating your business, this is an option you should discuss with your attorney and your accountant.

Although sole proprietorships and partnerships present more of a risk to the budding entrepreneur, they continue to be the dominant legal structures for small startups. They present a relatively safe and reasonable option, provided you have done your homework on adhering to zoning laws, having sufficient capital to launch your new venture, securing your business name, and insuring yourself against catastrophic losses and unavoidable injuries. All these provisions plus the training to perform well in your new occupation should put you in a favorable position to start your business. True, you are not launching the *Queen Mary*, but you need to know your small craft is seaworthy as you set sail on this exciting new voyage.

# Chapter Four

# Creating Your Workspace

Now comes the fun part, putting in place the doors and walls, the cosmetic touches and the shiny new equipment that will give your new business a home of its own. This is where the dream takes shape and becomes a reality. But before you open your doors and invite the world inside, make sure you are in compliance with your local zoning ties and have taken steps to ensure that your presence will not present a problem to your neighbors.

## Are You Zoned for Business?

Your town's zoning officer is one of the first people you should talk to when you are considering a home-based business. In many small towns, this person is the building inspector. Zoning laws are unique to every town and city. They are also subject to interpretation by the local powers that be, so what is allowable in your hometown may not be permitted in mine.

Within each town's zoning bylaws is a chart called the Schedule of Use Regulations. It lists the various zoning districts and spells out in great detail just what is allowed and what is not permitted within each category. The street—or portion of the street—where you live may be zoned as residential only or mixed use (residential and professional or commercial use). My town has nine different zoning districts: Residential A; Residential B; General Residence; Rural, Parks, Schools, Recreation and Conservation; Business; Central Business District; Limited Manufacturing; and Industrial. A home office is usually allowed in any residential zone, but you can not assume that it is.

For the aspiring pet sitter whose business operation would not bring traffic or animals to the location, there should be no problem. You would usually be allowed the same usage under the umbrella that allows a doctor, dentist, lawyer, real estate broker, or insurance agent to have a business office in the home. The law stipulates that office use would need to be secondary to the property's primary use as a dwelling. It is often required that the external appearance of the building should conform to the residential character of the neighborhood. An "accessory sign" identifying your business is permissible in most cases.

The same regulations would apply to a professional obedience trainer operating out of the home. However, if you are a groomer envisioning a home salon or a trainer who plans to hold classes at your home, you need to investigate any laws pertaining to the number of persons gathering for the purpose of instruction and the number of vehicles allowed on the premises at any one time. Restrictive parking regulations have put some home-based groomers and trainers out of business.

In general, operating a home business within a residential zone in which clients would come to the home for services requires a special permit or a variance from the specified use regulations. In urban or suburban areas, getting such a permit could be a long shot. In rural areas, zoning regulations are not usually as strict. Even if it looks like your plans would conflict with the zoning ordinances, maintain a positive and professional attitude. You may wish to explore your options in seeking a variance or changing the zoning regulations. When you contact your local zoning department, also ask if a home occupation permit is required to do business out of your home.

If your plans would violate the zoning bylaws, find out if there have been similar situations in which a person was successful in obtaining a zoning change or variance. Carefully document the information, getting answers to such questions as: What are the procedures for pursuing such a change? Will I need a lawyer? How long does the process usually take from petition to decision?

Bear in mind that establishing a business is beneficial to the community. As a local merchant, you will be paying taxes at the local, state and federal level. Document your membership in local business organizations and your current or planned areas of community involvement. Be prepared to discuss issues such as traffic, noise, and good housekeeping.

To obtain a special permit, a hearing would be held before the zoning board. All abutters to your property would be notified so they could attend to be informed of your plans, ask questions, and possibly voice their objections. The board would then take the matter under advisement before issuing its decision. You usually don't need a lawyer at this hearing, but it is wise to present your case properly. You will need legal help as you proceed with your plans, so you might as well involve your attorney in this vital stage of development as well.

If your request is turned down, the zoning board's decision can be appealed in court. Again, you may choose to represent yourself at this juncture, but I would recommend the services of an attorney. Knowledge of the local laws and your options is necessary as you proceed with your plans.

Of course, there are many home-based businesses of all stripes that operate without knowledge of the laws governing their existence but ignorance is not bliss, nor is it an excuse for an illegal operation. The risk involved is not worth it. A written complaint from a disgruntled neighbor or a business rival can lead directly to a cease-and-desist order, effectively shutting you down.

It would be devastating to invest the time and money in setting up your home-based business only to discover that you are operating in violation of the law. Finding out the zoning laws of your community is a necessary step in turning your dream into a reality.

## Licenses and Permits

Once you have satisfied the zoning requirements and have been issued a special permit—or in some localities, a home occupancy permit—by your local or county zoning department, you will need to find out if a license to do business is also required. Most communities issue such a license for a small fee, usually requiring that it be displayed at your place of business. If the business is to be opened within city limits, the city would issue the license; if outside a city, the county may be the licensing agent. You can find out what is needed by contacting the city, town, or county offices in your area or by going to the SBA Web site specializing in businesses startups: www.sba.gov/starting/regulations.html. This section offers links to state Web sites and home pages where the information you need is only a click away.

A word of clarification: This license to do business has nothing to do with the type of services you plan to provide. It is simply a stamp of approval that you operate a business. Issuing it also generates tax revenue for your city, town, or county.

Unlike barbers, hairstylists, or day care providers for children, in most states pet care professionals are not required to have specific licenses to perform their services. (New Jersey requires that pet groomers become licensed to handle pesticides.) Through industry associations and organizations, however, voluntary accreditation and certification exist in all three occupations. This is something you may wish to look into in the future, as a mark of achievement and to boost your self-confidence.

A groomer, obedience trainer, or pet sitter who has earned certification or accreditation has completed a course of study and mastered certain skills, passing written examinations and demonstrations of those skills. Having such an official title to feature in your advertising and a certificate to hang on your wall is impressive to your clients and a great source of pride to you.

As pet care occupations become more professional and recognized as part of the mainstream, it is possible that we could see legislation requiring licensing in the future. Pet care professionals who have already proven their ability and motivation by obtaining certification or accreditation within their field may have the advantage of being covered by a "grandfather clause" if and when licensing laws do change.

Within the grooming industry, feelings about mandatory licensing are mixed. A 1999 on-line survey conducted by Petgroomer.com indicated that 55 percent of professional groomers favored vocational licensing; only 8 percent were against it. The rest indicated that they either had no interest in the subject or lacked sufficient information to make a decision. For the time being, licensing requirements remain the subject of heated discussions within the world of pet care providers.

## Being a Good Neighbor

Once you've gotten your permits and licenses in order, you'll probably feel like heaving a big sigh of relief. Go ahead—you're entitled! You have cleared some hurdles on your path to success but there may be some other potholes on the road ahead. To be specific: What's the status of your Good Neighbor Policy?

If your pet care business will be bringing clients to your home, there could be a potential problem right where you live. If yours is a grooming business, parked cars blocking the street and driveways, increased traffic, dog poop on the sidewalk, or the sound of a roomful of dogs competing to see who can bark the loudest could all spell trouble. A series of irate phone calls to the police department or the board of health could soon close down your business.

To address traffic and parking concerns at your home-based grooming shop, you could stagger drop-off and pickup times so they will not become a problem.

To combat problems underfoot, meticulous dedication to keeping your property and the adjacent streets and sidewalks free of dog droppings is an absolute must. Dog feces not only produces unsavory sights and smells, it can also harbor parasites transferable to small children who play in the area. Be vigilant. No matter what the weather, all outdoor areas need to be patrolled and picked up on a daily basis.

After all my years in grooming, it still amazes me that dog owners feel free to let Rover relieve himself outside my front door, then hop in the car and go merrily on their way. One way to address the situation is to have a basket of free plastic "poop bags" on your counter with a little sign telling clients that these are provided for their use—and thanking them for helping you to be a good neighbor. Positive reinforcement works as well on people as it does on their pets.

Noise control can be handled before you open your doors by soundproofing your workspace during the construction process. If dogs will be on the premises for grooming, training, or occasional visits, you should also have a big enough area to walk them and work them. Unfortunately, horrific dog attacks continue to make the headlines and the evening news. Although you may not envision such nasty four-legged patrons, your neighbors' fears and their desire to protect themselves and their children must be addressed. Your backyard, or at least part of it, should be fenced.

## Your Home Office

So your home-based business is a go. Now where are you going to put your office? Organization should be your watchword here; a pile of papers on the dining room table and a shoebox full of cards in the dresser drawer just won't do. Your office needs and deserves a home of its own.

A spare bedroom, a basement room, a heated garage, or even a section of a room partitioned off with a movable screen could fill the bill. If no extra room is available, it's time to do some serious rearranging. Can you sell or store some furniture to open up some space? Can you do some remodeling to make room for your new base of operation?

Your office will be "command central," the place where you devise strategies, conduct interviews, receive prospective clients, store your records, set up your computer and phone system. It is the heart of your business from which you connect to the outside world, and so it should be well organized, attractive, and private.

Beyond the highly attractive fact that you don't need to pay rent for this space, there are tangible tax advantages to operating your business from home. Tax laws do change, so it's always a good idea to check with your attorney and/or accountant ahead of time, but in general, the IRS home office rules state that a home office deduction is allowable if you use an area in your home exclusively and regularly for business. To have current tax information sent to you, contact the IRS (800–829–1040 or www.irs.gov) to make sure your home office operation falls within specified guidelines.

## Drawing the Lines

You are well on your way to establishing your legal boundaries—how about your personal privacy zone? One of the greatest challenges you will face in operating a home-based business is drawing that fine line between your personal and professional lives. If you are a workaholic Type A person, this may mean a struggle to "leave work" and a corresponding lack of private time for yourself and your family. The more laid-back individual might be tempted to take too casual an approach, going in late and leaving early, finding lots of excuses to avoid getting down to business. After all, you're the boss, and every day can be casual day. Your new commute involves stepping across the hall.

In either case, self-discipline is the only answer. In starting your new business, you have chosen a career you love. The workaholic must draw the demarcation line by first installing an answering machine and voice mail. Rule Number One: Your personal phone number and your business number are not interchangeable! For the potential slacker, it's time to tone up your work ethic. You need to be relentless about keeping a schedule. You also need to think of your office as a bona fide workplace with its own hours. As far as distractions go, you need to make family and friends aware that even though you're wearing those comfy slippers, you really are at work!

# Action Checklist for Your Business

1. Choose a name and/or logo for your business then check at library and at secretary of state's office to make sure they are not already trademarked. . . . . . . . . . . . . . . . ☐

2. Make sure all permits are in order. Check with zoning board and health inspector to determine existing restrictions. Contact lawyer if you need to schedule hearing to go before zoning board for a special permit. . . . . . . . . ☐

3. Line up your advertising with yellow pages and local newspapers. (See Chapter 14.) . . . . . . . . . . . . . . . . . . . . . . . . . . . ☐

4. Visit other pet care professionals in your area (veterinarians, kennels, shelters, other groomers, trainers, and pet sitters) to introduce yourself and swap business cards. . . . . . . . . . . . . . . . . . . . . . . . . . . . . . . . . . . . . . . . . . . . . . ☐

5. Apply for a D-U-N-S number from Dun & Bradstreet to help with credit references. . . . . . . . . . . . . . . . . . . . . . . . . . . . . . . ☐

6. Complete the setup of your office area and workspace, including installation of phone, computer lines, and signage. . . . . . . . . . . . . . . . . . . . . . . . . . . . . . . . . . . . . . . . . . . . . ☐

7. Prepare a complete list of products and equipment you will need to start your business. Research prices on new and used equipment. Visit distributors and order catalogs. . . . . . . . . . . . . . . . . . . . . . . . . . . . . . . . . . . . . . . ☐

8. Set up accounts with distributors and suppliers for equipment and products needed. . . . . . . . . . . . . . . . . . . . . . . . . . ☐

9. As deliveries arrive, check the invoices against your order. Make sure goods and equipment are not damaged. Arrange products on shelves in workspace. . . . . . . . . . ☐

10. Start booking appointments! . . . . . . . . . . . . . . . . . . . . . . . . . . . . . ☐

# Chapter Five

# By the Numbers: Accounting and Taxes

Becoming a business owner means that you will wear a lot of hats. Being the boss requires a major shift in your mindset. No longer will you look to someone else to tell you what to do. You will always need to focus your attention on the bottom line. When it comes to the roles of manager, employee, public relations specialist, customer service representative, quality control person, financial director, and supervisor, guess what? The buck stops with you!

It does sound intimidating, but to help you plan ahead and sleep nights, professional help from an accountant will prove to be a sound investment as you approach this major transition in your life.

## Choosing an Accountant

Unless you are a bookkeeper or an accountant yourself, this is another expert you will need to add to your team. One thing I have noticed about pet care professionals in general is that they would rather watch paint dry than delve into the financial aspects of their businesses. I hate to generalize, but some of the most wonderful animal care people I know do not have a head for business. They are so enamored of their profession that they would just as soon ignore the financial side, but as people in the pet care industry continue to become legitimate players in the business world, it's time for this to change. The sad fact remains that hundreds of pet care businesses fold every year because their owners did not plan ahead and get the expert advice they needed before they joined the ranks of the self-employed. Their dream boats crashed upon the rocks of hard cold reality and financial ignorance.

You may think of yourself as a small potato, but you still need a fully qualified financial professional to help you navigate the waters of taxes, payroll, record keeping, and planning for your future, both personal and professional. You need someone who specializes in small businesses. Your accountant will help set up your books and obtain the necessary tax identification numbers. He or she will save you time by providing the tax forms you need to file and conform to your legal obligations.

With the ever changing tax laws and the transition to computerization in all things financial, it's important to find an accountant who is up-to-date on current laws and technology. Here's a hint: If he or she is still using a pad of paper and a calculator, this person may not be the one for you! Look for someone who takes advantage of educational seminars, professional publications, and other continuing education opportunities in the field.

You can find an accountant by asking other small-business owners for a recommendation or simply by looking in the yellow pages. You could also ask your attorney or your banker, or contact a state accounting association for a referral. A likely candidate might be found teaching a course at the evening adult education program at your local high school. Interview a few people before you make your choice. You need a person with whom you can communicate well, someone who has the patience and commitment to answer all of your questions, even if you feel silly asking them. (Get over your embarrassment—the only stupid question is the one you don't ask!)

Accounting costs and levels of expertise vary, so don't be shy about requesting fees, credentials, and references. Make sure this is an individual you can trust and that you feel you are being treated with respect. If you find yourself being ignored or feeling like the low man on the totem pole when it comes to information or deadline notification, it's time to find another accountant.

A certified public accountant (CPA) is a person who has passed stringent state tests to obtain a license and a title. This individual can perform audits and issue financial statements. There are public accountants practicing who have not yet gotten their state licenses, and there are certified masters of accountancy (CMA) who have a master's degree in their field. Your accountant should be an enrolled agent (EA), licensed by the IRS to prepare tax returns.

As a cost-cutting strategy, some budding entrepreneurs prefer to employ both an accountant and a bookkeeper. The bookkeeper keeps the books in order and reconciles bank statements, then those materials are delivered to an accountant at tax time. Your accountant should keep you informed about filing quarterly estimated income tax payments, both state and federal, in a timely manner.

Your accountant will work with you to establish accounting and reporting systems, cash projections, tax planning, and financial strategies for the future. He or she will be your guide through a jungle of red tape. As your business matures, you will call upon your accountant for guidance in helping to meet your financial objectives, seeking his or her assistance with strategic planning, cash management, cost reduction, and management information systems as well as retirement or profit-sharing programs.

Your accountant will format your business information into monthly, quarterly and annual financial statements. Your profit and loss statement will track your income according to bank deposits and list your expenses by category. When the grand total of operating expenses is subtracted from the amount of money generated by your business, you will arrive at your bottom line, the profit or loss incurred by your business for that period. In addition to this record of your income, the accountant will prepare a balance sheet showing your current assets, liabilities, and equity, a general picture of your overall financial health apart from your ongoing cash flow. At year's end, he or she will also prepare an annual financial statement for your business, a valuable tool in helping you to measure your progress and plan ahead. You will want to sit down and go over this data together. Your financial records are open to review by tax authorities, so keeping them accurate and up-to-date is extremely important.

Down the road, complete and orderly financial records will provide you with the data you need if you wish to expand your business, seek a business loan, decide to purchase another piece of property for your business, or make other investments with its financial proceeds. It seems far-fetched at this stage of the game, but if someday you are considering mergers or acquisitions or you need an appraisal to sell your business, you will need to turn to your accountant for expert advice.

If you are seeking a loan, either for startup or for expansion in the future, you will need to have a business plan detailing every aspect of your business to show the bank. (See Creating a Business Plan in Chapter 3.) Your accountant will help you with the financial aspects of this plan so you will be fully prepared.

## The Importance of Keeping Records

There's much more to running your pet care business than grooming, training, or pet sitting for your furry customers. You need to document every expenditure you make as well as every payment you receive for your services. Each month, these figures will be transferred to your accounting ledger or entered on your computer spreadsheets.

I've heard it said that when you're in business for yourself, your whole life is a write-off. Your accountant and the IRS would adamantly disagree with that statement. Even though yours is a home-based operation, it is important to keep your personal and professional accounts separate. To succeed as your own boss, you will need to become a stickler for record keeping.

When you have no one to answer to but yourself it's easy to get sloppy about the crossover between personal and business expenditures. The good news is that a surprising number of the day-to-day expenses you will incur will indeed be legitimate business deductions. When in doubt, ask your accountant. He or she is paid to keep you on the straight and narrow so you will stay out of trouble with Uncle Sam.

## Will You Need a Receipt for That?

The first rule of thumb is always get a receipt. If your job involves driving to service your clients, you need a receipt every time you put gas in your tank. You need all receipts related to automobile maintenance. Keeping your vehicle presentable is also a business expense. Get a receipt when you go to the car wash or have your van detailed. If you pay for parking or pay a toll in the course of business travel, ask for a receipt or push the button dispenser at the toll booth or parking garage and get it yourself.

If you buy stamps for business mailings, including routine bill paying, get a receipt. Every item you buy at the office supply store for your business needs to be tracked with receipts, even if it's just a box of paper clips! Yes, it's always worth the hassle. It's amazing how fast those little expenses add up.

Receipts need to be kept for tuition for courses and seminars you take to develop your business skills, travel and meal expenses when you attend such functions, promotional materials including greeting cards and holiday cards, uniforms you wear to work, and those T-shirts you had printed with your logo on them. If you hold a staff meeting and get bagels and coffee or pizza and soft drinks for your staff, get a receipt. These are bona fide business meetings.

Your annual party or a business-sponsored trip to the bowling alley or amusement park for your hardworking employees is also a legitimate write-off. Your family excursion to Disney World, on the other hand, is not! Check with your accountant about allowable deductions for meals and entertaining. Outlandish expenditures in any category will throw up a red flag to the IRS. You need to ensure your actions are completely legal from Day One.

Your daily planner probably has a handy little pocket for storing your receipts. If you always put them in the same place, it will do wonders for your record keeping. If your tax returns are ever audited, the IRS will require receipts as proof of business activity. You also need them to track your expenses. Your paper trail will help you to run a profitable business.

## Your Balance Sheet

Your balance sheet should be prepared on a monthly basis. It will give you an overall picture of what your business is worth at any given time by documenting your assets (cash, inventory, and equipment), liabilities (whom you owe and how much), and your net worth (the difference between your assets and liabilities). It is an important document to maintain not just for your own knowledge but as part of the financial package that may be needed down the road. Accurate records will be helpful in convincing outside investors and banks of the soundness of your business should you ever seek capital or a business loan for expansion.

The sample balance sheet shows how the asset accounts are documented, including accumulated depreciation. Any major piece of equipment you purchase for

### Know Your Numbers

Even if you hire a bookkeeper or accountant to keep track of your financial paperwork and reconcile your checkbook, having a basic knowledge of bookkeeping yourself is extremely helpful for several reasons:

- If you cannot afford a bookkeeper or the one you have quits or moves away, you will need to keep track of your own records.
- Leaving everything up to the bookkeeper is not a responsible way to run a business. You should know how your business is doing, otherwise you could be susceptible to fraud or embezzlement. It's just good common sense to track your own growth and the health of your bottom line.
- Taking a night school course in bookkeeping in your local adult education program or community college will help build your confidence as a businessperson. Knowledge is power!

**Expense Analysis Spreadsheet**
**Fur Magnolias Grooming**

**For the period ending October 31, 2002**

| Description | May | June | July | Aug | Sept | Oct | TOTALS |
|---|---|---|---|---|---|---|---|
| **Grooming supplies:** | | | | | | | |
| Shampoos | | | | | | | |
| Conditioner | | | | | | | |
| Cologne | | | | | | | |
| Coat sprays | | | | | | | |
| Ear cleaner | | | | | | | |
| Ear powder | | | | | | | |
| Styptic powder | | | | | | | |
| Ribbon | | | | | | | |
| Cotton rolls | | | | | | | |
| **Grooming tools:** | | | | | | | |
| Scissors | | | | | | | |
| Blades | | | | | | | |
| Brushes | | | | | | | |
| Combs and rakes | | | | | | | |
| Nail trimmers | | | | | | | |
| Forceps | | | | | | | |
| **Advertising** | | | | | | | |
| **Subscriptions** | | | | | | | |
| **Telephone** | | | | | | | |
| **Office supplies:** | | | | | | | |
| Computer paper | | | | | | | |
| Printing cartridges | | | | | | | |
| Envelopes | | | | | | | |
| **Internet access service** | | | | | | | |
| **Travel:** | | | | | | | |
| Tolls/parking | | | | | | | |
| Meals | | | | | | | |
| Gas | | | | | | | |
| Hotels | | | | | | | |
| **Bank service charges** | | | | | | | |
| **Merchant account fees** | | | | | | | |
| **Education** | | | | | | | |
| **Computer software** | | | | | | | |
| **TOTALS** | | | | | | | |

**Balance Sheet**                                    **June 30, 2002**
**Fur Magnolias Grooming**

## Assets

| | | |
|---|---|---|
| Cash | | $6,670 |
| Accounts receivable | | 0 |
| Inventory | | $500 |
| Office equipment | $800 | |
| Less accumulated depreciation | $80 | $720 |
| Grooming equipment | $2,450 | |
| Less accumulated depreciation | $245 | $2,205 |
| **Total assets** | | **$10,095** |

## Liabilities

| | | |
|---|---|---|
| Accounts payable | | $575 |
| Loan payable | | $135 |

## Owner's Equity

| | | |
|---|---|---|
| Jane Smith, capital, June 1, 2002 | $6,000 | |
| Net income, June | $1,650 | |
| Subtotal | $7,650 | |
| Less withdrawals | $250 | |
| Jane Smith, capital, June 30, 2002 | | $7,400 |
| **Total liabilities and owner's equity** | | **$8,110** |

## Notes

Office equipment:
  printer, $300
  phone, $100
  cash register, $400

your business—a computer, a printer, a dryer, or an electric table, for example—can be depreciated over a five-year period (60 months). In the example provided, Fur Magnolias Grooming Salon purchased a printer, a phone, and a cash register for $800, as well as dryers, tubs, and grooming tables for $2,450. Depreciation on the office equipment is $13.33 per month ($800 ÷ 60 months) or $79.98 through June ($13.33 x 6 months), rounded up to $80, the nearest whole number. Depreciation on the grooming equipment amounts to $40.83 per month ($2,450 ÷ 60 months) or $244.98 through June ($40.83 x 6 months), rounded up to $245, the nearest whole dollar. These values would be deducted from your assets.

The owner's equity section shows how a cash withdrawal is deducted from the capital account during the month. It also records the owner's income. But it's only part of the picture. The balance sheet measures the overall health of your business, the assets minus the liabilities. With assets of $10,095 and liabilities of $710, Jane's balance looks pretty healthy. But like all shrewd business owners, she needs to keep a healthy amount in reserve as a financial security blanket.

## Your Income Statement

In running a business, it's not how much you take in, it's how much you keep! Your income statement provides you with this information by detailing the month's total revenue and expenses to arrive at your net income. You can make your income statement as general or as detailed by category as you want it to be. Ultimately, you arrive at your net income after deducting all operating expenses from the revenue your business took in.

Jane's accountant arrives at her monthly bottom line (profit or loss) using a detailed income statement in which every expenditure she made during the month constitutes a line item. For the month of June, Jane made a profit of $2,009.

## Cash Flow Projection

A cash flow projection is an estimate of all cash you expect to earn and spend during a specific period of time. This projection will help you with the delicate balancing act of collecting payment for your products and services and managing your credit before paying your bills—to prevent the dreaded negative cash flow that can result if you do not plan ahead. As you begin your business, anticipating your cash flow involves a lot of guesswork; once you have become established, you

**Income Statement**
**Fur Magnolias Grooming**

**For the month ending June 30, 2002**

**Revenue**

| | |
|---|---|
| Sales (grooming) | $2,400 |
| Interest earned | $20 |
| **Total revenue** | **$2,420** |

**Operating Expenses**

| | | |
|---|---|---|
| Selling expenses: | | |
| Cost of products/supplies | $120 | |
| Advertising | $80 | |
| Total selling expenses | | $200 |
| | | |
| General and administrative expenses: | | |
| Telephone | $48 | |
| Depreciation of office and grooming | | |
| equipment per month | $74 | |
| Other expenses | $89 | |
| Total general and administrative | | |
| expenses | | $211 |
| **Total operating expenses** | | **$411** |

| | |
|---|---|
| **Net income** | **$2,009** |

will have a better handle on how much you can expect to bring in on a monthly basis, which seasons are busiest, and which ones are usually slower. Then you can plan your expenditures accordingly.

# Taxing Issues

Chances are you've been a tax-paying citizen for years, but once you start your own business, you will need to start paying a different set of taxes to both the state and federal governments. These taxes will be determined by the type of business structure you are starting. Let's look at the list of pertinent taxing issues.

## Federal Identification Number

If your business is a sole proprietorship with employees, a partnership, or a corporation with or without employees, the first thing you must do is obtain a federal identification number for federal and state tax purposes. This is sometimes referred to as an EIN (Employer Identification Number). To obtain this number, you must file Form SS-4, Application for Employer Identification Number, with the IRS. This form can be downloaded directly from the IRS Web site at www.irs.gov, or you can call the IRS at (800) 829–1040 to request one. In the states of Massachusetts, Connecticut, Maine, New Hampshire, Vermont, Rhode Island, and parts of New York, you may fax your completed form to the IRS at (978) 474–9774, or you may handle the entire matter over the phone by calling (978) 474–9717.

Sole proprietorships without employees are not required to have this Federal Identification Number. Instead, the owners can use their Social Security numbers for business tax purposes.

## Sales Taxes

Unless your state does not have a sales tax, if you are going to sell retail products along with your services you will need to pay a sales tax on these goods to the state. To do this, you must register with the State Department of Revenue as a sales tax vendor, receive a sales tax permit, and file the appropriate returns. You will be legally required to maintain detailed financial records of everything you sell. With very few exceptions, services that you perform—like grooming, training, or pet sitting—are not taxed.

**Six-Month Cash Flow Projection**
**Fur Magnolias Grooming**

May 2002–October 2002

| | May | June | July | Aug | Sept | Oct | TOTAL |
|---|---|---|---|---|---|---|---|
| **INCOME:** | | | | | | | |
| Grooming | 2,000 | 3,000 | 2,500 | 3,000 | 3,000 | 3,000 | 16,500 |
| Retail | 400 | 500 | 500 | 400 | 400 | 400 | 2,600 |
| **TOTAL INCOME** | **2,400** | **3,500** | **3,000** | **3,400** | **3,400** | **3,400** | **19,100** |
| **EXPENSES:** | | | | | | | |
| Rent | | | | | | | |
| Supplies | 225 | 150 | 125 | 150 | 150 | 125 | 925 |
| Utilities | 75 | 75 | 75 | 75 | 75 | 75 | 450 |
| Telephone | 200 | 200 | 200 | 200 | 200 | 200 | 1,200 |
| Advertising | 50 | 50 | 50 | 50 | 50 | 50 | 300 |
| Accounting | 60 | 60 | 60 | 60 | 60 | 60 | 360 |
| Legal | | | | | | | |
| Permits and licenses | | | | | | | |
| Repairs and maintenance | | | | | 200 | | 200 |
| Laundry | 10 | 10 | 10 | 10 | 10 | 10 | 60 |
| Seminars | | | | | | | |
| Dues and subscriptions | | 35 | | | | | 35 |
| Office expenses | 50 | 20 | 20 | 20 | 20 | 20 | 150 |
| Bank fees | 8 | 8 | 8 | 8 | 8 | 8 | 48 |
| Depreciation | | | | | | | |
| Postage | 10 | 10 | 10 | 10 | 10 | 10 | 60 |
| **TOTAL EXPENSES** | **688** | **618** | **558** | **583** | **783** | **558** | **3,788** |
| **PROFIT** | **1,712** | **2,882** | **2,442** | **2,817** | **2,617** | **2,842** | **15,312** |

In my state of Massachusetts, I must pay a monthly sales tax of 5 percent on everything I sell, with the exception of clothing (for people) valued at less than $175 per item. T-shirts, hats, and sweatshirts for my human customers fall well below that ceiling, but interestingly, dog apparel *is* a taxable item. The payment requirements in this state vary with the amount of products you sell. If you collect less than $100 from the sales of goods in a year, you need to file annually. If your sales receipts total between $101 and $1,200, you need to file quarterly. Because I usually have sales above this figure, I must file monthly, twenty days after the end of the filing period (e.g., February 20 for the month of January). Software is now available from the state for electronic filing.

To avoid paying retail sales taxes on goods that you are buying for resale, you will also need to obtain a resale certificate. You need to be a registered sales/use vendor to get this exemption. Your state Web site will tell you how to obtain this, or you can phone the customer service bureau at your State Department of Revenue to request the necessary forms. Click on your state to find out about how to conform to sales tax laws that apply to you at www.sba.gov/starting/regulations. html. A more comprehensive guide to all of your state's business tax requirements is also available at www.sba.gov/hotlist/statetaxhomepages.html.

The IRS also offers a publication called *Your Business Tax Kit*, which includes data and forms for obtaining your EIN and a tax guide for small businesses. Call its Forms and Publications Department at (800) 829–3676 or drop by your local IRS office to request a copy.

## Income Taxes

Federal income tax is a pay-as-you-go tax. An employee usually has income tax withheld from his or her pay. Our federal government receives 70 percent of its personal income tax revenues this way. As a business owner, an employer is no longer withholding these taxes for you. Now the responsibility for paying them will shift entirely to you. In most cases, you must make quarterly estimated tax payments if you expect to owe at least $1,000 in taxes for the year, after subtracting any credits due and income taxes withheld on your behalf from any sources of employment. Actually, you will probably find that the requirement of paying income taxes on a quarterly basis is a lot less stressful than having to come up with a whole year's tax payment at once. From now on, you will pay both your federal and state taxes on a quarterly basis.

Like all other income-earning individuals, businesses and/or their owners are required to pay taxes on their income. The types of taxes they need to pay and the forms required vary according to the business's structures. If you are a sole proprietor, you are required to file estimated tax payments for income you will draw from your business. Because you and the business are one and the same, this means paying taxes on your profit or your bottom line. If your accountant is calculating correctly, your quarterly income taxes to both the state and the federal government should provide a pretty close assessment of the annual taxes that will be due, so when April 15 rolls around, you will not be floored by a big tax burden.

You will now need to file the "long form" when paying your annual income tax. In addition to this Form 1040, you will need to file a Schedule C (profit and loss itemization) from your business. If you are a groomer, part of this may include a deduction for depreciation on your equipment as well.

> **Your Taxes Are Your Business**
>
> As far as your business income is concerned, the form you use when paying your taxes will depend on its legal structure. Here are some general guidelines:
>
> - If your business has only one owner, it will automatically be considered a sole proprietorship unless you elect to be treated as a corporation. A sole proprietorship files Form 1040, U.S. Individual Income Tax Return, and will include Form 1040, Schedule C, Profit or Loss from Business. As previously stated, your business income is treated as your personal income.
> - If your business is an S Corporation, Form 1120, U.S. Corporation Income Tax Return, is filed according to the same deadline as unincorporated companies, by April 15.
> - C Corporations must file their annual corporate returns within two and a half months after the close of their fiscal year.
> - If your business has two or more owners, it will automatically be considered a partnership. A partnership files Form 1065, U.S. Partnership Return of Income, by April 15.

## Social Security

You will also need to file a Schedule SE (Social Security payments for yourself, which you now need to make as a self-employed taxpayer). If you are a sole proprietor with no employees, your Social Security number will be used when you file your tax documents. Everybody must pay Social Security taxes, but yours will now be made through this Self-Employment Tax. You will need to file Schedule SE quarterly as well.

When you file your annual income tax return, the total of those quarterly Social Security payments you have made previously will be deducted from your final tax assessment. Currently, the self-employment tax rate on net earnings is 15.3 percent (12.4 percent Social Security tax plus 2.9 percent Medicare tax). Quarterly estimated income tax payments for the current year are due April 15, June 15, and September 15, and January 15 of the following year.

If you eventually hire employees, you'll be responsible for withholding federal and state income tax as well as Social Security from their pay. For more information on taxes, see Chapter 16, "Watching Baby Grow."

# Chapter Six
# Insuring Your Success

The details of starting your own business may seem daunting, but one area that you should not neglect is insurance coverage. Many different types of insurance exist, including property and casualty, automobile, liability, group health, business interruption, disability income, workers' compensation, life, including "key man" insurance and others. "You can insure against everything and anything," says Gene Fairbrother, lead small business consultant for the National Association of Self Employed. "The most important thing is to know the risks you are taking."

## Property and Casualty Insurance

Your business will need protection from fire, theft, or any other unexpected or uncontrollable losses. If it's a home-based business, the first thing you should do is to contact your insurance agent to find out if riders can be added to your homeowner's policy to cover your new venture. Coverage for a home-based business is not automatically included in a standard homeowner's policy. If your business involves a home office only, ask if your existing homeowner's policy can be updated to include replacement coverage for your office equipment.

When it comes to property and casualty insurance, there are many levels of coverage available. You need to figure out how much money you would need if you had to rebuild or replace your business. This policy would include fire, theft, and loss from weather-related disasters. Working with your insurance agent, you need to educate yourself on limitations and/or waivers of coverage. For example, in most states, losses resulting from flooding are not covered in a standard property insurance policy. You need a separate policy or a rider to an existing policy to protect yourself in the event of flood-related damages.

Some insurance companies offer special policies that cover both your home and a business run from your home. Taking this route may be less expensive than adding riders to your homeowner's policy or buying separate policies for home and business. Check the coverage carefully. If you are providing services or manufacturing goods at your home business location, these policies would probably not be suitable for you.

## Automobile Insurance

If you will be using your vehicle as part of your business, as would be the case with a pet sitter, trainer, or groomer who does pickup and delivery, it will be necessary to obtain auto insurance for any damage or liability that could result during such usage. If you are a mobile groomer, your new business on wheels must be totally insured as well.

## Liability Insurance

This type of insurance is usually easy to obtain, but when it comes to pet care occupations, liability insurance coverage has been difficult to find. These are relatively new professions with their own unique requirements. Groomers need protection to cover loss of or injury to the animals in their care as well as persons on their premises: pet owners, employees, delivery persons, and visitors. Pet sitters need protection at each and every location where they go to care for their four-legged, finned, or winged clients. Trainers need to insure themselves against harm, both at home if they do business there, and on the premises of their dog-owning clients. If a trainer is holding classes, insurance is needed to cover class participants, both human and canine.

If your insurance agent tells you that no such coverage is available for your business, go shopping for an insurance broker. An agent works for one insurance company; a broker can select from a wide range of providers to come up with tailor-made coverage for you.

You will need to describe your business operation clearly so that your insurance professional can assess your risks and needs. More and more pet care professionals are seeking the equivalent of malpractice insurance in case a pet is injured, lost, or its death occurs while in their care. Until recently, pets were evaluated only as property. What you paid for the puppy at the breeder or the pet store established its dollar value.

However, as the importance of pets to their owners' health and well-being becomes an acknowledged fact in our society, or if your four-legged client happens to be a champion show dog or a working dog, you could end up liable for thousands of dollars in damages if a pet is harmed or lost while under your care.

As a general rule, it is advisable in today's world to have $1 million of liability coverage for your business. It sounds like a huge amount of money, but for the protection and peace of mind you will receive, it really is not that expensive. It will protect you if someone slips and falls on your premises, if a dog jumps off a table and breaks its leg, if a child is bitten, or if a pet escapes and is hit by a car. These are all worst-case scenarios, but Murphy's Law is alive and well, so prepare for the worst and then do everything in your power to make sure it doesn't occur.

I was able to secure $1 million in liability coverage plus all the property protection I need through my agent with The Travelers Group. Because my policy covers a large grooming shop and retail store, it costs more than it would for a small home-based operation, but I pay in monthly installments, making it easier to manage along with my other expenses.

If you find it impossible to get coverage you need, consider going through one of our industry associations. For groomers, such insurance packages are available to members of the National Dog Groomers Association of America located in Clark, Pennsylvania. Call them at (724) 962–2711 or e-mail them at ndga@nauticom.net. The NDGAA Web site can be found at www.nauticom.net/www/ndga. For pet sitters, insurance is available for members of Pet Sitters International (PSI) at www.petsit.com and from the National Association of Professional Pet Sitters (NAPPS) at www.petsitters.org.

As far as professional trainers go, I was unable to find such association benefits available. This is subject to change, so you should keep abreast of the situation. Contact the Association of Pet Dog Trainers (APDT) of Springfield, Massachusetts, at (800) PETDOGS to make inquiries on this matter, or log on to its Web site, www.apdt.com. The Association of Companion Animal Behavior Counselors (www.animalbehaviorcounselors.org) is interested in having a carrier create such an insurance product when enough members show an interest, according to its spokesperson, Robert DeFranco.

No one should be working with animals or their owners without a liability policy. Although many trainers require their students to sign a waiver releasing them from liability in case of injury, this is something that needs to be checked by your lawyer to determine if it would hold up in court.

# Business Interruption Insurance

Another type of insurance you may wish to obtain is business interruption insurance. Your property insurance policy would pay you to replace damaged or destroyed equipment or buildings, but you would still be required to pay taxes, utilities, and other expenses if your business had to be shut down for repairs. Like disability insurance, this kind of insurance provides you with income when you are unable to earn your living.

# Workers' Compensation

If you have three or more employees (counting yourself unless you are a sole proprietor), you will also need workers' compensation insurance. This type of insurance pays the medical expenses and lost wages of an employee who is injured or becomes ill as a result of his or her job. It actually includes two types of protection: the coverage for employees, plus liability coverage for the employer to pay the cost of defending lawsuits filed by an employee or an employee's family.

Workers' compensation insurance is required by law in all fifty states. Without this coverage, an injured worker could sue your business to recover medical costs, disability costs, and damages. This could effectively put you out of business.

Last year, injuries in the workplace affected thousands of employees and cost U.S. companies in excess of $110 billion. Workplace injuries occur in all types of businesses. The unfortunate fact is that if you are in business long enough, it is likely that you will eventually have to deal with a workers' compensation claim.

There are differences among the states as to what types of employees qualify for benefits, how much coverage a firm must provide, and what percentage of an injured worker's wages must be paid. Check the regulations for your state either directly with the secretary of state's office or through a link provided on the SBA Web site at www.sba.gov/starting/regulations.html.

Insurance sales methods for workers' compensation policies also vary from state to state. A few states require employers to purchase this insurance through a single state agency; others allow private insurers who sell business insurance to offer workers' comp policies. Many states also offer "insurance pools" for firms that cannot afford standard coverage, often those with poor safety records or a long history of workers' comp claims.

If an employee is injured on the job, you must immediately file a claim with your insurance carrier. The carrier will then notify the state department that oversees such claims, and the case will be reviewed to determine whether the claim is valid and what benefits the worker should receive. Usually, employees will not start receiving workers' comp benefits until they have been out of work for five days.

Workers' compensation premiums depend on the nature of your business. Each type of job is assigned a classification code. Riskier work is classified accordingly and charged a higher premium. For a store clerk, you may only pay 48 cents for every $100 in payroll. Again, pet care workers do not have their own categories. My current policy classifies groomers as "hospital—veterinary and drivers" and I am charged $1.13 for every $100 of remuncration.

You can review your classifications with your state workers' compensation rating bureau to make sure you are receiving the codes closest to the jobs performed. You may also choose to have a deductible. More than half of the states allow small companies to reduce premiums by paying a deductible on workers' comp claims. Ranging from $100 to $1,000 per claim, they can reduce your premiums considerably.

## An Ounce of Prevention

The best way to prevent a high rating and the inconvenience and stress that workers' comp claims involve is to make your workplace as safe as you can. No matter what area of pet care you are involved in, when you hire workers, make sure you train them thoroughly.

Prevention is the best medicine when it comes to job safety. If spills occur in bathing or dogs leave "pee puddles," make sure you mop up immediately. Train your staff in proper lifting techniques to prevent back injuries. Install tub ramps to assist bathers when placing big dogs in the tub. Vary the types of grooming each worker must perform; overuse of the hands and wrists required in precise scissoring can lead to carpal tunnel syndrome.

Instruct workers to use muzzles and help each other out when dealing with uncooperative and unruly pets. Identify aggressive dogs and keep them segregated from other canine clients to cut down on the risk of dogfights. And while you're at it, practice safe work habits yourself. A good safety program for you and your employees is vital to the success of your business.

Employers are required to post a notice to employees in a suitable place outlining workers' compensation coverage and workers' rights. This is public information, and must be readily available to any person who needs it. This official notice, which is available at your state Department of Industrial Accidents (DIA) offices and downloadable from many state Web sites, must indicate the insurance carrier, the address, the policy number, and a contact person to whom injuries or incidents should be reported. Failure to provide the information to employees is a violation of the law, leaving you, the employer, subject to a fine.

Becoming an informed pet care provider and practicing safety in the workplace will help to minimize your risks. When you insure yourself against losses and protect yourself, your employees, and the pets in your care through wise business practices, you will be keeping your business healthy as well.

# Chapter Seven

# Banking on Your Future

A s a small-business owner, how should you choose a bank or financial institution? Like the choices of your lawyer and your accountant, selecting the right financial institution and learning how to access its resources can play a major role in your success.

## Your Business Bank Account

You will need a business checking account for your pet care business. Before you choose the bank that's right for you, it's a good idea to shop around. If you already have a history and a personal rapport with a local bank, that might be a great place to start. It's always good to establish a relationship with a banker before you need money!

It's important to find people you feel comfortable with. As you chat with bank tellers and officers, you will find out if you feel a personal connection. The bank personnel may already know you, but chances are they know precious little about the pet care industry; be prepared to answer their questions knowledgeably. Don't be shy about telling them why your business is unique and letting your enthusiasm show!

Talking to your fellow business associates may also help you make your decision. Your accountant, attorney, and even the local chamber of commerce are all good places to look for a referral. Attend meetings of the chamber or other service organizations to find out which banks are active in your business community.

These days the banking business is more competitive than ever. Sometimes a new bank in the community that is aggressively seeking customers will offer special deals and packages for your business. Bigger is not always better. A smaller bank may give you more personal service and have more relaxed rules when it comes to loan procedures.

Some factors to consider when making your selection are convenience, cost, and the range of services the bank has to offer.

Is it conveniently located? Can you bank by phone or on-line? When it comes to running your business, time is money. You don't want to waste it by driving a long distance or standing in line for long periods of time while you wait to make your transactions.

Will the bank offer you a line or credit and overdraft protection for your business account? When you need to purchase equipment or launch an advertising campaign, drawing upon a credit line can help you manage your cash flow, and knowing you won't be embarrassed or inconvenienced if one of your checks does not clear will add greatly to your peace of mind.

Does the bank accept federal tax deposits? Will your business be issued its own ATM and credit card? What will the monthly charges be for your account? Can your business checking account have a companion savings account that pays you interest? Can you easily make transfers between the two accounts? (I like to keep money for tax payments in a savings account until such payments are due. I'm collecting interest on these savings and it makes me feel more secure to know my tax money is set aside.)

Is there a minimum balance you can maintain to avoid monthly bank fees? In these days of giant bank mergers, some of the larger banks attach charges to everything you do, from using an ATM card to making an on-line inquiry about your account, even making an after-hours deposit in the lock box. Look for other hidden charges, such as fees for using a teller or writing more than a certain number of checks per month.

Does the bank provide special loan programs for small businesses, including SBA loans or other government-guaranteed loans? Will loan officers walk you through the application process if you decide to seek such a loan?

Although price alone should not be the determining factor in choosing a bank, you should at least compare interest rates on deposit accounts and basic consumer loans. (Because most business loans are negotiated, rates on these will not be posted.) Don't be afraid to ask for references and ask questions. Business is business. Bear in mind that you are trying to establish a long-term, mutually beneficial business relationship.

You will turn to your bank for help with cash management, payroll assistance, credit counseling, even investment products. Nowadays most banks have their own Web sites. Check them out to educate yourself on the full range of products they have to offer.

# Paper or Plastic? Credit, Charge, and Debit Cards

With consumers increasingly turning to credit and debit cards instead of cash and checks, you should also consider accepting credit cards in your business. Many small-business owners shy away from credit card transactions because they don't want to pay handling charges or they think credit card sales are just too much of a hassle, but processing plastic has become an everyday fact of life. It's a convenience that will make life easier for your customers and more profitable for you.

## Credit Cards

The average American now has four bank credit cards. The volume of sales done through these cards has been expanding by 15 percent per year for the past five years, three times faster than the increase in overall purchases in the United States.

For increasing numbers of American consumers, plastic is the preferred method of payment. Why are credit cards so popular? Let's look at the reasons:

- People don't want to carry cash.
- They wish to avail themselves of rewards, such as airline miles.
- They find it easier to manage their finances by paying one monthly bill.
- They want a record of every purchase.
- They don't want the hassle of providing identification or a phone number and waiting around for verification of a check.

## Charge Cards

Charge cards, such as American Express and Diners Club, also known as travel and entertainment cards, are another popular form of plastic. They differ from credit cards because they have no credit limit. To avoid paying interest, owners of these cards must pay off the entire balance when the bill comes in. If charge card owners opt to pay off a large bill over time, the balance can be spread out, but typically they will pay 18 to 21 percent interest. Charge card companies make their money by collecting big annual fees. They will also charge you, the merchant, a higher percentage for processing when your customers use them to pay for goods or services.

## Debit Cards

More recently, debit cards have been added to the mix. More than 60 million of us now carry these cards, and the number is expected to grow by leaps and bounds as their popularity increases. In fact, debit card purchases are growing at the rate of more than 50 percent per year. What makes debit cards so popular? These potent little pieces of plastic combine the functions of a credit card, an ATM card, and a check all in one.

In addition to their use in ATMs for making deposits, withdrawals, transfers, balance inquiries, and even loan payments, debit cards are now used just about everywhere in place of cash, checks, or credit cards.

What makes them more attractive than credit or charge cards? Cost, for one thing. For all the convenience they offer, credit cards are in reality expensive loans on which consumers pay interest, sometimes up to 26 percent. Banks love us to use credit cards. That interest accounts for 75 percent of the profits earned by banks that issue credit cards. In addition to high interest on unpaid balances, many credit card companies charge an annual fee for their use, late payment penalties, and fees for going over the stated credit limit. Finally, credit card processing companies profit by charging business owners and service providers (like you and me) a fee for every transaction made by our customers.

Enter the debit card, offering all the convenience of credit and charge cards and far less intrusive and time-consuming than writing a check. Unlike credit and charge cards, a debit card does not use the bank's money; you must have a sufficient amount in your checking account to cover every purchase you make when you use it.

What are the downsides to debit cards? For the consumer who needs three to four weeks to pay the bills, credit cards and charge cards are preferable. Also, because debit card amounts are removed immediately from the consumer's checking account, the customer does not have the option to withhold payment or cancel a check if a dispute arises over the goods or services paid for.

Not all debit cards are created equal. Those bearing the MasterCard or Visa logo can be used worldwide for purchases and ATM transactions. Most issuers do not charge fees for debit card purchases, and the rate charged to merchants for processing them is much lower than that for credit and charge card processing.

Debit card transactions are treated like cash. They are processed for a flat fee, usually around 30 cents per transaction regardless of the amount spent. From the merchant's standpoint, the risk factor is virtually eliminated. The possibility of credit card fraud or of receiving a bad check is removed, along with the potential loss of revenue, inconvenience and embarrassment that goes with it.

## Opening a Merchant Account

In order to accept credit, charge, and debit cards, you must open a merchant account with a bank. If you are just starting your business, you will need to have your credit reviewed before you are issued this merchant account. If you have no business history, the strength of your credit will depend on your personal credit history.

Not all banks handle credit card transactions but don't be deterred if your bank does not provide this service. Many farm out their credit card processing to a specialized processor or independent sales company, commonly referred to as an ISO. Whether your bank provides this function directly or you use an ISO, you still need a merchant account to receive credit, charge, and debit card transactions as payment for your goods and services. If this is an in-house function of your bank, its representative will set you up with a data machine and teach you how to use it. You can buy, lease, or rent this machine, with costs varying between $100 and $1,000, depending on your equipment and needs. If you are going through an ISO, its sales representative will handle equipment installation and training.

If you do not have an electronic data terminal to process your plastic, you would use a hand-operated machine that imprints the proper numbers and charges on paper forms in triplicate: one copy for you, one for the customer and one for the bank. My advice? Get the electronic data machine. For the time and trouble it will save you, it's well worth the expense, and your money will get into your bank account a lot sooner.

## The Pros and Cons of Plastic

Of course, nothing is for nothing, and processing all this plastic comes at a price. The fee charged per credit and charge card transaction varies according to the type of card used and the volume of sales. The transaction fee on cards charged by your processing company (ISO) or individual companies like Discover Card or American Express, is called a discount rate and will be itemized on your monthly statement. For a small-business owner whose credit sales total less than $5,000 in charges per month, this rate would usually vary between 1.5 and 3.5 percent per transaction.

Offering credit and debit card sales is a convenience you can offer your clientele and a potential moneymaker for you. Love 'em or hate 'em, credit cards and debit cards are here to stay. They will account for 33 percent of all purchases by 2002 and 43 percent by 2005.

If your business does retail sales, very often people will do more "impulse buying" when they are using a card, especially around the holidays. According to one recent estimate, if you sell retail products, you stand to lose up to 80 percent of consumer impulse buys if you don't accept credit cards. When your business provides this service, it also gives you a certain legitimacy and clout as an up-to-date member of the business community.

There is a downside, however. (Isn't there always?) With the use of credit and charge cards comes the possibility of a "chargeback" if a customer disputes a transaction that appears on his or her monthly bill. Chargebacks can occur when a customer is dissatisfied with merchandise or services, questions the amount of the charge, or in some cases, simply forgets making the transaction.

This dispute leads to a "retrieval," the process of gathering proof that the transaction was indeed a valid one. When one of your customers disputes a charge made by your business, your merchant account number is debited for the funds in question while the transaction is investigated. If you cannot prove the sale was a valid one, the unfavorable result will be a chargeback—or deduction of that sale amount—from your account.

Chargebacks result in a headache involving time and paperwork for the small-business owner, but there are steps you can take to prevent them from happening. Make sure you comply with all transaction requirements issued by the credit card companies, such as checking the cards for signatures, holograms, and expiration dates. If you suspect fraud, call the Voice Authorization Center indicated on your terminal and speak to an operator.

Remember, a sale authorization indicates only the availability of credit at the time of the sale. It does not guarantee that the person presenting the card is the rightful owner, nor does it protect you against chargebacks or credit card fraud.

## Corporate Cards

You may also find your own corporate credit card to be a valuable tool in managing your business expenses. The biggest boon in using a corporate card is that it consolidates your bills. If you engage in business-related travel, for example, your company will receive one bill broken down into hotel, rental car, airline tickets, and restaurant costs. Your monthly statement will allow you to analyze your expenses and help you to budget and plan for your business's future.

If you have a partner or a key employee, you may want to consider issuing this person a duplicate corporate card as well. That person will then have a line of credit in an emergency, and your bookkeeper or accountant will appreciate the record of expenditures your monthly statement will provide. Of course, you would need to review every charge made and make sure the privilege is not being abused by use of the card for personal expenses not related to the business.

Another benefit of using your corporate credit or charge cards may be additional travel insurance. For example, with American Express, you can obtain up to $200,000 in travel accident insurance and $1,250 in baggage insurance to cover lost luggage.

As small businesses continue to blossom all over the landscape, credit card companies are starting to recognize their clout. Keep your eyes open for deals and offers that can benefit you and your business as well.

Paper or plastic? What will it be? I think the choice is clear. The way you handle charge, credit and debit card sales for your customers and the way you use them yourself to manage your business can make a big difference. They can be tools for increasing your success.

# Chapter Eight
# The Basics of Working at Home

Are you ready to call your own shots? When you are your own CEO working out of your home, it's all up to you. How you design your office, keep track of clients, how high-tech your operation will be, the climate you will provide for your customers—this brand-new universe is yours to create. Blending it seamlessly into your family life may pose a few problems but you have come this far and you are up to the challenge.

## Equipping Your Office

Beyond the usual clerical accoutrements—desk, chair, telephone and answering machine, calculator, pens, pencils, paper clips, scissors, ruler, tape, stamps, stapler and staple remover, file folders, hanging files, and labels, you will need the following:

- Schedule book or reservations calendar. The most common one of these is a dated deskpad. From now on, your life will revolve around this item!
- Bookcase and shelves for storing notebooks, computer software, and office supplies as well as your personal library of books and videos on pets and their care. You'll be amazed at how quickly you'll fill it up.
- Filing cabinets for all paperwork, records, and business forms
- First-aid kit for people and pets
- Stationery, custom printed with your logo, name, address, and phone number
- Matching envelopes
- Plain business-size envelopes

- Brochures to hand out to prospective clients
- Notepads with your name and address for writing personal notes to clients
- Business cards
- Rubber stamps and inkpad for imprinting checks for bank deposit, return address on correspondence, and preaddressing invoices for clients' convenience in paying bills
- A paper shredder. Once you have retired your client forms and records, destroy them before they go out in the trash or recycling pile.
- Accounting ledger. Unless you are using a computer program like Quicken, MYOB, or a similar program, you will use this to furnish your accountant with a monthly report of your financial information. This can be a notebook, a One-Write checkbook system, or a customized software program.

Don't forget to keep a receipt for everything you purchase for your office. It will pay off at tax time.

## Client Cards

You will need to maintain a record of every pet that you deal with. This can be a simple index card listing the owner's name, address, and home, business, and cell phone numbers, along with the pet's name, age, breed, sex, and color. You also need the name and phone number of the pet's veterinarian as well as the expiration dates of its vaccinations. It's a bad idea to take pets that have no shot records. You are putting yourself, your employees, and the other pets at risk. Kennels have been requiring this information for many years, and it's time for all pet care businesses to make it a requirement as well.

On your client card you will also need to note any health problems the pet has, such as seizure disorder, heart

> **Proof of Vaccination**
>
> Inform prospective clients when they book their appointments that you will need to see proof that the dog or cat is up-to-date on its vaccinations. The three basic canine vaccines are (1) rabies, (2) a combination called DHPP that protects against distemper, hepatitis, parainfluenza, and parvovirus, and (3) an intranasal vaccine against Bordetella (commonly known as kennel cough). Cats need rabies shots too, as well as vaccines against feline leukemia and feline panleukopenia, also known as feline distemper.

# Groomer Worksheet

**Client:** Jones, Duncan

**Breed:** West Highland Terrier          **D/C:** D     **Sex:** M     **Color:** White

**Remarks:** Flat rate $38                                              **Age:** 3

**Notes:** Barker — out early, rebook 6 wks.                            **Schedule:** 6

**Profile:** #4 on Back, regular Westie trim


**Appointment:** 08/01/02

**Time:** 9:00 A.M.

**Groomer:** Jane                         GCD:


| | | | |
|---|---|---|---|
| Complete Groom | $ _____ | Deskunk | $ _____ |
| Handstripping | $ _____ | Medicated Bath | $ _____ |
| Flea/Tick Bath | $ _____ | Deodorizer Bath | $ _____ |
| Tough Strip Charge | $ _____ | Dematting | $ _____ |
| Special Handling | $ _____ | Anals | $ _____ |
| Teeth | $ _____ | | |

---

## Groom Profile

Reg. Groom - Blade # _____     Overall/Strip - Blade # _____     Other _____

Legs: Scissor _____     Demat _____     Bands _____     Tail _____

Body: Bands _____     Poms _____     Other _____     Ears _____

Face: Cf _____     M _____     G _____     M/G _____

Other Face/Head _____

Feet: Pf _____     Tf _____     Other _____

Collar/Lead: _____


Groomer Remarks:

# Client Card

Last: _____ First: _____ Title: _____

Address: _____

Town: _____ State: _____ Zip: _____

Phones: Home: _____ Work: _____

Emergency: _____ Contact: _____

Comments: _____

Pet name: _____ Breed: _____ Color: _____

DC: _____ Age: _____ Sex: _____ Weight: _____ CC: _____ Vet: _____

Preferred groomer: _____ Schedule: _____ Last: _____ Pending: _____

Remarks: _____

DHLLP      /   /          Rabies      /   /          F/Leukemia      /   /

Bordetella   /   /          Lyme      /   /          Corona      /   /

**Sample client card (front)**

# Client Groomer History

**Client:** Jones, Duncan          **D/C:** D          **Breed:** Westie

**Date:** 06/15/02          **Groomer:** Jane
**Profile:** same
**Full groom:** $38

**Date:** 04/02/02          **Groomer:** Jane
**Profile:** #5 Westie, letting hair grow out a bit
**Full groom:** $38

**Sample client card (back)**

## Carefree Pet Caregivers Client Card

**Name:** _Brown_     **First:** _John & Susan_     **Title:** _Dr. & Mrs._

**Address:** _44 Robin Road_

**Town:** _Plainfield_     **State:** _MA_     **Zip:** _02011_

**Phones: Home:** _(508) 555-9876_   **Work:** _(617) 354-1200_

**Cell or pager:** _(222) 444-6677 (John)  (444) 543-7888 (Susan)_

**Emergency:** _Mary Clark (508) 333-9988_   **Relationship:** _Susan's mother_

**Directions:** _Rte. 1 South to Green St. Take first right on Meadowlark Dr. then second left on Robin Rd. House is at end of road in cul-de-sac on right (#44)_

**Pets: (1) Name:** _Peaches (F)_   **Age:** _10_   **Type:** _Golden retriever_

     **(2) Name:** _Butch (M)_   **Age:** _3_   **Type:** _English bulldog_

     **(3) Name:** _Ming (F)_   **Age:** _4_   **Type:** _Siamese cat_

**Vet:** _Dr. Black_     **Phone:** _(508) 555-9090_

**Address:** _Plainfield Animal Clinic_

**Referred by:** _Laura Peters (client)_

**Sample client card, filled-out**

disease, allergies, hip dysplasia, arthritis, skin problems, or injuries from accidents. On the reverse side, you will record special instructions for each visit. For example, a groomer might note "short summer teddy bear clip" or "schnauzer trim, short feathers." Here you might also record the price once the job is done, detailing any extra charges (flea shampoo, dematting, anal glands, etc.). Likewise, a pet sitter might add notes to the client cards about special feeding and care, while a trainer might jot down behavioral problems.

This client card will serve as the pet's history, giving you a record of every visit, the services that were performed, and what the customer was charged. Available through its *Groomer to Groomer* magazine (online at www.barkleigh.com) Barkleigh Publications offers "Klip Kards" for groomers, as well as many other printed products. Keep them in alphabetical order in a metal file box in your office or reception area. Whether you are a groomer, pet sitter, or trainer, your card file will become one of your most valuable possessions.

# Computers and You

Computers have ushered us into the Information Age, some of us kicking and screaming all the way. How you handle the information that applies to your business is vitally important to the efficiency of your operation and your success. More and more pet care pros are now relying on computers in the day-to-day running of their businesses.

There are now wonderful software programs available to keep track of appointments and client histories. In 1983 Rick Smith of Kennelsoft in Elk Rapids, Michigan, developed one of the earliest versions for groomers, Top Groomer. He has continued to improve upon it, developing new systems for the pet care industry, including the most recent version, Atlantis, adaptable to groomers and kennel operators alike. You can learn more about Kennelsoft's products and download a free demo disk at www.gtii.com/knlsoft.

Other software systems are available from Blue Mountain Data Systems, www.staubassociates.com; The Groomer's Write Hand, www.GroomersHand.com; OBS-Soft, www.groommanager.com; Blue Crystals Software, www.bluecrystalsoftware.com; K-9 Bytes, www.ktdinc.com; KenlPro 2001, www.kenlpro.com; and Kennel Suite, www.planesoftware.com.

It's all about data. Whether your client histories are maintained on index cards in a file box or in a computer system, you will want to include basic information—the client's name, address, and phone number, pets' names, vet name and phone number, and health and vaccination information—plus any special notes that will help you in your work.

If you are a pet sitter, you can keep track of individual pets' likes or dislikes (Rollie likes sticks; Max is afraid of cars). A trainer's client cards would include specific training goals and problems. As a groomer, you might want to know when Mrs. Miller last came in with Clancy, her Irish Setter. Your client card will tell you that, as well as how much she spent and a brief description of how Clancy was groomed. With a software reservations system, you can find out all that and a lot more. It can tell you how many Irish setters are in your clientele, how many clients rebook on a six-week basis, your history of price increases, the dog's health history, and the idiosyncrasies of that pet as well as those of its owner.

Both systems provide information, but the computer provides a lot more of it a lot faster without the reams of paperwork that have always been part of doing business. A computerized system will give you a lot more information in a lot less time, freeing you up to do what you like best: taking care of your furry customers.

With the right software package you can schedule appointments and track customers, pets, revenues, employees, and client histories. Some systems also offer accounting packages to track income and produce needed reports. If your client reservations program does not offer sufficient financial management capabilities, there are several applications that will handle everything from check writing to financial reports. Microsoft Office for Small Business is the leader in this area. Another favorite is Quickbooks; it will handle all aspects of your data, including checkbook and payroll operations. MYOB offers programs to adapt any small business to computerization. Check out its capabilities at www.MYOB.com.

When considering a software program for your pet care business, here are some important questions to consider:

- Does the system offer point-of-sale capabilities if you have a retail operation?
- Is it user-friendly? We are probably the last generation that will need to pose this question, but if the system is too complicated for you or your employees, keep shopping!
- How about customer support? Is it offered 24-7 or must you call within limited hours? Is it free of charge? Are there time limits attached? Will the company help install the software? Will they help train you and your staff?
- How much will it cost? Are upgrades available?
- Do you know anyone who currently uses the system? Ask for their feedback.

My client files have been maintained by computer for years and I love the system, but when a client comes in for the first time, I still record the pertinent information on a card before I enter it in the computer. I only do this the first time; the data for each subsequent visit becomes part of that client's history in the computer files.

For people like me, computerizing the business caused much fear and trembling, but once you get used to running your business via the computer, you won't look back. With the time you will save on booking and managing your financial data and the wealth of information you can glean with just a keystroke, I think you will find that your initial investment will pay for itself within the first year.

# The Telephone:
# Your All-Important First Impression

No matter which pet care business you choose to open, the telephone will be your lifeline to your clients. The majority of your business will involve bookings done over the phone.

Clients call to inquire about your services, prices, methods, products, and schedules. Because you will be dealing with their beloved pets, they also want to "feel you out," to get a reading on whether or not you are the type of person they can trust with little Spunky. You will probably occasionally get phone calls from other pet care providers disguising themselves as customers. (It's a dead giveaway when you have to strain to hear over the chorus of barking dogs in the background and the "prospective client" asks the prices on three or four different breeds.) Thankfully, because many of us now have Caller ID, that technique of price-shopping is not so common anymore. Besides, you should have a good enough relationship with your colleagues to be able to pick up the phone and ask such a question outright.

## Telephone Etiquette and Techniques

Your customer gets a first impression of you and your business over the phone. If you sound rushed and stressed, that client will certainly not feel comfortable and appreciated. If you answer questions as if it's a big bother, he or she will not be encouraged to book your services. Simply put, good telephone techniques reflect common courtesy. Here are some do's and don'ts of phone etiquette:

- When you answer the phone, give your business name and your own name as well. "Good morning, Fur Magnolias Grooming Salon. This is Jane speaking. May I help you?"
- Answer the phone as quickly as you can. People do not like to be kept waiting, and many will hang up after four or five rings. Unless you have Caller ID or want to pay for a "Star 69" identification, an unanswered phone call is a lost opportunity.
- Provide all the information you can about your services and your background. If your service involves home visits, it's only natural for people to have reservations about inviting strangers into their homes. They need to be reassured you won't make off with the silver. Don't just dryly state your

prices, explain them. "Yes, that is our price to groom a cat. It can be a tricky process and it takes lots of patience and skill. If you would prefer, I could sell you the shampoo and the tools you need so you could do it at home." (Most cat owners will gasp at the prospect and book an appointment!)

- Get as much information as you can over the phone. Write it down on your daily desk calendar or begin filling out a client card while you are talking. This will save time and build an instant bond when the person uses your service.

- Personalize it. "Oh, Jake is a golden retriever. We love that breed. Our family has had four goldens over the years. Aren't they wonderful?"

- Speak in a warm, friendly tone, not in a bored monotone or in a rushed, stressed voice.

- Smile as you speak! The inquiring customer can hear it in your voice. Besides, it's a proven fact that smiling has an immediate physical and physiological impact on you. It increases circulation, lowers your blood-pressure, changes your metabolism, and sends healthy hormones into your system to counteract stress.

- If you are using an answering machine, personalize your message. It's nice to sound like you love your work and take good care of your clients:

  "You have reached Carefree Pet Caregivers. This is Mary speaking. I am probably out taking care of my furry friends at the moment, but if you leave a message, I will return your call as soon as I can. Thank you for calling Carefree Pet Caregivers, and have a great day!"

  "Good Morning! This is Fur Magnolias Grooming Shop, Jane speaking. I can't take your call at the moment. I am probably up to my elbows in bubbles giving the puppies a bath right now, but if you leave a message, I will return your call as soon as I can. Thanks for your patience, and have a great day!"

- Do not argue with people who are rude or disrespectful about your policies or prices. ("I never had to get all that shot information from the vet before! Why can't you call him yourself?" or "Thirty-five dollars to groom my little Schnauzer? That's outrageous!") Inform them courteously that maybe your service is not the one for them and thank them for calling. When dealing with the public, you are bound to run into some difficult people, but you don't have to allow them push your buttons!

- Return your calls promptly. Potential customers like to feel valued. If they feel ignored, they will shop for services elsewhere.
- If you are making reminder calls from your grooming salon, get away from the barking dogs to do so. All that noise in the background sounds chaotic and unprofessional. People won't want to leave their pampered little pooches in what sounds like a doggie insane asylum.
- If yours is a home-based business, do not let small children answer your business phone. Most folks will not appreciate your toddler's gibberish when they call to make an appointment, no matter how adorable you may find it. If you have older children or teenagers, please train them to be courteous if they answer your phone.

## Answering Machines

In your absence, I would recommend an answering machine over an answering service because you can give the message your personal touch. Clients tend to get annoyed when they reach a person who can only take a message but not answer questions about prices, availability, or services. It is also far more cost-effective to have an answering machine or voice mail system.

As these phone answering systems become more sophisticated, you can also provide a menu option on your machine: "Press 1 if you would like information about our services. Press 2 if you are a Carefree Pet Caregivers client who is returning home. Press 3 if you would like us to mail you a brochure. Press 4 if this is a personal call," and so on.

Your personalized message also allows you to add or change information about your office hours, vacation closing, or holiday information. "Happy Holidays! You have reached Fur Magnolias Grooming Salon and we are busier than Santa's elves! We are completely booked until after Christmas, but if you would like to leave your name and a number where you can be reached, we will be glad to put you on our cancellation list. We are taking appointments after January 1, so please leave us a message if you want a return call. Have a great holiday!" (Try to be nonspecific about holidays to accomodate today's diverse population.)

Having "Jingle Bells" or some such festive music playing in the background—softly—adds a nice touch. In any season, instead of the ubiquitous beep, have callers leave their message after a pet sound, a bark or a meow. When you're in the pet care business, people delight in humorous little touches like this.

In cases of inclement weather, you may leave a message letting clients know whether or not you will be making your pet-sitting rounds. Groomers and trainers may leave a message informing clients to call before they leave home to see if you will be open for business. (One of the blessings of having a home-based business is that you don't need to drive anywhere during weather emergencies!)

## Pagers and Cell Phones

Pagers and cell phones are another boon to service businesses today. For the pet sitter who walks alone in an unfamiliar neighborhood, enters a dark empty home, has car trouble, or encounters a health crisis with a pet, it's a relief to know that help is just a phone call away. For the trainer, pet sitter, or mobile groomer running late for an appointment or an interview, it provides a way to handle the situation in a thoughtful manner.

A pager costs less than a cell phone and lets you receive messages when you are out of the office. Before you put that pager number on your business card or in the yellow pages for all to see, make sure you really want to be reachable at all hours of the day or night. "Our pager is for emergency use only," says pet sitter Ken Clark, "not because someone wants to book a trip to Florida six months from now." He and his wife, Catherine, turn their phone ringer off after 8:00 P.M. and use the pager system for emergency calls. You may also devise an emergency code with family members or partners that tell you when, like E.T., you need to phone home!

## Should You Have a Toll-Free Number?

If you draw clients from a wide area or from across state lines, it may be wise to install a toll-free number. Installation is now easy and affordable, and it's a good selling point for your business. Having a toll-free number that has to do with animals is an added perk. (My toll-free number is (800) 439–PETS.)

All long-distance carriers provide toll-free numbers. Call your provider to ask about their service, rates, and whether those rates fluctuate during the day, evening, or weekends. Also find out if you will have to pay for wrong numbers. (For a while, we got countless calls on our toll-free line for one of the big pet food companies!) Ask how long the service must be in effect and if there are penalties if you decide to cancel before that time is up. Ask about harassment calls. Will they trace such nuisance calls for you? Will you be charged for them?

Having a toll-free number is a great promotional aid in all your advertising—print, Internet, radio, and TV. Keep an eye on your bill to make sure it's cost-effective and that you are not being charged for someone else's calls if your toll-free number was previously used by another business.

## Office Hours

If your working hours have always been dictated by somebody else—your boss or the timetable imposed by your nine-to-five job—working from your home will be a huge change for you. You may find that there is always something to distract you from the job, whether it's the demands of family or unexpected interruptions from friends or your own emerging talent for discovering distractions. The weather is gorgeous and you would much rather go outside and plant some flowers. The mall is beckoning with its siren song of a big clearance sale. It's dark and gloomy today and you want to pull that comfy quilt up over your head and stay in bed. This is where the need for self-discipline kicks in.

Even though you are working from home, you need to keep regular hours. It's easy to procrastinate—to fix a snack, throw in a load of wash, start cleaning that hall closet. You need to establish a schedule and to have your family and friends recognize that just because you are on the premises does not mean that you are not working. Don't be surprised if things get a little bumpy. When you're just starting out, sometimes your relationship with your significant other will take a back seat and resentment will build up, but you can set aside time for your mate even if it means "penciling in" a special dinner or evening walk after supper.

Sometimes it helps on these special "mini dates" if you limit the shop talk and focus on each other. You want to let your mate know how important his or her support is to you and you need to use those ordinary everyday moments to nurture your relationship. Neglecting your husband, wife, or special someone can become a habit, so give yourself a priority check from time to time to make sure a failed relationship is not a by-product of your new entrepreneurial zeal.

The telephone can be another huge distraction when you are working at home. You get that sinking feeling in the pit of your stomach when you pick it up and it's your long-lost aunt or garrulous girlfriend about to launch into an hour-long chat. It's not the time or the place, but it's not always easy to disengage. The greatest remedy for this particular problem is that marvelous and inexpensive innovation known as Caller ID. Once you clock the time you waste making excuses as to why you can't get into the details of your niece's wedding shower plans or why you don't need another credit card no matter how low the rate is, believe me, this service will pay for itself!

What's more, you now have a business phone. Let your friends know from Day One that personal calls should be made to your personal phone number. Leave your home answering machine on and head for your office or your shop. The reverse is true as well. When you are not available to clients, your answering machine will let them know that they can expect a prompt reply. If your particular pet care service warrants it, you can also let them know how to reach you by pager or cell phone in an emergency.

## The Yin and Yang: People-Pleasing and Setting Your Boundaries

Another important skill you will need to develop to keep your work schedule intact is the ability to say no. It's crucial to both your work and your family time. Say no to yourself when you're tempted to raid the refrigerator or watch that TV talk show instead of returning phone calls or doing your paperwork. Learn to say "I'm sorry, but I'm working now" when a neighbor pops in just to chat. Print up a NOT NOW— I'M WORKING sign to hang on your office door to discourage such interruptions. When your husband asks you to pick up his dry cleaning during your work time, gently but firmly tell him you can't do it. If you take your job seriously, you will teach others to do so as well. No one can walk all over you unless you lie down!

As you take on this new responsibility, it's important to recognize that there is a difference between being a nice person who takes care of your responsibilities and being a people-pleaser who goes way overboard to accommodate others' needs at the expense of your own. Chalk it up to "mother's guilt" or society's conditioning, but this type of approval-seeking behavior is far more common among women than it is in men. The stress of never saying no, of feeling that it's your job to make everything work and keep everybody happy, can take a toll on you physically and emotionally and hinder the success of your business as well.

## The Kids Are All Right

One of the reasons you want to start your home-based business is so your schedule will be more flexible. If you have small children, you'll be more available to their needs. This sounds great in theory, but you'll learn that things change every day, and it's not so easy in practice. As you take joy and pride in the fact that your pet care business is growing, you'll realize you must master a whole new juggling act.

Most home-based moms try to work around their children's schedules, making appointments in or out of the home when the kids are in school. On weekends, they may rely on their husbands to do the child care while they groom, train, or make pet sitting calls. The work hours and child care coverage you end up with will be unique to your work situation and the needs of your family. The more you can get done when you have built-in child care or when the kids are in preschool or elementary school, the better for you, but there will probably be times when you will need the services of a reliable baby-sitter. Thankfully, it won't last forever. Paying a sitter can be costly; it's also a great incentive to get as much done as you can when the kids are at school or summer day camp. Once in a while, you may even reward yourself and the kids with an afternoon trip to the playground or the beach! It's good for your own mental health.

As your business grows, those kids will be growing too, and eventually the child care demands will diminish. They may even end up helping out with the business! In the meantime, try not to become so obsessed with your work that you lose sight of why you made this career switch in the first place. In a business based on personal service, you have the power to schedule your time so that you can get to your son's soccer game or be on hand to take pictures of your daughter and her date as they head for the prom. Years from now, you won't remember that last dog you squeezed in that kept you working late, but you'll never forget those important family moments.

## Friendly Relations

When you operate a grooming business out of your home, you develop a personal relationship with your clients. This is one of the perks of pet care work. You want to be warm and friendly, but there is still a fine line between clients and bosom buddies. Even if you socialize, it's usually wise to maintain certain boundaries between you. Dishing the dirt about your relationship problems or having them unload their true confessions can come back to haunt you. If your client friend later has second thoughts or feels embarrassed about revealing too much, your relationship could suffer and you could lose business.

If you live and work in a small town, you will also find that when you run to the store for groceries, your clients will usually be in line behind you at the checkout counter. There's no getting away from them, so you always have to be "on," smiling and pleasant even on days when you wish you were on a desert island. When you are a local businessperson, you need to look presentable at all times. Every meeting is a business opportunity. I've booked dogs for grooming in the dentist's office and at a church rummage sale.

If you are driving around town in a vehicle bearing your business name, you can't get caught speeding or losing your temper at someone who just cut you off. You're somebody in your community now, and you must always be aware of the image that you project. Your face may get sore from smiling at all those cute pet stories, but it goes with the territory. After all, folks think of you as a caring person in the extreme, someone who will cherish every little tidbit about Fluffy's daily activities. And you know what? It's good for business!

That personal relationship with clients also kicks in when it comes to your business hours. There is nothing wrong with letting customers know that your family is a top priority with you. "I love my business, but I'm working around my family," says Elaine Belrose of Kibbles & Klips in Blackstone, Massachusetts, whose grooming and boarding business has grown right along with her children, now ten and twelve. "Ninety-nine percent of my clients know this and they bend their schedules around mine. The kids are in sports and I want to be there. They grow up too fast!"

Carrie Prest of The Bub'ly Bow Wow in Milbury, Massachusetts, has won more than her share of awards. A professional groomer who has been operating out of her home for the past seven of her twenty-four years in the business, she has been on GroomTeam USA and has won gold and silver medals in Italy and England. She now acts as a grooming consultant for the Andis Corporation. Prest groomed at a commercial location for many years. Her life changed drastically after her son's major health problems and the subsequent birth of two daughters made keeping a daily schedule in the shop all but impossible. Now divorced, she bought a house zoned for business where, with the help of her father, she built her grooming shop in the basement. She says the home-based salon was one of her best decisions.

"You can be there for your children and your clients as well. I have a lot of doctors and nurses who work 7:00 to 3:00, and it's not a big deal to have them drop off their dogs at 6:30 A.M., but my number one concern is people not picking up on time. My clients know that at 6:00 P.M. my doors are locked and I'm with my children."

Diane Betelak of Heads and Tails Professional Grooming in Liverpool, New York, echoes this sentiment. Named American Groomer of the Year in 1997, this international medalist and GroomTeam member recalls the easy convenience of a short walk across the yard to nurse her baby daughter during her first year and later the security of being there when the bus dropped her off from school. "It's the perfect situation for any mother," she says. Because she recently purchased a building, her business will soon relocate to a 3,000-square-foot facility where she will offer doggie day care as well.

## Chapter Nine

# Constructing Your Home Grooming Shop

Constructing a grooming salon in one's own home is a dream for many. It's a dream that takes a lot of planning and consideration, as well as a fair amount of start-up capital. You'll be completely renovating an area of your home—upgrading it's plumbing, electrical, heating, and air conditioning systems—and furnishing it with grooming equipment such as tubs, tables, clippers, dryers, and cages. In this chapter, let's go ahead and plan your ideal grooming shop. Then we'll deal with the reality of financing your dream—and making the necessary compromises—in Chapter 10.

## Room to Grow

The space considerations for constructing a home-based grooming salon may be less than those required for a commercial location, but it's wise to give your operation room to grow. My current grooming space takes up 1,000 square feet and features six grooming stations, two tubs, and crates and cages to accommodate forty-five pets. In addition to this large room, I have a small soundproofed area for noisy dogs, a laundry/break room and a rest room. A separate retail area in the front of the shop is equal in size to the grooming room. Guess what? I could use more space! Most of my grooming colleagues would agree. Even if you are starting as a one-groomer operation, you should allow a minimum of 500 square feet for your work area.

# A Warm Reception

Once clients come through your door, the reception area is where they get a first impression of your business. It's not all that different from a guest's first visit to your home. Make sure it is well organized, attractive, clean, and spacious enough so that people and their pets will not be tripping over each other, causing congestion and confusion as well as presenting a safety hazard to two- and four-legged customers alike.

My reception area is not included in my main work area. Clients are checked in and out at the counter in the front room, the 1,000-square-foot area that also serves as my retail store. The key word here is "reception." You want your physical surroundings to convey the same warm welcome you personally strive to communicate to your clients.

Whether you are grooming in a home salon or a commercial space, the requirements are similar. You need to put the same amount of thought into layout and design for both types of grooming businesses. Because of the time and expense involved in creating your salon, chances are you will be living with the results for a long time to come, so plan wisely.

The appearance, atmosphere, and efficiency of your salon layout will speak volumes to your prospective clients. The first thing to keep in mind is that you will be dealing with animals. This is not your doctor's or dentist's office where folks sit quietly and read a magazine while they await their turn. Many of your canine clients will come bounding through the door with their owners in tow. Most are happy and excited to see you, and eager to meet and greet each other. Such unbridled exuberance is wonderful, but it's like a kid's birthday party—you need to keep it under control.

Other pets may be timid, hiding behind their owners or trying to fade into the woodwork. They really don't want to be there at all. Perhaps they are experiencing separation anxiety or maybe they're just plain shy, but the last thing these timid canines need is some happy-go-lucky doggie pal jumping all over them, covering their quaking bodies with slobbers and sniffs.

Your reception area should be separate from your work area, which can sometimes be a noisy and hectic place in its own right. Dogs can become very excited when they see people coming and going. There is nothing more difficult or frustrating than trying to groom a pet that is jumping and spinning on the grooming table as it reacts to the presence of an onlooker. It's not a safe situation for pet or groomer. You need to manage traffic flow efficiently, with the comfort and safety of both pets and their owners in mind.

Your desk or countertop where you do client intake should be spacious enough to allow you to wait on a couple of clients at once. I consider safety gates a must. They should be installed at the entry to your grooming area to keep dogs from entering or escaping. The entry to my work area features a Dutch door, the top and bottom of which open independently into the groom room. The top half of this door has a Plexiglas window, allowing clients to see into the groom room. If we are working on a hyperactive or unruly pet or if an owner arrives early to pick up a dog still on the grooming table, both portions of the door can be closed for the groomer's peace of mind and the dog's protection.

Your front desk or counter should be roomy enough to feature some display materials and a few impulse items—dog cookies, flea and tick collars, and promotional materials and brochures. If you plan to sell collars, leashes, toys, and treats, these should be displayed nearby on Peg Board or in bins. Fancy gift items like ceramic dishes and pet-related art objects are best displayed in well-lit glass cases, keeping them free from pet hair and dust, unending by-products of your grooming operation. Ask any groomer: Pet hair ends up in the darndest places, from ceiling fixtures to your undies!

In my opinion, the need for client seating is debatable. Some groomers like to offer a regular waiting room, complete with comfortable couches and refreshments like bottled water, coffee, and tea. When my husband and I opened our second salon, I couldn't wait to offer ample seating on attractive patio furniture. I felt "house proud" about our shiny new quarters. As traffic picked up and our product lines increased, it soon became obvious that this lovely area had to go. You really only need a couple of chairs. If you make your reception area too comfy, people will use it as a social gathering spot, lingering for extended visits and cutting into the time you need to do your job.

Your reception area should have room for your computer terminal, phone, cash register, adding machine, electronic credit card machine, and filing systems. You can store office supplies and some retail items under the counter or in a nearby storage closet. Like the floor of your grooming area, the reception area floor should be an easy-to-maintain, nonslippery vinyl surface. Ceramic tiles are too expensive and, like pebbled or distressed linoleum surfaces, tile grouting is too hard to keep clean. As for carpeting, forget it. Except for a mat by the front door to wipe muddy feet and paws on stormy days, rugs have no place in a grooming salon.

# Room to Groom

Your grooming area also needs a smooth, nonslippery floor. Rolled vinyl flooring works best. A light color on both the floor and the walls brightens the room. When you are grooming, you need all the light you can get! Fluorescent overhead lighting fixtures that provide illumination as close to daylight as possible should be located directly over each grooming station. We use 8-foot warm fluorescent bulbs hung in pairs lengthwise and crosswise over our grooming tables. Some salons add spot lamps to better illuminate each groomer's work station and eliminate shadows. If you have windows, don't cover them up. Natural light is good for both pets and people, but you will probably need blinds to keep the sun from shining directly on the groomer's work area at certain times of day.

Starting out, you will need two grooming tables. Hydraulic tables work best, allowing the groomer to raise and lower the table to accommodate each dog as well as rotating to reach each area of the pet as they work. Tables should be standard size, 24 by 36 inches. They are usually priced from $450 up.

When it comes to handling large dogs, nothing beats an electric table. These are larger, usually with 24-by-42-inch tabletops. Their most impressive feature is that they lower to around 18 inches, allowing the bigger dogs to step right on. They can be raised as high as the groomer needs to work comfortably, safely holding up to 250 lbs. They range in price from around $800 to $1,500. This may seem like a hefty investment as you're starting out, but bear in mind the fact that groomers make more money on large dogs, and lifting them is hazardous to your back. In my shop, we do a lot of large dogs, and I would not be without an electric table. Shop around, and check manufacturers' warranties.

Rubber "fatigue mats" at each grooming station will make standing much more tolerable. Another item to make this labor-intensive job easier on the body is a stool. Many groomers like to sit while doing their job, a skill not everyone can master, but one that makes this career a lot easier on the body. A simple bar stool will do, with or without a back support, but if you want something more ergonomic, check out beauty supply companies and price the stools they provide for the hairstyling industry.

# Tools of the Trade

When it comes to grooming, time is money; organization of your tools and your workspace is key. Each groomer needs his or her own workstation. If you went to grooming school, you probably graduated with your own "kit," a toolbox full of supplies needed to do your job. Most schools estimate that you need to spend between $1,000 and $1,500 for the tools necessary to begin your career.

Now that you have your own shop, you don't need to lug this tackle box around anymore. Get yourself a high-quality plastic caddy on wheels with its own drawers to store tools and supplies, or have shelving built and Peg-Board hung so everything you need is within easy reach. Caddies are available from grooming equipment manufacturers like Petlift or Edemco. For a lot less money, the ones you find in the household goods department of the major discount stores can also be adapted to fit your needs.

Some groomers like to install mirrors, giving the grooming station the look of a human beauty salon. Take some field trips to other grooming shops and, if possible, attend seminars on shop design at industry trade shows to familiarize yourself with various design options for your grooming stations.

On top of your rolling cart you will want to keep items you will use for each grooming: liquid ear cleaner, ear powder, styptic powder to stop bleeding if you nick a dog's nail, coat sprays, and cotton balls. My favorite cost-cutting solution for keeping a supply of cotton on hand is to purchase it in boxed rolls at a beauty supply store. Handy little items like nail files, nail trimmers, elastics for bows, tweezers, stripping knives, and first-aid supplies can be kept in the caddy drawers, along with brushes, combs, and mat-splitting tools. Protective devices such as muzzles and animal handling gloves as well as larger rakes and shedding blades can be hung on Peg-Board at your grooming station.

Each groomer will need two clippers and two sets of blades of every size. A backup clipper is needed in case you run into mechanical difficulties with one; the blade duplicates will allow you to send one set out for sharpening and still do business. You will also need the full spectrum of snap-on comb attachments, a great time-saver for today's groomers. Supplies for maintaining your clippers are also important. You will need blade wash solution, lubricating spray, grease, or oil, and an old toothbrush for cleaning blades. If you employ other groomers, they will probably bring their own tools, now the norm for grooming professionals. For bather-brushers and grooming assistants, providing the tools of the trade would be your responsibility as the shop owner.

As an artist working on a living canvas, your scissors are the paintbrushes you use to create your masterpieces each and every day. You will need a 9- or 10-inch heavy-duty pair for "roughing," the prep work you do prior to the bath. These scissors are wider than your finishing shears and sometimes referred to as "88-style." You also need two straight and two curved 8½-inch scissors for your fine finish work; two pairs of thinning shears for debulking, shaping, and blending; one pair of blunt-tipped scissors for work around the face or fanny, and a smaller pair (5½ to 6½ inches) of straight shears to trim ears and footpads. Optional items include 10-inch straight or curved shears, which are great time-savers when working on big scissoring jobs like sheepdogs or standard poodles.

Scissors come in a wide price range, but you do get what you pay for. Carbon steel is durable, holding a good edge, but it can rust if you don't keep it dry and oiled. Stainless steel, sometimes combined with chromium or other metals, is rust-resistant. Ice-tempered steel has been subjected to subzero temperatures, changing the metal so it becomes much harder and holds an edge longer.

Blade edges differ as well. Honed and razor edges are so sharp they leave no marks when you use them on a pet's coat. Serrated edges have tiny grooves to hold the hair as they cut. Hollow blades are ground inside to reduce their weight and provide a smooth cut. Like major-league baseball players with their bats, every groomer has certain preferences about how scissors should feel and perform. Because each pair differs widely as to weight and tension, it's best it to try before you buy, sampling the scissor displays offered at grooming trade shows and conventions or visiting a grooming supply house.

Be good to your scissors and clippers and they will be good to you. Don't leave your precious and expensive equipment on the grooming table where it can be dropped or kicked to the floor. Place your scissors and clippers out of harm's way. You can get a hanging organizer or a leather holster for your shears, with built-in pockets for each pair. When you put your scissors away, don't just stick them in the drawer with their edges unprotected. Store them in their own individual cases. Pamper your clippers as well. Learn the basics of clipper maintenance—cleaning, lubricating, replacing brushes—and make it part of your weekly routine.

## Holding Patterns

Crates or cages to hold pets waiting to be groomed, sitting under a dryer, or ready for their owners to pick them up are best arranged against the walls of your grooming shop. For safety reasons, they should be in full view as you work. Some dogs get stressed in cages and try to dig or chew their way out, injuring their noses, mouths, or paws. Nervous pets sometimes urinate or defecate in their crates—usually after the bath, of course! Pets also need to be closely observed during the drying process. Heat stroke is a groomer's worst nightmare; unfortunately, some dogs have succumbed to it at grooming shops.

Cages and crates are available in many styles and sizes. Multicage units usually feature six to nine spaces of varying size, stacked in three tiers. Some multi units come on wheels, making it easier to clean your shop and rearrange your system. Stainless steel cages with removable floor pans and wire racks are expensive, but they can be cleaned and disinfected easily and they last for decades. Fiberglass cages are another alternative. With them you can design your own stackable units. Besides being easy to clean, this material comes in pretty colors and is highly resistant to germs, stains, and odors. The major cage and crate manufacturers—Clark, Snyder, Petlift, and Edemco—will help you plan your salon and meet your needs in this important part of your overall design.

You can also custom-build your own stacked units using individual wire cages placed inside homemade wooden frames that can be painted with washable enamel in bright colors. In my shop, in addition to multicage stacked units, we use custom-built crates that resemble stalls, better described as "cubbies." They were designed by my husband with Formica floors for easy cleaning. Stacked in two tiers, the bottom rows offer larger units for dogs like Labs and German shepherds, with smaller ones for dogs like poodles and schnauzers on top. Dogs are secured in their cubbies by vinyl-coated cables attached to hooks on the back wall. For dogs that panic when confined to a cage, these cubbies offer a great alternative, and they were relatively inexpensive to install. Are you lucky enough to have a carpenter in the family?

## Pipe Down!

Right up there with pet hair, noise is another by-product of a busy grooming operation. Your neighbors will definitely not want to hear dogs howling, yapping, and barking every day. You can reduce noise levels by installing sound-absorbing ceiling tiles when you build your shop. My grooming room features a soundproof cubby area, visible through heavy glass sliding doors, for the very vocal members of our canine clientele. Noise is stressful for the groomer and the other pets as well. Schedule your little yippers to get them in and out as quickly as possible, cutting down your own stress level and helping to keep peace in the neighborhood while you're at it!

## Plug It In

When planning and constructing a grooming salon, the need for electricity is a major consideration. Think about all the things that require electricity: lighting, clippers, dryers, heating, air-conditioning, computers, vacuum cleaners, air purifiers, even your radio, coffeepot, or a microwave oven. They all call for "juice" and lots of it. You will need an electrician to help determine the number of outlets you will need and where they should be placed.

When consulting with your electrician, you will also need to examine the load requirements of all your equipment to make sure your electrical panel can handle it without blowing fuses or tripping circuit breakers. Will standard plugs do the job or will you need special 20-amp outlets for heavy-duty dryers and air-conditioners? Upgrading your electrical panel can be a costly proposition, so do it right when you design your salon to avoid expensive alterations down the road.

## Keeping It Cool

One of the biggest draws on your electricity will be your air-conditioning system. In the grooming shop, it is absolutely necessary to the comfort and safety of yourself, your coworkers, and the pets in your care. Even in New England, mine is operating nine months out of the year. Every day there is a duel between the hot air of the dryers and the cool air of the AC.

How can you reduce the load? It stands to reason that the less time your dryers are operating, the less hot air they will be producing. Never put sopping wet dogs in a cage or a crate to dry. Towel or force-dry them first until they are merely damp, not dripping. Change your air-conditioner filters often. Pet hair clogs up everything in a shop, from air-conditioning filters to computers! Use exhaust fans in your tub area. Consider augmenting your array of dryers with newer units that recirculate room-temperature air rather than using heating elements. In warm weather, turn all dryers to the "cool" setting. Consult with an air-conditioning contractor as you plan your shop to make sure your system will operate as efficiently as possible.

In the grooming shop, the bathing and grooming areas heat up the fastest, but you need to air-condition your entire shop, including the reception and retail areas. Yes, it is expensive to install it and pay those monthly utility bills, but it's essential for the professional groomer. Learn from my mistakes: I have had to upgrade the air-conditioning system in my latest salon three times to bring it up to speed, with a considerable cost outlay each time. Bite the bullet and build it in from Day One. You'll save yourself money and headaches down the road.

# Fluff and Buff: Dryers for Your Salon

There are three types of dryers to consider when outfitting your grooming salon.

## Standing Floor Dryers

You will need two standing floor dryers for finish and fluff drying your canine and feline clients. These are the workhorses of the grooming industry, used for blow-drying pets on the table or as they sit in a cage or crate. Their prices usually reflect the amount of power they have to offer; you need to determine how many amps they will take to operate. Heavy-duty ones may require a 20-amp plug and receptacle; most will use the regular 15-amp service.

Generally, it's advisable to have a heavy-duty high velocity model for thick-coated dogs as well as one that produces an average flow of air for the smaller breeds and cats. Some stand dryers deliver a variable airflow, between 107 and 250 cubic feet per minute (CFM), giving you the option to adjust the power according to the size and coat of the animal being dried. Stand dryers range in price from around $250 to $700, and different manufacturers offer different warranties.

In my busy shop, we shy away from plastic housing on dryers because it tends to break easily if the machine gets tipped. Because these dryers are top-heavy, some tip more easily than others, another factor to consider when making your selection. The dryer stand should be sturdily constructed with well-balanced legs on casters that roll freely and can be cleaned easily of that pesky substance that gums up everything in no time: pet hair!

A standing dryer should have a long arm with an adjustable nozzle that can rotate to 360 degrees to direct the airflow in any direction. It should also be adjustable for height. Shop your shows and ask any veteran groomers you know what works for them. Buying a "bargain" dryer that doesn't hold up can be an expensive mistake.

## Cage Dryers

Cage dryers are a boon in a busy shop. They clip on to the front of the cage or crate to blow-dry the pet. Some have temperature-selection knobs and timers that alert the groomer when the pet has been dried long enough. I use an "octopus" dryer with three hoses that blow warm air to three cages at once. This multicage unit does not have a heating element, eliminating the danger of "cooking" a dog.

*Safety Note:* If used properly, cage dryers are safe. They become unsafe if used in poorly ventilated areas or if dogs are left under them too long. The potential for heat prostration exists for any dog that is not closely monitored under the dryer, especially those who are elderly, have health issues such as heart, trachea, or lung problems, or those whose breathing may be compromised by very short muzzles, like pugs or Pekingese.

Cage dryers are relatively inexpensive, ranging in price from $140 to $400. Some manufacturers now offer a dual-purpose stand dryer with a hose attachment for cage drying. Used properly, cage dryers will increase the efficiency of your grooming operation.

One of the greatest innovations in the grooming industry in recent years has been the arrival of the force dryer. This high-velocity dryer uses a nozzle that sweeps excess moisture from the coat, usually while the dog is still in the tub. As the airflow is directed at the coat, the water blows off the hair shaft, drying the coat without brushing. The animal still needs to be dried for finishing, either in the crate or on the table, but the time required is enormously reduced, cutting down on your electric bill in the process. In my shop, two such 20-amp dryers are placed next to the tubs; each can generate 45,000 feet per minute (FPM) of air speed.

## Force Dryers

Although force dryers have greatly improved grooming speed and efficiency, they are not without drawbacks. Manufacturers are starting to produce quieter models, but most are still quite noisy. In addition, some sensitive pets cannot tolerate their "wind tunnel" effect. For this reason, they should never be used full-force on small, elderly, nervous, or aggressive dogs, nor should they be used at full power on cats. On all pets, one should avoid using their powerful airflow on faces, ears, or genitals. Put yourself in the pet's place; you probably wouldn't find this a pleasant experience either! Towel-dry these sensitive areas of the pet's anatomy instead.

There is a right way and a wrong way to use force dryers. If used improperly on long-coated breeds, their powerful airflow can actually tangle and mat the coat. For such dogs, use the force dryer hose without its nozzle, sweeping the hair in one direction only. Otherwise, you may find yourself spending twice as much time, having to demat the dog both before and after the bath.

Force dryers vary greatly in price, from the small "vacuum cleaner" model that starts around $100 to the 20-amp box units priced around $600. In my opinion, no grooming shop should be without one.

## Splish Splash

Many modern shops separate the "befores" from the "afters" when it comes to canine customers. Keeping unbathed pets in a separate area prevents them from soiling clean pets or passing on fleas or ticks. If you cannot do this in your workspace, at least have one area for dogs who come in with parasites or have been sprayed by a skunk, keeping them away from other pets.

Place your bathing area near the back of your salon—the more self-contained, the better. Keeping this vital component of your operation separate reduces noise and heat in both your reception area and your main grooming room. When adapting your space to accommodate your home grooming shop, have a vent installed in the bathing area to get rid of excess hot air and humidity. An exhaust fan can draw it out through the roof or an exterior wall. This also helps to cut down on the demand for air-conditioning.

If you can provide a grooming table next to the tub, prebath brushouts can be performed there, cutting down on those piles of dirty hair rolling around like tumbleweeds in your main grooming area. This table will also be a great help for force-drying pets before they go into a cage or crate for additional blow-drying.

Ideally, you should have two bathtubs: one standard size for most pets, and a smaller one (the size of a laundry sink) for cats and small dogs. I have used porcelain and fiberglass tubs, but I recently made the switch to stainless steel, which can be cleaned and disinfected easily. My new tubs are self-contained units that have their own backsplash panels and foldable ramps to help bathers get the big dogs in and out of the tub. Each one has a specially installed hair trap to prevent clogged pipes. Hair and soap can combine to jam up your system, creating a potentially huge expense and inconvenience and possibly affecting the entire neighborhood as well!

Inside each tub are vinyl-coated racks to keep pets from standing in soapy water as they are being rinsed, which speeds up the drying process. Unless you buy such self-contained units, you will need the services of a carpenter to frame and build a support system for your tubs.

# The Plumber's Friend

Consult with a plumber as you plan. The closer you can place your bathing area to existing water pipes the less costly it will be. Plumbing work can quickly become very expensive. If I were constructing my dream salon from scratch today, I would include a floor drain to accommodate spills and save the floor from water damage.

Grooming uses lots of water, much of it hot. Today's automatic bathing systems, such as the Hydrosurge, aid greatly in water conservation and help cut down on water bills. A standard-size 40-gallon water heater may be adequate if yours is a small operation. In my salon, we require a 75-gallon heater to keep us in hot water all day long.

Your bathing area should be tiled or walled with plastic or fiberglass panels. Tubs should be installed at waist level, eliminating unnecessary bending for the bather. You will need shelving for shampoos, conditioners, and towels as well. Like your grooming area, the bathing area needs to be well lit and well maintained for the safety and well-being of workers and pets alike. Spills must be mopped up as soon as they occur. Pets must not be left unattended in a tub. Safety practices really boil down to good common sense, but it's important to make them part of your routine from the day you open your doors to your first customer.

# Incidentals

Every grooming salon needs basic supplies like waste containers, trash bags, paper towel dispensers, a shop vacuum cleaner (preferably one that can be used for wet and dry cleanup), fire extinguishers, smoke detectors, locked cabinets for storing toxic cleaning supplies and pesticides, brooms, dustpans, mops, pooper-scoopers, light bulbs, extension cords, and a basic tool kit including a hammer, pliers, and screwdrivers.

You will also need a first-aid kit for people and pets. Check out the OSHA regulations and make sure yours is in compliance.

Nothing makes owners happier than a pretty bow on their freshly groomed pet! A ribbon rack will help organize and manage this decorative little item. Save yourself a bundle by learning how to make your own.

# When Nature Calls

Your salon will also need a rest room for you and your future employees—nothing elaborate, just a toilet, sink, medicine cabinet, and storage for paper products and cleaning supplies. The needs of your furry customers are another matter.

Like it or not, your clients will inevitably allow their furry friends to relieve themselves on and around your property. If only you could install a pet porta-potty! A special "potty walk" area is the next best thing. It will make life a lot easier for all concerned. Include a small signpost to let owners know where to walk their pets. On the counter in your reception area, offer a basket of plastic "poop bags" for clients to use, and station a trash can in the potty walk area.

Even with all this encouragement, some folks just will not pick up after their pets or confine their elimination to a designated area; you must be extra vigilant to do "potty patrol" each and every day. Dog waste is unsightly and can be harmful to your health. Urine stains buildings, kills grass and plants, and smells awful. To maintain your property and keep good relations with your neighbors, keep your potty walk clean. In addition to your daily pickups, wash it down with a sterilizing agent at least once a week.

# Read Any Good Books Lately?

Here's a nifty little area that won't bust your bankroll: your own personal grooming library. Start off with just one shelf. You will need a place for those wonderful reference books that no groomer should be without. First and foremost, you should have the AKC's *Complete Dog Book,* now in its nineteenth edition. This all-time best-selling dog book offers the official standard for every breed within the AKC's registration. It also contains a wealth of information on breeding, health issues, training, registry, and events within the world of dogs, a wonderful sourcebook for the serious pet care professional.

Other important books for your grooming library include *From Problems to Profits: The Madson Management System for Pet Grooming Businesses* by Madeline Bright Ogle, *The Stone Guide to Dog Grooming for All Breeds* by Ben and Pearl Stone, *The All Breed Dog Grooming Guide* by Sam Kohl, *The Art and Business of Professional Grooming* by Dorothy Walin, and *The Complete Poodle Clipping and Grooming Book* by Shirlee Kalstone. I treasure my monumental *Atlas of Dog Breeds of the World* by Bonnie Wilcox and Chris Walkowicz. Two delightful and informative books by Myrna M. Milani, D.V.M.—*The Body Language and Emotions of Dogs* and *The Body Language and Emotions of Cats*—are fantastic for gaining an understanding of the animals we care for every day. A comprehensive book on first aid is also a must.

Having your own personal library is important to your sense of pride in what you do. You may also wish to stock some videos on grooming the various breeds. Having a combination TV and VCR would be another item to add to your wish list. You can learn to groom each breed from some of the industry's most accomplished groomers like Sarah Hawkes or Joan Anderson in the privacy of your home or shop.

## Dress for Success

When I first started grooming back in the seventies, most of us wore jeans and T-shirts to work. At that time groomers' uniforms consisted of nylon smocks that could have doubled as maternity wear. No more! Today's groomers can pick and choose from a wide variety of stylish uniforms that are highly attractive and practical too. In wash-and-wear fabrics that repel pet hair and look sharp, they are another indication of our newfound professional pride.

In my opinion, one of the best things about being a groomer is that you can kiss the power suit, pantyhose, and high heels goodbye. Men, you can ditch the buttoned-down shirt, pinstripe suit and best of all, the necktie! However, that does not give us permission to look sloppy. Ripped jeans that fit like you were poured into them, T-shirts with X-rated slogans, bare midriffs, halter tops, short shorts, coffee-stained sweats, and tons of jewelry or long dangly earrings are no-nos. Your personal style is an indication of your pride and professionalism. The clothes you wear tell others who you are. They can serve to enhance your image or detract from it.

Uniform manufacturers are always present at industry shows and conventions to show off their latest fashions, and their products are surprisingly inexpensive. To request a catalog, contact Lange Industries in Conroe, Texas, at (800) 542–7113 or www.langeind.com, or Stylist Wear in Garland, Texas, at (800) 288–9327 or www. stylistwear.com. Major distributors also carry groomers' uniforms. Dress for success in your grooming career, proudly portraying the image of a professional in the community.

# Oodles of Options

While we're at it, let's include a sound system to serenade yourself and your furry clients with the soothing sounds of classical, New Age, soft rock or smooth jazz—no raucous rock or rap, please! It's hazardous to the stress levels of both humans *and* animals!

There are countless options when it comes to equipping your dream salon. You probably won't include them right away if you are keeping your eye on your bank account, but isn't it fun to dream? Eventually you may want to add an automatic shampoo system with a central pump dispenser or tanks to deliver the shampoo of your choice right to the pet's coat in the tub, cutting down considerably on the waste and spillage that can occur when you pour from bottles.

My own wish list includes an air purifier system to improve the quality of air for pets and humans alike and to alleviate odor problems. A dehumidifier placed in the bathing area would also cut down on moisture and temperature, allowing dryers to do their job more efficiently.

While we're on the topic of air quality and your health, a vacuum attachment for your clippers, such as the one made by Clipper-Vac, will remove most of the hair from the air you breathe as you clip dogs. Groomers ingest hair every single day, another occupational hazard, and nobody wants to wear a mask. This device would be a worthwhile investment in your health and longevity in the grooming profession.

A central vacuum cleaner system is also a good idea—no clunky canister to trip over, and instant cleanliness at the flick of a switch! One of my innovative fellow groomers had her husband rig up a homemade version, installing a commercial vacuum in the basement with an extra-long hose attachment accessible through wall vents in her salon.

An emergency generator like the ones used by veterinary hospitals is another item on my wish list. Can you think of a more frustrating situation than having the power go out in midclip or finding yourself surrounded by a roomful of wet dogs that can't be dried? Murphy's Law applies everywhere, including the grooming shop!

If you have the room and the resources, consider adding separate laundry facilities for your grooming business. One of my proudest purchases was an industrial capacity washer/dryer. The units are stacked on top of one another to take up less room. I never liked taking doggie towels to the laundromat or putting them into the same washing machine I use for family laundry, and the convenience of having a laundry system on-site can't be beat.

My salon also features a break room for the groomers, with a coffeemaker, microwave, and a small refrigerator. Having a place to sit and eat your lunch out of the hairy environs of the grooming salon is a dream come true. We also placed a picnic table in the outside area in back of the shop so employees can take a well-deserved break in the fresh air in warm weather.

It pains me to admit it, but many grooming shops of yesteryear were sweatshops, dingy places where everything in sight wore a fuzzy coat of dog hair. Thankfully, as the industry has come of age, that image is fading away. Pet owners will no longer settle for second-rate when it comes to caring for their beloved pets. Today, our shops vary widely in character and design, but they do reflect our pride in the grooming profession. As a home groomer, your workplace will be where you live. That's the best reason of all to plan it wisely, make it efficient and attractive, and keep it clean as a whistle!

## Chapter Ten

# Financing Your Grooming Business

Do your homework before you begin the process of constructing and equipping your grooming salon. You'll want the most bang for your buck but you'll need room to grow quality equipment that will stand up to heavy use. If you are on a tight budget like most budding entrepreneurs, you'll probably be living with your choices for a long time!

## What Will It Cost?

OK, now for the reality check and the compromises. What will your dream grooming shop cost? When it comes to estimating the cost of starting a home-based grooming business, there are countless variables. First of all, there is remodeling the space your operation will use. Construction costs will vary according to what you need and will be different for every budding home groomer. The cost will also depend on what hired professionals will charge—carpenters, plumbers, electricians—as opposed to labor provided by you, your family, and friends. One word of caution: Unless your cousin or your neighbor is a licensed plumber or electrician, to satisfy the building inspector you will need the services of these pros.

If you are adding on to a structure, of course you will need a building permit. As far as carpentry, painting, and floor installation go, a do-it-yourself project can save you a bundle. Whether located at home or in a commercial setting, grooming operations usually need to upgrade the capacity of their building's electrical, air-conditioning, and heating systems. You will need a separate water heater. In a commercial location, the landlord often shares in leasehold improvement costs, but at home, you're on your own.

Either way, remodeling and system upgrades could cost as much as $10,000 to $15,000. So you'll want to plan very carefully, determining what you absolutely need to start with and what can wait until later. And you'll want to take advantage of all the "free" family labor you can get! Of course, rather than start your grooming business in a home-based shop, you can choose to begin in a mobile grooming van. For more information on mobile grooming, including the costs, pros, and cons, see "Taking Your Show on the Road: Mobile Grooming," on page 139 of this chapter.

And then there's the equipment. It's easy to go overboard when purchasing equipment for a new salon. Pardon me if I drag out that old chestnut, "Rome wasn't built in a day." You could blow all your cash on state-of-the-art stuff for the shop of your dreams and quickly find yourself out of money. Planning is key. Stick to your business plan and begin with the essentials. As your business and your bottom line grow, you will be able to make those special purchases to improve your salon without jeopardizing your solvency in the process!

The basic cost of equipping a salon with two tubs (one large, one small) and two grooming stations is between $6,000 and $10,000, depending on the amenities you provide. "Six thousand is 'bare bones,'" says Carol Visser, technical support adviser at New England Serum. "It's folding tables, one all-purpose dryer, and a regular bathtub, possibly used, as opposed to stainless steel." A former grooming school instructor and professional groomer both in her home and at commercial locations, Visser told her groomers-in-training to start out this way. "Let your clients buy the good stuff," the industry veteran advises. "Let the dogs pay for it."

This estimate does not include a computer or other office equipment and supplies, nor does it include the costs of licensing and advertising. Most importantly, it does not include the cost of supporting yourself while the business is being built.

So what will you need for your office and reception area, if they will be one and the same? A desk and chair, a phone with an answering machine, a cash register, stationery, and office supplies ranging from rubber stamps to a calculator are bare bones essentials. Your final cost will be affected by variables such as whether you already own a personal computer and printer you can use for your business as well as whether you plan to purchase software, a fax machine, shredder, and copier. The estimated cost of equipping your office can vary between $1,500 and $3,000.

Many home groomers don't give up their "day jobs" for a while, working part-time at something else while they are building their clientele. The sad statistic regarding new businesses is that half of them fail within the first four years. The main reason they go belly-up is undercapitalization. Again, your best tool for ensuring your success is a good business plan. This document outlines your resources, projects your cash flow, and helps you set goals so you can make decisions based on reality, not wishful thinking. Of course, if you are seeking a bank loan to start your business, you will need your business plan tucked under your arm when you go to meet the loan officer. Even if you do not plan to seek outside financing, your business plan will be an important management tool in making every business-related decision you will face.

Business experts tell us that it's generally advisable to have enough cash on hand to take yourself and your business through one full cycle, typically one year. I don't know many groomers who have been able to do this. One of the good things about grooming is that our typical clients come in at four- to eight-week intervals, providing us with a great turnover rate. Rebooking those clients is absolutely essential to the health of your operation.

## The Importance of Rebooking

When I started out, a lot of our dogs were once-a-year clients—big, furry outdoor dogs who got clipped down every spring. "Once a year, whether they need it or not," we used to joke. Thankfully, in most locations, times have changed. Dogs have moved inside and their owners like them to be nice. Our animals are family members, and people are getting accustomed to the pleasures of sharing their homes with a well-groomed pet.

Longhaired breeds and mixes should never be allowed to "winter over" in a mass of matted hair. Not only are they unsightly and smelly, but when they get wet, it can take days for them to dry, leaving them susceptible to chills and illnesses. Your people skills will be called into play as you recommend rebooking to your clients. As a professional pet care provider, it's up to you to educate them about how often their pets should be professionally groomed.

## Shop Till You Drop: Where to Buy It

As you plan your equipment purchases, it would be wise to review industry trade magazines such as *Groomer to Groomer*, *Pet Product News*, *Pet Age*, and *Pet Business* as well as the catalogs of major suppliers, all of which now offer on-line shopping. Among the top distributors are New England Serum of Topsfield, Massachusetts, www.NESerum.com; Ryan's Pet Supplies, Phoenix, Arizona, www.ryanspet.com; American Pet Pro Wholesale Grooming Supplies, Hayward, California, www.americanpetpro.com; LNC Pet Supply, Sun Valley, California, www.lncpetsupply.com; The Animal House of Pet Supplies, Kansas City, Missouri, www.animalhousepetsupply.com; LDC Professional Pet Products, Waukesha, Wisconsin, www.a1petsupply.com; Petfood Warehouse, East Rockaway, New York, www.pfwh.com; and Nolan Enterprises, Inc., Kingsville, Ohio, www.nolanet.com.

These are national companies, but there are hundreds of smaller vendors and distributors that serve a regional clientele. These are the folks who will fill your weekly orders for shampoo, flea and tick collars, brushes, and combs. They usually have a sales rep deliver the goods; the bigger outfits will ship your order. Again, your fellow groomers will be a good source of recommendations on where to buy supplies.

A Web site listing all major vendors and manufacturers can be found at www.PetGroomer.com. This comprehensive Web site also features a wealth of grooming information, plus calendar listings for upcoming regional, national, and international grooming conferences and trade shows. These events offer a great opportunity to equip your salon while pumping up your motivation in the process. Some of the major equipment manufacturers like Petlift and Edemco sometimes offer seminars on salon design at these shows. Their reps are always available to answer your questions and assist you in the planning process.

Subscriptions to magazines like *Groomer to Groomer* are provided free to professional groomers. They often feature articles on salon design and management, grooming products, and the latest equipment trends. Last but definitely not least, before you shop, pick the brains of those who have gone before you, people who make their living in the grooming profession. Arm yourself with knowledge before you whip out that checkbook or credit card!

## Obtaining Credit with Wholesalers

When you go shopping to equip your salon, you will usually need to pay up front for your grooming equipment—tubs, tables, dryers, clippers, etc. Unless you already have a personal relationship with these folks, your initial transactions will be paid for with cash or a credit card. Once your business is up and running, you can obtain credit for purchases with the balance to be paid according to the distributor's terms—within ten, fifteen, or thirty days. This is standard practice for items you intend to sell as retail goods to your clients. You buy them wholesale, usually double the price for your retail, then pay the distributor according to the terms agreed upon.

As you are just starting out, you will need to build a relationship first, starting with a small credit balance that will be increased once you have proven to be a reliable customer. Your first few orders for flea collars and dog biscuits, for example, will probably be C.O.D. or paid for by credit card. After a few such orders, call the company and ask if you can establish an account. This means they will ship merchandise to you without payment, then bill you according to the terms they've stated.

The distributors will most likely have you fill out a credit application. If they ask for a credit reference sheet, provide this information on your own letterhead. At this stage of the game, you might never have heard of such a thing, but if you have a D-U-N-S number, include that too. Dun & Bradstreet, an information services firm that provides business information to companies that make marketing, insurance, or other credit-related decisions, issues this number at no charge. You can register your business by contacting Dun & Bradstreet and answering a series of general business questions regarding ownership, projected revenues and business history. Why bother? A Dun & Bradstreet number will allow you to register for certain business-related events. It will also give you clout when you go looking for additional credit. To find out more, call Dun & Bradstreet at (800) 333–0505 or apply on-line at www.d&b.com.

If you do not have any business references to list on your credit application or credit reference sheet, use personal references. A company likes to see five or six references listed to verify your creditworthiness, but if you can provide only three or four, do so. If you are turned down, explain to the distributor that you intend to purchase products often and ask if there is any other way an account can be opened. If you are told to reapply in the future, then it's up to you to prove yourself by paying your bills on time before you come back to ask for credit again. Remember to conduct yourself like a businessperson. Don't take rejection personally. Everybody was the new kid on the block at some point in time, and if you maintain your winning attitude, you will eventually get what you want.

# FUR MAGNOLIAS GROOMING

## Credit Reference Sheet

D-U-N-S No. 22-333-4444

### Bank
Prosperity National Bank
1415 Main Street
Plainfield, MA 02011
(508) 555–1500
Checking Account #09-123456-0

### Credit References

Peterson's Pet Products
899 Jefferson Boulevard
Clarkville, MA 02789
(508) 555–9876
Account # 604115

Dodson's Doggie Duds
44 Bridge Road
Springdale, MA 02033
(782) 555–1317
Account # 123777

Fido's Factory
85 Rolling Terrace
Southport, RI 00543
(401) 555–0099
Account # 25-888

Sunshine Pet Shampoos
88 Bridge Road
Eastview, MA 02077
(781) 555–1122
Account # 566791

Leo's Leather Leads, Ltd.
2345 Lariat Lane
Sunset Pines, TX 80910
(603) 555–0099
Account # 157-903

402 Maple Lane, Plainfield, MA 02011
Telephone (508) 555–8770

# Managing Credit to Your Advantage

If you succeed in obtaining credit, make sure you understand the terms. Is there a minimum purchase or a special price for quantity buying? What is the company's return policy? How do you receive credit for damaged or missing items in an order? What if you are disappointed in a product? Can you return it for an exchange, a credit, or a refund?

Some vendors offer discounts if you pay by a certain date, usually 10 percent off the total cost. These are special terms, usually reserved for repeat customers.

Once you have established a relationship, however, your distributors can be your best friends. Sometimes they will give you special terms on a major purchase—an electric table, for instance. They may allow you to pay it off in three monthly payments. This is because you are now a known commodity. As a startup, you just don't have this sort of mutual relationship . . . yet.

Why do they make it so tough? Unfortunately, many distributors and vendors in the pet care field have been burned. Many people start their pet care businesses with very little knowledge of how a business should operate. They fly by the seat of their pants, hoping for the best, then they crash and burn, leaving their creditors holding the bag. Don't be one of them. Use your credit wisely and responsibly. It's one of the best things you can do for your professional reputation and the future of your business.

You should also obtain an American Express corporate card for business use. Your responsible use of this card will open up a line of credit for you to use to manage your cash flow, allowing you to stock up on inventory, buy a new piece of equipment, or make needed improvements as your business grows. This is a very flexible credit line for the small-business owner in good standing, and it's a whole lot easier than going to the bank for a loan. It allows repayment in installments instead of when the monthly bill arrives. Contact American Express Small Business Services to find out more. Check their Web site at www.americanexpress.com and click on "Small Business."

# To Sell or Not to Sell?

I firmly believe that you should offer some retail items in your salon. When little Fluffy and Max come in to get groomed, their devoted owners often think about buying a treat to reward their pets or a new collar and leash to dress up their glamorous doggies. Their shopping lists may include flea and tick products, poop bags, dental health and breath items, ID tags, chew toys, stain and odor removers, lint brushes, ear and eye cleaners, vitamins, nail clippers, and brushes and combs to maintain those pets between appointments. You can add substantially to your income with impulse items like these.

Why send your clients elsewhere to find these products? As a pet care professional, you carry a high degree of credibility with these clients. After all, they entrust you with the care of their beloved pets. In providing these retail products, you are helping them to take better care of their animals. You are acting as a problem-solver for them. Learn to listen for cues in conversations with your clients and recognize them as sales opportunities. Tell them about a product, lead them to it, and put it in their hands as you explain how it will help them. Don't be shy! Adopt a businesslike perspective. You are not taking advantage of these folks; you are helping them and making a profit in the process.

Of course, if you decide to sell goods, you will need to keep track of your sales taxes. Most states have a sales tax, and you need to register with the state Department of Corporations and Taxation to receive your sales tax number. See Chapter 5 for more information on collecting and paying sales taxes.

## Ask and You Shall Receive: How Your Distributors Can Help You

If you do opt to sell pet products, there are ways around spending big bucks on displays. Many distributors that deal primarily with treats and toys offer displays with minimum orders. My daughter Missi manages my retail operation, and she has spent no money on displays in our 1,000-square-foot retail area, yet our displays are always fresh and attractive. How does she do it? She makes deals! Just like you and me, all of those good folks out there selling products are trying to make a profit, so make them work for you! It's a win-win situation!

Let's eavesdrop on a couple of typical conversations between Missi and the sales reps:

> "I see your product doesn't come with a display, but I know I can get a display from this other company. I just really wanted to do business with you because I've heard so many good things about your company."
>
> "I'll buy the deal, but you have to throw in a display and I'll only

feature your product in the display! That means I *have* to buy from you again, right?"

Develop relationships with your sales reps. Being in business is all about interacting successfully with people. A nice display sells more, so you'll make more money and so will they!

# Buying in Bulk and Product Storage

It's in your best interest to become a wheeler-dealer. That's part of the fun of being in business! You can get some great deals when you buy products in bulk, whether it's flea collars or gallons of shampoo. The case price always beats the individual price. Of course, you will need a place to store these bargains. Remember as you design your salon that you can never have too much storage space!

If the products you are purchasing by the bushel are edibles, long-term storage could also present a problem. Even dog biscuits have a shelf life. They can get moldy or attract moths if stored too long, so what appears to be a big bargain might not turn out that way after all. Learn to read product codes, especially if you plan to sell pet food and snacks.

Date codes for shelf life on dry pet food, cookies, and snacks are pretty straightforward, stating the product is "best sold by" a particular date. Canned goods are another matter. Each company does it differently, some clearly indicating an expiration date, others using numbers indicating the code of the plant where it was produced, the number of the batch, and the number of the day (from 1 to 365), and year when it will be out of code. In case of a recall, these numbers would identify the product. The pet food company sales

> **Never Pay Retail!**
> One of the best things about being in business is that when it comes to business purchases, you don't have to pay retail! When buying products from a company that sells retail as well as wholesale, all you have to do is provide your state tax ID number and you can avoid paying sales taxes on your own purchases. Suppliers are sticklers for this tax ID number, so be sure to have it handy. The success of your business is measured by profit margins. To win at this game, you should try to squeeze every penny you can out of every purchase, keeping your eye on that all-important bottom line.

representative should inform you about these codes when you agree to sell that product line.

As a "little guy" you might not think you have much buying power, but one organization offers discounts and rebates for pet care professionals from hundreds of participating companies. It is the Groomer's Club, now operating under the auspices of Barkleigh Publications. To find out more about this potential money-saver, e-mail barkleigh@aol.com.

If you have a friendly relationship with other groomers in your area, find out if they would be interested in forming a buying cooperative. That way you could all get those quantity discounts and increase your buying power. Of course, this would only work if co-op members can shelve their distrust of "the competition" and join together with a mutual spirit of camaraderie.

## Inventory Control

If you have chosen to do some retail, you will need to keep track of your inventory. When that consists of a dozen flea collars, some cookie treats, and slicker brushes, it's pretty simple. But as the number of products you carry grows—and sells—you will need to know what you have in stock so you can keep up with customer demand and not lose valuable sales because you don't have an item in stock.

To keep an accurate count and make sure you are getting what you pay for, inventory items should be examined and counted as you unpack the boxes. By law, a count of your inventory is required once a year for tax purposes. You will need to provide it to your accountant. For insurance purposes, you also need to document the value of everything you have in stock as well as your grooming and office equipment. Keep a list of every product you sell and record the quantity on hand for accurate record keeping. Your inventory's value is a combination of each item's cost plus any shipping charges you paid.

Here is an example:

| | | | |
|---|---|---|---|
| 12 flea collars | @ $4.50 | = | $54.00 |
| 12 flea powders | @ $3.50 | = | $42.00 |
| 12 flea combs | @ $1.00 | = | $12.00 |
| | Subtotal | | $108.00 |
| | Shipping | | $9.00 |
| | Total cost | | $117.00 |

The cost of shipping ($9.00) divided by the total number of products shipped

(36) equals 25 cents. You would add this 25 cents to each product to get the true cost for your inventory as well as to arrive at the price you will decide to sell it for.

Some people like to keep their inventory on a spreadsheet to document each product, the quantity available, wholesale price, and quantity sold to date. Others use software programs like Mind Your Own Business (MYOB) or Quickbooks. Until recently, we used a simple ledger in my salon, but as our retail has grown, we needed to install a point-of-sale cash register system with a pricing gun that scans the bar code on every item, much like the ones used in supermarkets. Among the many features this system provides is an inventory tracking system that produces a weekly order for each vendor and tracks our profits as well. I realize that for someone just starting out, this is monumental overkill; it really performs the same function as we did when we walked around the front room with a list and a pencil.

## Taking Your Show on the Road: Mobile Grooming

Another option for the groomer who wants to operate out of his or her home is mobile grooming. This is a business that has really come of age in the last decade. With today's demand for convenience and individual service, there is plenty of room for the mobile groomer. Many pet owners, including the elderly and those with disabilities, have trouble transporting Fido to the grooming salon. For clients like these, having a grooming shop on wheels roll right into the driveway to provide care for their pets is just what the doctor ordered!

Once you have completed your training, all you need to go mobile is a fully outfitted van. These vans come in all sizes and models, from brand-new custom-built units to converted RVs or trailers. They can be extremely attractive and luxurious, featuring state-of-the-art grooming equipment like clipper vacuum systems, hydraulic or electric tables, dryers, ramps, carpeting, cages, and even stereo systems, TVs and VCRs. Until you step inside and check out what they have to offer, you can't imagine how efficiently and attractively they are designed.

Being mobile gives the groomer flexibility. From raising kids to showing dogs, the mobile groomer builds a work schedule custom-made to fit his or her needs. New units are priced in the $40,000 to $50,000 range, but your initial investment can be as little as 10 percent down. Financing is available through the major auto manufacturers like Ford and Chrysler or through a conventional bank loan.

When you consider the initial cost of starting a shop, the mobile looks even better. In a commercial location, you must pay first and last month's rent as well as leasehold improvements, which can easily total $10,000 to $15,000 once you get through with remodeling, electricity, and plumbing costs. Once your van is paid off—typically within five years at $800 to $900 a month—you will have an asset worth $25,000 or more if you have taken care of it properly.

While experienced shop groomers typically groom ten to twelve pets in a day, the mobile groomer usually grooms no more than six. However, when you consider the higher cost per job the mobile operator charges for such personalized service, you end up doing fewer pets and taking in the same amount of money. According to Dina Perry, President of Wag'n Tails Mobile Conversions of Elkhart, Indiana, the average mobile groomer makes at least $50,000 a year. Perry, who has also owned and operated grooming salons, a grooming school, a dryer company, and a boarding kennel, once had a fleet of twenty vans on the road. This innovative woman who has been such a force in the mobile grooming industry was named Groomer of the Century at the Cardinal Crystal Achievement Awards ceremony this year at Intergroom—akin to a Lifetime Achievement Award at the Oscars.

When investigating the purchase of a mobile grooming van, you should educate yourself by checking out manufacturers' Web sites on-line. For Perry's company, now run by her son Dennis Gnetz, check www.wagntails.com. For J. T. Custom Works, Inc., also of Elkhart, visit www.customvehicles.com. Odyssey Mobile Pet Grooming Vehicles of Wharton, New Jersey, building mobiles since 1979, is on-line at www.odysseyauto.com. Frank Weag, Odyssey's mobile van sales representative, runs the Mobile Van Roundup Rodeo at Groom Expo in Pennsylvania every September, a great place to check out makes and models. Another major manufacturer, Ultimate Groomobiles, Inc. of Sarasota, Florida, can be visited on-line at www.ultimate-groomobiles.com.

You've heard the pros but what are the potential cons when it comes to mobile grooming? First, downtime for the mobile groomer's vehicle means no income! You'll want to check carefully the service and support options that are available.

"If the company truly cares for your business they will send you replacement parts overnight and deal with vendors and repair shops themselves," says Terry E. Minix, President and CEO of J. T. Custom Works. "Some conversion companies require you to have written authorization before repairs can take place. Most responsible manufactures have a policy that will allow the customer to choose where they would like to have repairs made to their vehicle."

You also need to be aware of the quality of the conversion. The mobile industry has been known to make things look good cosmetically while cutting corners on materials, equipment, and workmanship. Talk to other mobile groomers; most manufacturers will be glad to furnish references.

Mobile grooming also has a self-contained ceiling as to the number of pets you can groom. In a mobile business, there is no room for expansion unless you purchase more vehicles. It can be done. You can make your business a family affair, with your spouse or adult children hitting the road in another van of their own. One of the most accomplished groomers in the industry, Melissa Verplank, started with a single mobile van and grew her business to six units. A national and international grooming champion, Verplank has been a member and National Coordinator of GroomTeam USA. She currently operates her own grooming school, which is under contract to train groomers for the PETsMART chain.

Tailor-made insurance policies are now provided for mobile operators by Gibson-Governor Agency, Inc. of Vienna, Ohio (www.gibsongovernor.com). Mobile groomers even have their own organization, Professional Mobile Groomers International, (PMGI). Find out more on-line at www.yourpmgi.org.

If you are an independent spirit who desires the freedom of the open road while running your own grooming business, a career as a mobile groomer may be just the ticket!

# Chapter Eleven

# Pet Grooming Potpourri

One of the best and worst things about grooming is that in this job, no two days are alike! You can cut down on stress and keep things running smoothly if you adhere to routine operational procedures from Day One. You will soon develop your own policies regarding shop upkeep, scheduling, client relations, safety and health issues. To keep your batteries charged and continue to learn and grow, it's also important to attend seminars and network with your fellow groomers. When you're working alone, isolation can become an occupational hazard.

## Good Housekeeping and Antiseptic Procedures

When I'm in my shop, you will often see me with a broom in my hand. As I have said, a business owner wears many hats, including that of the janitor! I've even overheard the staff joking that the broom is my primary mode of transportation. In a grooming salon, hair is a plentiful by-product. If we could sell it by the bagful, we could all retire early. Just as in a beauty salon for humans, when a stylist is giving a haircut, there is bound to be hair on the floor. But in a beauty parlor, it gets swept up after each and every client. Can you imagine how you would feel if you had to wade through someone else's hair to get into the stylist's chair? It would be like having the hostess at an expensive restaurant show you to a table piled high with the previous patron's dirty dishes—not very appetizing!

It's the same story in the grooming salon. I can't tell you how often busy groomers who are "on the clock" keep grooming dog after dog without sweeping or vacuuming the floor around their tables, totally oblivious to the fact that they are working knee-deep in hair! Can you think or a more unattractive sight for clients who pop their heads into the groom room to ooh and ahh at all those cute little critters?

Okay, I'm done ranting. The professional groomer should sweep up the hair and clean his or her table after each dog. End of story. If you can't get to it yourself and you have employees, use a little teamwork and help each other out. At least once a day, the place should be vacuumed thoroughly. Hair builds up in corners, on dryer filters, on top of and under the water heater, under the tubs, even migrating into the reception area. The stuff seems to have a mind of its own. It would be a shame to spend all this time and money planning and building your dream only to give the impression that you don't give a hoot about keeping it clean. Clients will appreciate the cleanliness of your shop and they will want to keep coming back. After all, they are entrusting you with their precious pets, their surrogate children, and they need to feel that you are a responsible professional who provides a safe and sanitary environment for the animals in your care.

One of the nicest compliments a visitor can pay me is to remark on how fresh and clean my shop smells. It makes my day. Grooming can be a messy and smelly business. Dirty dog hair, "accidents" that occur on a daily basis with nervous pets, dogs that have just had a personal encounter with a skunk, wet towels, anal gland secretions, ear odors—you name it, bad smells come from myriad sources. Keeping them under control is a challenge.

Your grooming area must be cleaned and disinfected daily. If dog hair builds up in the crates or under the tub, it can provide a breeding ground for fleas, ticks, mange mites, bacteria, and mold. Sweeping and vacuuming often is an important first step, but the floor needs a good scrubbing with a deodorizing and disinfecting cleaner at least once a week. The product you choose should not only make the place look and smell clean, it should also eliminate viruses, bacteria, and fungi. Dander and sloughed off skin from pets can harbor all manner of infectious materials. Feces, urine, and other body fluids can spread parvovirus and many other diseases.

Your grooming table should be cleaned of hair and debris after each dog. Keep spray bottles of antiseptic cleaner handy to speed up this process and for immediate cleanup when accidents occur. Use a scrub brush to clean out the grooved surface of your grooming table. Cages and crates should be washed down at the end of each day. If they get soiled or hold pets with skin conditions, of course they will need cleaning immediately. Your job will be made easier if your cages have removable pans in the bottoms or your built-in cubbies have a washable surface like Formica. The tub also needs a good scrubbing at the end of each workday.

Your clipper blades and scissors need frequent cleaning too. An old toothbrush works well for removing hair and dirt from the blade teeth. If you have been clipping a dog with a skin condition, soak those blades in a disinfectant made for this purpose. Wipe your shears down with a germicidal cleaner, dry them thoroughly, then lubricate the hinges. The forceps you use to remove hair from dogs' ears are another potential source of contamination. Disinfect them after each and every use to avoid spreading ear infections among your furry clientele. If an animal has fleas or ticks, keep it separate from all other clients, get it into the tub for flea or tick bath as soon as possible, and spray every area it has been in.

Beyond the cleaning and disinfecting of equipment, all groomers should learn basic clipper repair and maintenance. For students and veterans alike, hands-on workshops are held at every major grooming convention covering clipper care, the causes and correction of common problems, the tools needed for routine repairs, and the use of blade coolants. Mastering these basic chores is not difficult and can save you a bundle.

By educating yourself on the safe use of pesticides in the shop, you can also be your own pest control expert. During flea season, use foggers to eliminate those pesky parasites in your shop at least once a week. When ticks are removed, drop them into a container of alcohol or dip to kill them. Never throw them in the trash bucket; they can escape and hatch out their young. Never handle ticks without gloves. They cause several diseases, including Lyme disease, Rocky Mountain spotted fever, tularemia, ehrlichiosis, and babesiosis. If you have groomed a pet with fleas or ticks, get those bags of contaminated hair out of the shop immediately. Having a client tell you that a dog picked up fleas at your shop is not the kind of word-of-mouth publicity you want to get around.

A wide array of wonderful products is available to keep your workplace sanitary. Make sure the one you choose is effective against all viruses (including parvovirus), bacteria, and fungal spores. In a pinch, you can disinfect surfaces with a solution of one part chlorine bleach to thirty parts water, but if you splash this stuff on your clothing, you'll be wearing polka dots! Electric air purifiers work wonders keeping the air fresh and clean. Ours employs an ionizer to remove odor-causing particles from the environment. It works so well that my neighbor, a veterinarian, sometimes borrows it. We also freshen up the place up regularly with a spritz of citrus deodorizer.

Last but not least, wash your hands, preferably with an antibacterial hand cleaner. This will protect your own health as well as that of the pets in your care. Just like bad news travels fast, so does a good reputation. If your shop is clean and sanitary, the word will get around and you will receive recommendations from happy clients, veterinarians and fellow pet care professionals.

## Pet Health Issues

For groomers, it is vitally important to check the condition of every single pet that comes through your door when it is being dropped off for grooming. Ask the owner if there have been any changes in the pet's health since its last appointment. For new clients, ask if you need to be aware of any existing ailments or conditions. If a pet is under the care of a veterinarian, you need to know if it will be at risk during the grooming process. If you have any doubts or misgivings, by all means contact the vet to get the proper clearance before you groom the animal, or have the owner rebook and return with a letter from the vet to protect yourself.

There are many instances when it would be advisable to have the owner sign a release form to protect you in case the pet has an adverse reaction to the grooming procedure. "Red flags" include a coat so severely matted that clipping and/or brushing could cause skin irritation; dogs with heart conditions, seizure disorders, cancer, or joint problems; or dogs that are frail or elderly. You may not be aware that a dog has a disk problem in its back or a trick knee until it cries out in pain as it is being groomed or bathed. Take the time to ask the right questions and have the release forms signed and kept on file.

Observe the dog's skin condition as you go over it with the owner. If there are open sores, scabs, and obvious infections, you should not attempt to groom the pet; refer it to a veterinarian instead. This is not only for your own protection, but to avoid exposure to other dogs in your care.

You should also require that all dogs you take in to your establishment be up to date on their shots. Rabies, caused by a virus that attacks the nervous system, is increasingly more widespread. In the Northeast where I live, it has reached epidemic proportions. Although it is far more prevalent in wild animals than in the pet population, dogs and cats can get it too. After entering the body, the virus multiplies, causing encephalitis (inflammation of the brain.) Untreated, this disease is always fatal to pets and people. To protect yourself and your staff, gather vaccination information when you take dogs in and make sure you update your files.

# FUR MAGNOLIAS GROOMING
402 Maple Lane, Plainfield, MA 02011
Telephone (508) 555–8770

## Dematting

June 1, 2002

Dear Mary Brown,

Your pet's health and proper care are first and foremost in our minds and in our hearts here at Fur Magnolias Grooming. Due to the matting and tangling of Max's coat today, it will require extra work to complete his grooming. Dematting is not included as part of the base price, and there will be an extra charge today. The rate for dematting is $35 per hour in addition to your pet's base price for grooming.

Please understand that the process of dematting can be uncomfortable for your pet and may sometimes cause skin irritations. We will provide your pet with a medicated bath if it will increase his comfort. There is an additional charge for medicated baths.

If the dematting process is too uncomfortable or strenuous for Max, we will be in touch with you to discuss the alternatives. Please leave us a telephone number where you can be reached.

If you agree to this contract, please sign below.

I, the undersigned, grant permission to Fur Magnolias Grooming to demat my pet. I understand that there may be complications and I will not hold Fur Magnolias Grooming responsible.

_____     _____

Signature                                              Date

_____

Phone

**Client release form letter, dematting**

# FUR MAGNOLIAS GROOMING

402 Maple Lane, Plainfield, MA 02011
Telephone (508) 555–8770

## Stripping the Coat

Dear Mary Brown,

Your pet's health and proper care are first and foremost in our minds and in our hearts here at Fur Magnolias Grooming. Due to Max's condition of severe tangling and matting, we will need to shave him today. Please understand that it is our belief that this is the kindest and most humane thing to do for Max. The matting is too severe and the dematting process itself would be painful and leave the coat severely damaged.

We will perform this procedure with the utmost care; however, there is a possibility of skin irritation and nicking. If we feel a medicated bath will soothe the irritated skin, we will provide that service for your pet at an additional charge.

If you understand this contract, please sign below.

I, the undersigned, grant permission to Fur Magnolias Grooming to perform the necessary grooming procedure to remove the matting from my pet. I understand that there may be complications and I will not hold Fur Magnolias Grooming responsible for these complications.

_____          _____
Signature                                Date

**Client release form letter, stripping the coat**

Some clients perceive this information-gathering as a bother, but don't be put off. Proof of rabies vaccination is required by most states in order to get a dog licensed. Most pet owners will appreciate your diligence and professionalism. Even though rabies is a far greater threat to humans in developing countries, every year an estimated 35,000 people in the United States must receive postexposure prophylaxis (PEP) treatment, a twenty-eight-day series of shots, following exposure to this dreaded disease.

Be sure to check with your local health department on the laws regarding dog bites. In Massachusetts, a dog bite must be reported to the local health authorities and to the animal control officer in your community. Whether the dog is up-to-date on its shots or not, if it has bitten someone it must be quarantined at home for a ten-day period, after which it will be examined by the animal control officer to make sure that it is healthy before it is released from quarantine.

Pet animals become exposed to rabies when they tangle with wild animals, usually through a bite wound. When you are handling dogs that have been sprayed by a skunk or outdoor cats that hunt, you are putting yourself at risk if these pets do not have current rabies vaccinations. Rabies can be transmitted through bodily fluids, so if a pet's coat has blood or saliva from an infected animal, you could contract the disease through a cut or scratch on your own skin.

You must also exercise care when dealing with puppies. They usually start to receive their vaccinations at six to eight weeks of age, followed by three or four booster shots at two- to four-week intervals. These youngsters should not be exposed to other dogs until they have completed their second series of shots. Healthy adult dogs that are up-to-date on their shots are protected from infectious diseases like parvovirus, but in the case of an unvaccinated pup, such an illness could be fatal.

The three basic vaccinations all dogs should receive include a multipurpose one known as DHPP, which guards against distemper, hepatitis, parainfluenza, and parvovirus (if it also includes leptospirosis antigen, it is called DHLPP); Bordetella, the most common cause of so-called kennel cough; and the rabies vaccine. A rabies shot is good for either one year or three. Whether given annually or every three years, it's the same vaccine. Boosting it annually produces a stronger immunity for the pet. Most states require rabies shots for dogs and cats. Some states, such as New York and Texas, now require dogs to be vaccinated annually. Ultimately, it is the owner's responsibility to keep dogs properly vaccinated, but to be on the safe side and to protect your clients and staff, make this record keeping part of your regular intake procedure.

Having a good relationship with the vets in your area is vitally important for many reasons. When you are known as a conscientious and caring professional, vets will send their clients your way for grooming. You will also need to keep the lines of communication open. A client might tell you, "The vet said my dog was clipper-burned at your shop," or "The vet told me my dog picked up kennel cough the last time you groomed him." A personal and professional relationship with the vet will help you to discuss the situation in a professional manner. Unfortunately, some vets blame the groomer for everything from impacted anal glands to the common cold, but many times, clients' reports of what the vet said get severely distorted in translation. A mutually respectful relationship with the vet is your best insurance against unwarranted accusations.

Clipper burn is probably the most common complaint that groomers hear about. It is the result of shaving the dog with a blade that is too hot or cuts too close in a sensitive area like the face, tummy, or genitals. It can be serious, causing a second-degree burn or leading to a bacterial infection. The good news is that it doesn't have to happen. Make sure your blades are not overheated when you groom. Feel them with your fingers and change them often. Spray them with a cooling agent as you work. When clipping white or light-colored dogs like bichons, poodles, Maltese, or West Highland terriers, don't use a blade that cuts very close on sensitive areas. Instead of a #15 or a #10 blade, use a #9 or a #7F. Also make sure you are not grooming with dull blades, another potential cause of this condition.

Sometimes the groomer gets blamed for clipper burn if the animal's sensitive skin causes a reaction to the grooming. Other times, dogs whose coats have been badly neglected end up irritated and itchy after a clipdown. These pets may go home and start digging and scratching themselves to the point of self-mutilation, and the irate owner will call to accuse you of "cutting" the dog. Your best bet is to explain that some dogs, like some people, have highly sensitive skin and get a rash from shaving. If the animal was in rough shape before you even started, explain the need for more frequent groomings and resolve to examine all pets more carefully in the future. In the case of a supersensitive pet, tell the owner that the situation can be remedied if you leave the hair longer next time in sensitive areas. Offer a free medicated bath to soothe the pet—and the owner too.

A good working relationship with a vet is a blessing if an injury to a pet occurs in your shop. It is unfortunate and extremely upsetting, but occasionally accidents do happen. A nicked ear, a cut footpad, an eye irritation from soap, or a scissor cut—these situations require a vet's prompt attention. I have always been fortunate to have veterinary colleagues who would deliver that stitch in time or provide emergency treatment when such situations crop up.

The first rule to follow when an injury occurs is to tell the pet's owner. It's scary, but you have to do it. Nine times out of ten, it's a minor matter—skin irritated from brushing, a scratch or a nick—but as an honest professional, you must document the incident and let the owner know about it immediately. Offer a product to help heal it, at no charge, of course. Offer the next grooming "on the house." If you feel it is your fault, you should volunteer to cover any veterinary expenses, if needed. Your liability insurance should cover such medical care. Most people understand that a dog can wiggle or jump unexpectedly as you are working on it. They are living creatures, after all, not stuffed animals. Being honest and up-front in such situations is important for your own integrity and peace of mind as well. Follow up the visit by calling to see how the pet is doing.

No matter how upsetting a situation is, we can always learn from it. Grooming, performed with sharp instruments like shears, clipper blades, and dematting tools, requires total concentration. By paying attention and adhering to safe practices in the workplace, we can take steps to keep such instances from occurring.

Of course, there are times when you will detect an injury or a medical condition that has nothing to do with you. Because we examine and handle dogs all over their furry bodies, we often notice things the owner might miss when giving Fido a pat or a tickle once or twice a day. It is important to tell the owner of anything out of the ordinary you discover while grooming a pet. It is also important to document it. Occasionally, we all run into that problem customer who wants to blame everything on us. It's a worst-case scenario, but if such a matter ends up in court, you will need proper documentation to prove you are not at fault.

The most common causes for concern that groomers discover when caring for pets are tumors and growths. They are not hard to spot on short-coated dogs, but they can be easily missed under a thick or long coat. Older dogs are prone to warts, making the job of grooming without nicking them very tricky. Most fatty tumors you detect are probably not malignant, but those solidly adhering to bone may indicate cancer is present. Dogs get all the same cancers as people, including mammary tumors. Dogs that wince or cry when you touch their muzzle may have oral tumors or dental problems. If you see tartar buildup on the teeth or notice that the pet's breath has a foul odor, you need to convey this information to the owner.

You may notice that a dog is limping or doesn't want one of its paws touched. You may see a discharge from the ears, eyes, or genital area. The skin may have lesions or evidence of parasites like fleas, ticks, lice, or mange mites. You may uncover an abscess or wound the owner does not know about. A normally happy pet may appear listless or overly agitated on a particular visit. A dog may have a seizure in your shop. All of these conditions need to be brought to the owner's attention. In cases of serious illness, the sooner the pet gets medical treatment, the better its chances for a full recovery. It is so gratifying to have an owner thank you for noticing something he or she could have missed. It's fun to be a hero!

You must be careful informing the client about anything out-of-the ordinary you encounter while grooming. First, do not diagnose; that's a job for the vet. Even if you suspect something as common as ear mites in a cat, remember that those tiny organisms can only be seen under a microscope. Do not suggest treatment; merely tell the owner calmly and without drama that you think Fluffy needs to see the vet to have the situation checked.

Tact is essential. Owners may have financial problems and feel they are unable to afford treatment. They may be in denial or emotionally unable to cope with a pet's illness. They may react defensively, blaming the messenger, which in this case happens to be you. In any event, as a caring professional, you must tell them what you have observed and recommend they seek the proper medical help.

## Early Arrivals and Late Pickups

One of the most common complaints for all groomers, especially those who work out of their homes, is the customer who arrives early and picks up late. Having your grooming business where you live can be a blessing and a curse. Stories abound of impatient clients parked in the driveway with the motor running as you sip your morning coffee or emerge from the shower. Just because you work where you live, some folks think it's perfectly acceptable to drop off or pick up their pets any time they please.

Educating your clientele on your hours of operation is up to you. You should post a sign listing the hours your business is open. When animals are dropped off in the morning, be sure to say, "Last pickup is by six o'clock," or whatever time you deem appropriate. People need to realize that groomers have a life too. We have dinner engagements, kids' baseball games, evening courses to attend, and social functions, just like everybody else.

If owners pick up late more than once, it's up to you to tactfully tell them that you can no longer groom their pets unless they can pick up on time. Some groomers institute a "late fee," usually five to ten dollars per hour, for pets left after hours. In my decades of grooming, I have only had to take forgotten canine customers home with me on three occasions. Two of those three owners left me a generous tip, but I still missed out on family plans because they were tardy.

If John Q. Public pulls into your driveway while you're still in your pajamas, have the self-control not to go to the door until you are ready to open. People do not do that to their doctor, dentist, or hairstylist; why is it okay to do it to their groomer? When you do open your doors, again explain your hours of operation. Some folks need to hear it more than once.

In my busy salon, we open at 7:30 A.M. two days a week instead of the usual 8:30. We do this to accommodate commuters, and they appreciate it, but we still occasionally encounter the impatient patron banging on the door at 7:15, irate because we are not open yet. It is important to remain calm and professional. This is the customer's problem, not yours. You can be sure if you do open at 7:15 this time, the next time this guy will arrive at 7:00!

We make reminder calls to each client a day or two before the appointment, always stating our shop's drop-off times. We require the dogs to be in by 9:30 A.M. so each groomer will have his or her workload for the day and can get the "roughing" work out of the way before the dogs are bathed. If a person arrives an hour late without phoning to let us know, it can disrupt a groomer's schedule and cause a lot of stress. My daughter Missi has posted a sign informing the clientele of our policy:

> Dogs arriving after 9:30 A.M. may not be taken. We go to a waiting list at 9:30 to ensure our groomers a full day of work. Thank you for your understanding.

This gives us a little leeway to either take in the late arrival or reschedule the appointment for another day.

Of course, at times there are extenuating circumstances. We are happy to make an exception, but in such cases the client has usually called ahead to make special arrangements. We also write the arrival time along with the date on the appointment card when we rebook the pet. Walking that fine line between enjoying the customers' friendship and commanding their respect can be a challenge. You need to set your boundaries and stick to them.

# Groomer Health Issues

Grooming takes a toll on the body. It is a labor-intensive job. First of all, most groomers stand all day, straining the legs and contributing to varicose veins. Performing some grooming functions while seated on a stool will give your legs a rest. Use a cushioned mat under your table and move around as you work to lessen the strain and prevent blood from pooling in your legs. Some groomers wear support hose to prevent leg fatigue. All groomers need to wear comfortable shoes that offer support. Clogs and sandals do not fill the bill, and bare feet are a no-no in the shop. You could drop sharp tools on your toes or step on something highly unappetizing as you go about your work.

Today's groomers have the benefits of hydraulic and electric tables and ramps or folding stairs to help get big dogs in and out of the tub, but there is still a large amount of lifting you need to do in this profession. It's crucial to the health of your back that you learn to lift correctly, using your legs to do most of the work and asking for help when you need it. You are not Superman or Wonder Woman!

Scissoring is an activity that uses repetitive motion of the hands and wrists, a prime cause of tendinitis and carpal tunnel syndrome. The continual overuse of the fine muscles of the hands and wrists places a strain on a large nerve that extends from the wrist to the fingertips. Carpal tunnel syndrome is painful and debilitating; it can end a grooming career. It results in numbness of the thumb and fingers and a loss of muscle control as well as chronic pain. Working with the proper tools—scissors that are the right size and weight for your hands, clippers that are not too bulky and heavy—goes a long way toward preventing this occupational hazard. Many groomers wear wrist supports to prevent or relieve this condition. It is treatable through surgery, but that requires several weeks of incapacitation and recuperation, and it is not always 100 percent successful.

Our workplaces can be like obstacle courses. I was reminded of this recently when I ended up on the floor after tripping over the base of a dryer. Electrical cords attached to dryers and clippers are easy to trip over as well. Making sure we never touch electrical equipment with wet hands may seem like a no-brainer, but in the hectic rush of a busy day, one can easily become distracted and forget this fundamental safety rule.

Stress is another common health hazard to groomers. We work by the clock, and time is money. We strive to please a wide spectrum of the general public. Our work can be unpredictable and sometimes dangerous. We are not always treated with respect. To preserve your sanity, it is necessary that you learn to handle stress. Groomer burnout is a recognized phenomenon in this business.

We need to take good care of Number One. Good eating and sleeping habits go a long way toward preparing us for all the situations we face in a day of working with animals that can be uncooperative and owners who can be quite demanding. Groomers are notorious for their poor eating habits. A cup of coffee and a doughnut may constitute breakfast, while lunch is whatever you can grab in between dogs. I have been known to get through the day on coffee, candy bars, and soft drinks, but after a while, it takes a toll. Sugar gives us a quick energy boost but it fades fast, leaving us feeling more tired and "empty" than we did before. It is important to make the time to eat a nourishing breakfast and sit down away from the dog hair for a well-deserved lunch break.

I used to think that grooming dogs was all the physical activity I needed to stay in shape, but today I know better. Aerobic activity like walking, running, biking, or taking some classes at the gym protects our cardiovascular health, builds our endurance, and helps us deal with stress. Weight training improves our overall conditioning and strengthens our bones as it improves our metabolism. Going outside during the day for a breath of fresh air or a walk around the block provides a mental and physical respite from the harried routine.

Taking care of your physical needs is key, but to succeed in this field it is equally important to develop a healthy mental attitude. You need to learn to take things in stride and not sweat the small stuff. It's easier said than done, but once in a while, it helps to get a reality check. We are dealing with pet grooming, not brain surgery! We do our best to treat the animals with loving kindness, to improve our grooming knowledge and skill, and to style these pets to please their owners. We soon learn, however, that we can't please everybody. Some people have demands that we cannot fulfill. Sometimes things happen that are beyond our control. Anger over problems that we can't immediately solve, the hectic pace of our working environment, financial pressures, family issues, unreasonable clients—all of these things can overwhelm us, robbing us of our energy and our joy.

Keeping our problems bottled up inside does not make them go away. Having a trusted partner, friend, or family member to turn to can be a huge help. We may need to talk to a therapist or counselor to get to the root of our problems and start feeling better. One thing is certain: If you don't deal with your stress, it will manifest itself in physical symptoms like sleep disturbances, depression, anxiety, fatigue, or serious illness.

Taking the time to pamper yourself also helps maintain your mental equilibrium. Yoga, meditation, writing in your journal, reading, planting a flower bed, learning how to say no—there are many ways to counteract the stresses of everyday life. Laughter is a great stress reliever. No matter how overwhelming a situation feels, chances are you can find a humorous way of looking at it.

Groomers like to joke with each other, saying that we are "no-lifers." There is some truth to that. We sometimes focus on our jobs to the detriment of family life and friendships. We all need to achieve that balance between doing a job we love and nourishing ourselves with supportive relationships and fun activities that recharge our batteries and feed our souls.

## Transmittable Diseases

Pet care professionals also need to be aware of zoonotic diseases, those illnesses that are transmittable from animals to humans. We have already mentioned tick-borne diseases. The most important thing to remember is to wear gloves and use tweezers when pulling ticks off pets. Ticks spread their diseases to humans not only by attaching themselves to our skin but also through our contact with their bacteria-laden fluids.

Such internal parasites as hookworm, roundworm, heartworm, trichinosis, ringworm, and tapeworm can be passed to people who come in contact with animal feces. When you're working with animals, never pick up food without scrubbing your hands first.

Ringworm, a fungal infection, is more prevalent in cats than in dogs. You can pick it up through spores in the air as well as by contact with an infected animal. When you scratch the resulting ring-shaped lesions, the disease spreads as new spores are released. It is highly contagious to people you come in contact with and can eventually lead to kidney damage.

Learn to look for its symptoms. Pets with crusty sores behind their ears, small round scabby or bald patches on their bodies, and/or sparse hair growth around their eyes may have ringworm. I prefer to let the vet handle pets with this problem. If animals infected with ringworm have been in your shop, treat every area they have come in contact with, using a germicidal disinfectant or a bleach solution. These spores can linger in cages and on tables for as long as fourteen days.

Animal bites are the source of a variety of illnesses. Rabies, septicemia, and streptococcal and staphylococcal infections are all bacterial infections transmittable primarily through bite wounds. When working with animals, it is vital to maintain up-to-date tetanus shots. If you get bitten, bleeding should not be stopped immediately because your system rids itself of bacteria this way. Thoroughly wash the wound with an antibacterial soap, then assess whether you need to go to the hospital for stitches.

Canine brucellosis, another transmittable illness, causes symptoms similar to those of mononucleosis: fever, chills, headaches, joint pain, and fatigue. When seeking medical treatment for symptoms like these, be sure to tell your doctor that you work with pets.

Coccidia and giardia are microorganisms present in the intestines of cats and dogs. When pets get stressed, as they often do in grooming or boarding situations, they become symptomatic, resulting in vomiting, diarrhea, and eventually coat and skin damage. Keeping your shop cleaned and disinfected will protect you from catching these diseases.

Chlamydia is transmitted by cats that show symptoms through runny eyes, sometimes with the "third eyelid" elevated in the corner of the eye. Cats can and should be vaccinated against this illness. In humans it looks like conjunctivitis, but it can cause pneumonia and genital infections, transmittable by sexual contact.

Because of the danger of toxoplasmosis, no pregnant groomer should work on cats or clean their cages or litter boxes. Cats contract this disease from raw meat or garden vegetables. It is highly transmittable when humans come in contact with cat feces. It causes miscarriages and birth defects in mammals, including humans. Because it may be asymptomatic, the best way to protect groomers who are pregnant is to have them avoid cleaning litter boxes and cat cages at home and at work.

A somewhat rarer ailment known as cat scratch fever is another malady spread by contact with infected cats. Mimicking a case of the flu, it causes a general feeling of malaise as well as fever, swollen glands and lymph nodes, and pustules. It is carried in the animal's saliva or bacteria on its claws, and is transmittable through a scratch, bite, or lick from an infected cat. Left untreated, it can cause brain and liver disorders in humans. It can be diagnosed with a skin test.

Tularemia is a bacterial infection transmitted to humans through bites and scratches or bodily discharges of infected dogs or cats. Pets get it from fleas or ticks; outdoor pets can also pick it up from infected rodents when they hunt. It manifests itself in humans as sores on the hands, swollen lymph nodes, muscular pain, diarrhea, vomiting, and pneumonia.

Rabies is the most deadly of all the zoonotic diseases. It is diagnosed by euthanizing the suspected animal and having its brain tested. If you have been bitten by an unvaccinated pet that shows its symptoms, you need to begin an immediate regimen of twenty-one daily injections, administered in the stomach or back. To protect yourself and your employees, all animals in your care should be required to have up-to-date rabies vaccinations—no excuses and no exceptions.

## Chemical Contamination

To rid pets of fleas and ticks, groomers use pesticides. These highly effective products are a boon to pets and their owners, but their frequent use can be harmful to your health. Chemicals that spell doom to fleas and ticks can be absorbed through your skin, causing a host of debilitating problems over time. Some groomers have become disabled with severe and irreversible nerve damage caused by the improper use of pesticides.

It is important to familiarize yourself with flea and tick products. The safest ones use natural substances like pyrethrins, citrus peel, and other botanicals. Although these substances knock down fleas and ticks fast, they offer very little residual effect. It takes the more potent organophosphates to do that. These contain cholinesterase inhibitors, causing nerve damage to the parasite by suppressing its immune system. Unfortunately, they do the same to unprotected humans.

Wear gloves, goggles, and a heavy-duty plastic or rubber apron when dipping an animal. Make sure your bathing area is ventilated by an exhaust fan, preferably installed over the tub. Read the labels on all pesticides. Do not mix and match products; it can cause chemical overload to the pets you are treating. Dilute strictly according to directions and make sure you label everything! Be sure to ask clients what flea and tick control products they are currently using before you treat an animal.

The signs of chemical overload are the same in humans as they are in pets: muscle weakness, headaches, dizziness, salivation, thirst, frequent urination, fatigue, diarrhea, and nausea leading to coma, convulsions, and death. I don't mean to scare you out of the industry before you even begin, but you need to educate yourself on pesticide use and employ good old common sense to protect your own health and that of your four-legged clients.

# Honing Your Skills

It's important to keep up-to-date on all phases of your profession. Grooming styles change, equipment keeps improving, new techniques are constantly being introduced. In addition, there is no substitute for the camaraderie you experience when you gather with your peers.

## In-Service Training

Truly successful people in every field know that there is always room for improvement. The best way to continue your education as a groomer is through involvement in a grooming association and attendance at workshops and seminars. Working on your own as a groomer, especially when you are based at home, can sometimes be an isolating experience. When you join a groomers' association you will meet new friends and colleagues and keep up-to-date on what's happening in your industry. These associations have sprung up in every state and many foreign countries as well. Do not feel like a poor relation because you are a new kid on the block or a home groomer. Many of the industry's top groomers, speakers, and judges came from the ranks of home groomers just like you!

Become active in your association. As is the case with most professional organizations, there is always a dedicated core of volunteers who do the lion's share of the work on behalf of everybody else. Your help will be needed and appreciated, and you will advance yourself in the process. To find out more about national and state grooming organizations, make use of that remarkable resource, PetGroomer.com, at www.petgroomerdirectory.com/associations.htm.

There are also national organizations for professional pet groomers that offer benefits, hold conventions, competitions, and seminars, and offer professional certification. The largest one is the National Dog Groomers Association of America (NDGAA) with 2,500 members at last count. Established in 1969, it offers such benefits as health, disability, liability, and life insurance as well as retirement plans. Check it out at www.nauticom.net/www/ndga.

## Certification

When groomers get together, the question of whether to become certified always provokes a lively debate. Because we are not required to have formal licensing like professional stylists for people do, virtually anybody can advertise himself or herself as a professional pet groomer. Achieving professional certification is one way you can communicate to your clientele that you are a trained member of your profession who has passed certain tests to achieve formal recognition of your knowledge and skill.

Certification involves both written and hands-on testing of the correct way to groom the various breeds according to the official breed standard. The written test covers dog and cat health, anatomy, and breed information. Once you have become certified, you can and should advertise it at your place of business, in your yellow pages and newspaper ads, and on your business cards. You will gain the title of Certified Master Groomer or Master Stylist.

In addition to the NDGAA, there are other professional organizations that offer certification. Look into all the different programs before you decide. Becoming certified takes time, money, and effort on your part. You will need to travel to the sites where testing takes place and provide your own dogs for the practical parts of the test. (In my case, my clients were generous and trusting enough to let me use their dogs.)

Becoming certified is by no means a requirement to becoming successful in this profession. It does, however, carry with it a certain pride in the accomplishment of having completed the process. It boosts your confidence and self-esteem. In addition, if the day ever comes to pass when the grooming profession requires vocational licensing, being certified may give you a leg up on your fellow professionals who have not achieved this title.

Many groomers shy away from the licensing issue because they envision a dreaded tangle of bureaucratic red tape and governmental fees. Others have tunnel vision, wishing to avoid the issue entirely as they toil away in their own little cocoons. On the other side of the coin, some feel that vocational licensing may be a much needed step forward for our profession, arguing that it would bring more respect from the public and make it easier to command the prices that we deserve. Others feel that for the protection of consumers—in this case, pet owners—licensing would ensure that those to whom they entrust their precious pets have met minimum standards for proper care and safety. The debate continues. Because it could affect us so directly, this is one area in which professional groomers need to keep themselves informed.

## Grooming Shows and Competitions

Nationally and internationally, grooming conventions seem to get bigger and more numerous every year. These events combine grooming competitions, educational seminars, trade shows, and hands-on grooming demonstrations under one roof. In my opinion, they are well worth the price of admission. Some groomers save their tips all year long to finance their attendance at such events.

The trade show exposes groomers to the latest in grooming equipment, from shears to shampoos. Shop owners can upgrade their salons with state-of-the-art equipment offered at special show prices. The largest of these events are Intergroom in New Jersey, Groom Expo in Pennsylvania and California, Jerry Schinberg's All American Grooming Competition in Illinois (the oldest of these events, begun in 1973), the Atlanta Pet Fair in Georgia, the NDGAA shows in Florida and another southern or western state, the U.S. Pet Pro Classic in Texas, and the Southern California Groomers Association Show in California.

As a neophyte groomer, the first time you find yourself ringside at a grooming competition will be an unforgettable experience. There you will witness the talented fingers of skilled groomers performing their magic, transforming unkempt, overgrown furballs into exquisitely sculpted examples of the breed hiding under all that hair. Poodles, terriers, sporting breeds, even mixed breeds—grooming contestants compete in several divisions for cash prizes, trophies, ribbons, and medals.

Intergroom, the gala international convention held in New Jersey each April, is now in its twenty-second year. Begun by Shirlee and Larry Kalstone, this prestigious show is now owned and organized by Christine De Filippo, who estimated its total cash awards for 2001 were in the vicinity of $30,000. Its International Groomer of the Year competition features the top groomers from all over the world competing for $20,000 in prizes and awards. Groomers compete in six different classes: (1) Poodles, (2) Terriers, (3) Handstripping (dogs whose hair is plucked or stripped out rather than clippered), (4) Spaniels and Other Sporting Dogs, (5) All Other Purebreeds and (6) Mixed Breed/Miscellaneous (dogs of mixed-breed parentage plus any pedigreed dogs trimmed in styles other than the recognized breed standard). To compete in this event, a groomer must have previously been awarded a First Place at a recognized regional contest. This competition is considered by many to be the Olympics of the grooming world.

Intergroom now has a place for novices to compete as well. Beginning this year, De Filippo instituted the Rising Star Competition, an event open to novice and intermediate groomers. Cash prizes and ribbons as well as gift certificates and free attendance at industry educational events make this highly attractive to newcomers to the contest world.

Distinguished by its international flair, the Oster International Invitational Tournament of Champions brings thirty to thirty-five of the world's top groomers to Intergroom to compete for the title of "World Invitational Grand Champion" with a $4,000 top prize.

Groom Expo, held each September in Hershey, Pennsylvania, bills itself as the world's biggest educational seminar and trade show for pet care professionals. Last year it drew 1,900 attendees and featured 168 exhibitors' booths. It also features grooming competitions, including its Creative Styling contest in which groomers let their imaginations run wild with color, costume, and whimsy, dressing themselves up as part of their chosen theme. No longer limited to the grooming industry, this show, held by Sally Liddick of Barkleigh Productions, attracts professionals from the boarding, pet sitting, and training arenas as well.

To find out about such national and regional events, check the listings at www.Petgroomer.com or at the Pet Groomers Lounge (www.groomers.com). Trade magazines like *Groomer to Groomer* and *The Pet Stylist* also feature calendar listings of these events.

## The Contest Bug

Once you have attended a few grooming competitions, you may start thinking about competing yourself. Watch out: You've just been bitten by the contest bug! It takes time and effort to compete. There's a lot more to it than a few hours spent under the bright lights of the contest ring.

First of all, you need the right dog. Unlike AKC shows, which judge dogs on their conformation (how closely they conform to the breed standard), grooming competitions are judged according to how well the dog is groomed according to the breed profile. What's the difference? The breed profile is the correct visual appearance of that particular breed, based on the accepted grooming patterns established by each individual breed club. You still need a good example of the breed to begin with. A poodle or bichon needs a fluffy coat for scissoring; a cocker spaniel needs a full coat that falls well over its body contours. In other words, the dog needs good conformation with a good haircut on top of it!

Next, you need to grow that coat out to the correct length, usually six to eight weeks of growth, according to the contest rules. Make sure that you read the rules carefully before you fill out the entry form. If you have any questions, call the show organizer. Plan to get to the contest site in plenty of time; newcomers tend to get butterflies, and you will be calmer if you are not rushed.

Besides being beautiful, your contest dog must be well behaved. No matter how handsome he is, if he nips the judge, you'll be disqualified! You need to be able to finish grooming in the allotted time, usually one to two hours. Your dog must be bathed and fluffed before you enter the ring, either that morning or the day before. In the prejudging phase, the judge will examine the animal from head to tail to make sure it has sufficient coat growth and is clean, brushed out, and free from tangles, parasites, and skin diseases.

You should look your best when you enter the ring. Contestants should leave the jeans at home, choosing to look every bit as well-groomed as their dogs. You also need to have the right mental attitude. It can be nerve-racking to groom in front of an audience for the first time, aware of the clock ticking away precious minutes. You need a competitive spirit and a cool head. Even if you do not place, you will learn from the experience. Most judges are more than willing to evaluate your work when the contest is over, helping you to do better the next time out. If you've been bitten by the bug, you'll probably be back to compete again!

## GroomTeam USA

In 1987, a new program brought together the country's most successful groomers to represent the United States in international grooming competition. Thus was born GroomTeam USA. Groomers compete for their place on this team by piling up the points at sanctioned contests nationwide. The GroomTeam committee keeps track of contest results, tabulating point totals, and the six groomers with the most points win a place on the USA squad. Corporate contributions finance the team, covering everything from travel expenses to snazzy red, white, and blue uniforms. The USA team has brought home the gold on may occasions, intensifying the competitive spirit among the best of the best. Some of its illustrious members, such as Diane Betelak of New York and Marea Tully and Carrie Prest of Massachusetts, have sprung from the ranks of home groomers. There is nothing wrong with dreaming; if the idea of representing your country in international competition appeals to you, then while you're at it, dream big!

# Chapter Twelve

# Pet Sitting and Dog Walking

As businesses go, it is surprisingly inexpensive to launch a pet sitting service. Because you are home-based and don't need to rent or lease office space or invest in expensive equipment, industry experts estimate the cost of starting such a service at $3,000 to $5,000. As long as you have an optimistic attitude and good common sense, and you can always be counted on to be there for the pets that need you, the sky's the limit.

## Organization Is Everything

The general public may view pet sitting as a warm and fuzzy experience, heavy on the purring and petting, making your own hours, just a fun way to make a living outside the box of the corporate workplace. All that may be true, but what makes a pet sitting business successful is hard work and superb organization. Unless you are organized—from the way you set up your office to your filing system to your appointment schedule—you will get sandbagged by wasting time and duplicating your efforts. When you looked after friends' and relatives' pets as a favor, whether or not you got paid for it, that was a hobby. Things are different now. You are running a business.

I don't mean to imply that pet sitting is not a fun way to make a living, but to pay yourself and your bills, you need to make a profit. The only way to do this is to stay on top of all the money you take in as payment for services and all the money you pay out for expenses. To do this, you need to develop your own business policy as a day-to-day operating routine. You need to live by the book!

> **Where to Find Scheduling Sheets**
>
> Preprinted camera-ready scheduling sheets are available from both Pet Sitters International (800–380–7387 or www.petsit.com) and the National Association of Professional Pet Sitters (717–691–5565 or www.petsitters.org). Both organizations were founded by Patti J. Moran, the woman often credited with turning pet sitting into a recognized profession. Her book, *Pet Sitting for Profit,* is considered the bible of the industry.

Let's start with your office setup. In addition to the equipment and supplies described in Chapter 8, you will need business forms tailored to your pet sitting business. These include daily and monthly schedule forms, time sheets, daily report logs to be left for clients, service contracts, invoices, client evaluation forms for customer feedback, and separate notification forms for the vet, neighbors and police department. Notification forms are optional but highly recommended. They let others know you are authorized to care for the pets in question and to be present at the home in their absence. Neighbors can reach you if necessary, the vet will be authorized to provide emergency care, and the police will be aware that the owners are out of town. As a bonus, all of the above individuals will become aware of your services. In this business, every interaction is a marketing opportunity.

Because you will be traveling to your clients' homes, you should also have detailed maps of the areas you will serve.

## The Client Interview

Before you agree to provide pet sitting services, you will need to conduct a client interview. This is your opportunity to get to know the client and the pet. Allow at least a half hour for this visit; my pet sitter friends say their interview sessions sometimes run as long as two hours! This is a business call, not a social occasion, so keep it friendly but professional.

Before you try to interact with the pet, let it get used to you. This will be your opportunity to discuss your company policies (schedules, insurance coverage, fees, and payments), to obtain all emergency information, to learn about the pet's special needs and idiosyncrasies and to gather immunization records. You should also detail any additional services you may perform: watering plants, retrieving mail, yard pickup, etc.

**CAREFREE PET CAREGIVERS**

### Daily Service Report

Client(s): _____

Date: _____ Provider: _____

| Date | Arrival Time | Departure Time | Food | Water | Walk | Cleanup | Brush | AM Med. | PM Med. | Litter Box | Mail | Paper | Plants |
|------|------|------|------|------|------|------|------|------|------|------|------|------|------|
|  |  |  |  |  |  |  |  |  |  |  |  |  |  |
|  |  |  |  |  |  |  |  |  |  |  |  |  |  |
|  |  |  |  |  |  |  |  |  |  |  |  |  |  |
|  |  |  |  |  |  |  |  |  |  |  |  |  |  |
|  |  |  |  |  |  |  |  |  |  |  |  |  |  |
|  |  |  |  |  |  |  |  |  |  |  |  |  |  |
|  |  |  |  |  |  |  |  |  |  |  |  |  |  |
|  |  |  |  |  |  |  |  |  |  |  |  |  |  |
|  |  |  |  |  |  |  |  |  |  |  |  |  |  |
|  |  |  |  |  |  |  |  |  |  |  |  |  |  |
|  |  |  |  |  |  |  |  |  |  |  |  |  |  |
|  |  |  |  |  |  |  |  |  |  |  |  |  |  |
|  |  |  |  |  |  |  |  |  |  |  |  |  |  |
|  |  |  |  |  |  |  |  |  |  |  |  |  |  |
|  |  |  |  |  |  |  |  |  |  |  |  |  |  |
|  |  |  |  |  |  |  |  |  |  |  |  |  |  |
|  |  |  |  |  |  |  |  |  |  |  |  |  |  |

**CAREFREE PET CAREGIVERS**

Time Sheet

Name: _____

| Date | TIME | | | Name | Address | Begin | End | Total | Purpose | Fee |
| | Leave | Arrive | Stay | | | | | | | |
|---|---|---|---|---|---|---|---|---|---|---|
| | | | | | | | | | | |
| | | | | | | | | | | |
| | | | | | | | | | | |
| | | | | | | | | | | |
| | | | | | | | | | | |
| | | | | | | | | | | |
| | | | | | | | | | | |
| | | | | | | | | | | |
| | | | | | | | | | | |
| | | | | | | | | | | |
| | | | | | | | | | | |
| | | | | | | | | | | |
| | | | | | | | | | | |
| | | | | | | | | | | |
| | | | | | | | | | | |
| | | | | | | | | | | |
| | | | | | | | | | | |
| | | | | | | | | | | |
| | | | | | | | | | | |
| | | | | | | | | | | |
| | | | | | | | | | | |
| | | | | | | | | | | |
| | | | | | | | | | | |
| | | | | | | | | | | |
| | | | | | | | | | | |
| | | | | | | | | | | |

It's highly advisable to bring along a client book, including your business cards and brochures, copies of your licenses and credentials, references, your service contract, and some snapshots of your well-loved pets. If all goes well, this agreement will be completed and the keys exchanged before you go on your way.

## Security Is Key

Keeping track of client keys is extremely important to your success. Most pet sitters devise a number system for each key, storing them in a locked file or in a safe in their offices. Some charge a small fee for pickup and delivery of client keys; after all, it's your gas, your vehicle, and your time. Your established customers will provide you with a key of your own—two if you employ sitters. This really lets you know that they have faith and trust in you. It also saves you a lot of time and means you may require less notice from these "regulars" because you always have a house key at the ready.

A coded number system rather than a name label on the key works best and protects the client in case your office is ever burglarized. (Make sure you store this decoding chart in a separate safe place!) Having clients leave keys outside, under the mat, or beneath a rock in the garden is unprofessional and unsafe. Keys should be logged out of your cabinet as you begin your day, logged in at day's end. They should always be carried on a key ring that is clipped to your belt loop. You don't want to leave the key on the kitchen table, take the dog out to potty, and watch as a gust of wind blows the door shut! Knowing the client's alarm code if the home is outfitted with a security system is another important home security detail today.

## Routine Booking

All of your client bookings need to be recorded in several places: first, on your reservations calendar when the client contacts you, next on your monthly schedule, then on your service contract, and finally on your daily schedule. As I said, this business only functions when it is well organized, and this system allows you to cross-check all your appointments so no one will be overlooked.

The reservations calendar shows you at a glance who is booked and whether or not you can take more bookings. The monthly schedule gives you the details of your planned service visits. The daily schedule goes out the door with you in the morning as you set about your daily routine.

# Pet Sitter's Service Contract

Name: _BROWN, John & Susan_   Address: _44 Robin Rd._

City or town: _Plainfield_          State: _MA_   Zip: _02011_

Phones: Home: _(508) 555-9876_   Work: _(617) 354-1200_

Cell or pager: _(222) 444-6677 (John)_   _(444) 543-7888 (Susan)_


Pets:

1. _Peaches (F) 10 Golden Retriever_

2. _Butch (M) 3 English Bulldog_

3. _Ming (F) 4 Siamese Cat_


Date leaving: _02/14/02_          Time: _8:00 A.M._

Date returning: _02/21/02_          Time: _6:00 P.M._


You can be reached at: _Moonlight Bay Hotel, Sea Gardens, FL_

Phone: _(222) 666-3399_

Local emergency contact: _Mary Clark (508) 333-9988 (Susan's mother)_

Persons with access to your home: _Mary Clark only_

Vet: _Dr. Black, Plainfield Animal Clinic_   Phone: _(508) 555-9090_


Additional services to be provided by us: [ ] Mail  [ ] Newspaper  [ ] Water plants

Special instructions:

_Peaches: 1 Cosequin pill in morning with food_

_Both dogs: Add Omega Oils supplement to food_

_Ming: Feed separately — Butch loves cat food!_

**Sample service contract (front)**

**Location of food:** <u>*Bottom cabinet near refrigerator*</u>  **Recycle cans? yes / no**

**Other supplies:** <u>*Cat litter in closet by cellar door; stain and odor*</u>
<u>*remover under sink*</u>

Carefree Pet Caregivers hereby agrees to provide services from <u>*Feb. 14, 2002*</u>
through <u>*Feb. 21, 2002*</u> for the pets listed above.

Total number of visits: <u>*21*</u> at <u>*$12*</u> each for a total of <u>*$262*</u>.

Services to be performed in accordance with instructions outlined herein. The client

waives any claims against Carefree Pet Caregivers except if Carefree Pet Caregivers

fails to provide the services as agreed herein. Payment for services is due upon com-

pletion. (Please mail in your payment in the addressed envelope promptly upon your

return.)

Thank you for trusting Carefree Pet Caregivers to care for your pets. Travel safely, and

please call again when you need the services of Carefree Pet Caregivers!

_____        _____
Carefree Pet Caregivers                              Client


Date: _____

**Sample service contract (back)**

Once you have arrived at your appointment, you will also need to fill out a daily report that documents the client's name and address, your time of arrival, your mileage, duties performed, and so on. In addition, if you leave behind a personal note for the client, it will be greatly appreciated. It's a wonderful way to bond. I treasure these little notes that reassure me my animals were cared for with affection in my absence.

It's also important to update your records of payments and expenses on a daily basis. This information will be necessary when you undertake your monthly accounting report. Doing it daily takes only a few minutes and ensures that nothing is overlooked.

## Your Service Area

One of your first policy decisions will concern the area you wish to serve. If you are holding down another job or parenting small children at home while getting established, this might be as limited as a 5-mile radius of your home. Most pet sitters I know service three to five towns, but many added employees as they grew.

Gaining a thorough knowledge of your service area will familiarize you with the best travel routes, including shortcuts. As gas prices increase, it becomes easier to eat up your profits with gasoline costs. Make sure your advertising literature, including your business cards, spells out the areas you intend to cover. Otherwise, you will spend an inordinate amount of time telling callers you don't service their area. If and when you opt to add staff, you may eventually split your service area into territories.

## Insurance Needs

Professional pet sitters have unique needs when it comes to insurance. In today's lawsuit-happy society, you need to protect yourself and your business from claims resulting from bodily injury, personal injury, property damage, and negligence. Even if these claims are unfounded, you still need to defend yourself against them. Having the proper insurance is another selling point that will reassure your clients that you are indeed a professional. Sit down with your agent or broker and outline your needs. You will also need riders on your homeowner's policy to protect your home office and on your auto insurance because you will now be using your car for business purposes.

Your professional organizations also offer insurance benefits to members. Contact Pet Sitters International (PSI), which offers a liability policy package designed by founder Patti Moran, at www.petsitterinsurance.com or (336) 983–9222. The National Association of Professional Pet Sitters (NAPPS) offers liability, bonding, and health insurance for its members at special group rates. The agency they work with, Worldwide Insurance Services, Inc. of Northbrook, Illinois, can be reached by phone at (800) 955–0418 or on-line at www.wwins.com.

## Dishonesty Bonding

As the owner of a business service that visits private homes, you should obtain dishonesty bond insurance, especially if you hire employees. I know this term itself is enough to make you wince, but even if you are working alone, it is just another indication of good faith that identifies you as a pro. If you have employees that are ever, heaven forbid, convicted of theft from a client's home, your bonding company will pay to reimburse the client, then go after the employee in question to collect damages. Make sure this is the type of bonding insurance you purchase. You do not want to find out after the fact that the company will expect *you* to make good on someone else's criminal actions.

In most cases, bonding in the amount of $5,000 will be more than sufficient for your needs. Again, PSI and NAPPS have such coverage available to members,

### Tips from the Pros

Ken Clark and his wife, Catherine Flynn, operate Animal Works, a pet sitting service in East Walpole, Massachusetts. They've been in business for seven years, and offer novices the following hints:

- Always make double or triple checks on everything you do.
- Leave one to one and a half hours open each morning and afternoon just in case somebody needs to go to the vet.
- Use sturdy equipment. In your caddy or tote bag, carry extra collars, retractable leashes, a can opener, cleaner, household brushes, and a first-aid kit.
- Try to return all phone calls within twenty-four hours.
- You are a vacation service. As a safety precaution for your clients, don't mark your cars.
- Never offer information about your clients, such as answering the question, "Did they go away?"
- Wear durable clothing, waterproof socks, and good sneakers. Keep extra boots in the car. You will be out there in all kinds of weather.

including sole proprietorships, with information available at their Web sites or the phone numbers listed above.

## Tools of the Trade

Although it's true that every day is "casual day" when you're a pet sitter, jeans or chinos, T-shirts, golf shirts, and sweatshirts should be clean. Your company logo on the shirt is a nice touch.

Your tool kit or tote bag should include a pooper-scooper, dustpan and brush, paper towels, garbage bags, a flashlight, and flea spray. Always carry some brochures and business cards as well. Having a collapsible pet carrier and a towel or pillowcase in your vehicle will come in handy if you need to transport a pet.

A cell phone is another essential item in the pet sitter's bag of tricks today. It's a great time-saver as you make calls and check messages between appointments. It also makes your job safer. Program in the numbers of the police and fire department as well as the animal control officer of the towns you serve.

A pager is another way to keep accessible to your clients. Making unnecessary trips to the homes of clients who have returned early and have been unable to get in touch with you is a waste of your time and money.

## Why a Post Office Box?

It is highly advisable to use a post office box as your mailing address. Once people know you're an animal lover, letting them know where you live could invite surprise deposits of unwanted pets on your doorstep. It could also encourage drop-in visits from clients, invading your privacy and disrupting your routine. Use this box number as your return address on stationery, business cards, print ads, and business checks.

## Your Emergency Backup Plan

What if something happens to you and you can't keep your appointments? If you are a one-person operation, this could spell disaster. If you have a good relationship with fellow pet sitters in your area, you can fill in for each other during times of illness, emergency or even your own vacation. This is another argument for forming some kind of regional association. Networking among yourselves can be beneficial in many ways. There is one caveat, though. Make sure the sitter you choose as a pinch hitter is adequately insured and make prospective clients aware of your emergency coverage plans.

## Reliable Transportation

Your business and the safety and security of the pets in your care depend on your ability to get to your clients' homes on time, in all kinds of weather. For this reason, you need reliable transportation. In fact, having a second vehicle at your disposal should be part of your emergency backup plan. Batteries die, cars break down, and you are a pet sitter, not a mechanic. Keep your vehicle well maintained and make sure it's comfortable. Do your heater, air-conditioner, and radio work? Once you hit the road with your new business, this vehicle will become your second home!

## Accreditation and Certification

Although pet sitters need not be licensed, the two leading industry organizations offer programs that accredit or certify you in your chosen career. NAPPS has developed a certification program that includes courses on business management and properly handling the pets you will care for. These are supplemented with courses offered by the Pet Industry Joint Advisory Council (PIJAC) on certification for specific animal specialties. Studies are done at home for the two-level program, and applicants must pass a written exam to be certified. Detailed information is available at www.petsitters.org. NAPPS also publishes the *NAPPS Network* newsletter for its members.

PSI offers accreditation at four levels: Pet Sitting Technician, Advanced Pet Sitting Technician, Master Pet Sitting Professional, and Accredited Pet Sitting Service. Like the NAPPS program, home study and testing are involved. For complete information, visit the links at www.petsit.com. PSI also publishes the *World of Professional Pet Sitting* for its members.

Attaining credentials like these will sharpen your skills, increase your knowledge and provide formal recognition for your commitment to providing the best care possible for your clients. If you achieve accreditation or certification, be sure to feature it on your business cards and in your advertisements.

## Good to Go

Okay, you've got your ducks all lined up. You've done your homework on the need for in-home pet care in your community. You've gotten organized, networked and petworked, printed up cards and brochures, mastered the office setup and paper trail, secured that post office box, and even gotten the car tuned up. Your desire to offer pet owners a caring alternative when they must be away from home, fueled by your determination to generate an income from this labor of love, will stand you in good stead as you begin your new venture. You're good to go!

# Chapter Thirteen
# Obedience Training

Obedience training differs from grooming and pet sitting because you really need to immerse yourself in the world of dogs before you launch your career. There is no one clear-cut route mapped out for you as you embark on this journey. There are many paths to the mountaintop; your way will open as you proceed from self-training, to local dog clubs, to training schools.

Many dog trainers start out by visiting clients' homes for either basic obedience or problem correction. This low-overhead approach is a good way to get into the business. Some hold home-based classes in their basements, in their garages, or in their backyards. Some rent space elsewhere or eventually buy or build their own training facilities.

## Trainers Needed: Apply Within

At last count, we had 63 million dogs sharing our homes in the United States. What's more, this monumental figure continues to grow every year. The need for professional pet trainers goes hand in hand—or should I say hand in leash?—with this proliferation of pups.

We wouldn't think of bringing a child into this world and letting it grow to adulthood without providing any schooling. We would be branded unfit parents, and that child could even be removed from our care. Dogs need schooling too. The fact is that people should not consider bringing a puppy into their homes without training it to be a good companion. After all, that's why we have dogs in the first place, to be our companions and members of our family. As responsible owners, it's up to us to school them in the proper way to behave. Simply put, if you don't intend to train your dog, you shouldn't get one. Get a hamster or a turtle instead.

Whether it's a Maltese or a mastiff, an untrained dog is a problem waiting to happen. A dog that is aggressive and antisocial is a danger to people. A dog that does not come when it's called is always at risk. A dog that jumps all over Grandma and knocks her down the stairs is hazardous to her health. A dog that bites the baby when it crawls too near his food dish will soon end up at the shelter, probably to be euthanized.

The overwhelming majority of dogs that meet that unfortunate fate end up at shelters because of behavior problems. Untrained and destructive dogs cause neighborhood conflicts, injuries, lawsuits, needless expense, and painful losses for all concerned. Surely this is not what dog owners envision when they bring home that cute little puppy.

Obedience training is not just about teaching dogs to heel, come, sit, and stay. Professional trainers also train service dogs for the disabled, protection dogs, and therapy dogs. They teach them to perform search and rescue operations, intercept illegal drugs, hunt down criminals, sniff out bombs, even to be movie actors and models. We are still learning about the valuable role pets play in our mental and physical health as the use of therapy dogs increases in hospitals and schools and with the elderly.

Dogs are pack animals. Through training, they learn to follow their human leader. Untrained, they take that role for themselves, dominating the household and causing problems. The best trainers use positive reinforcement to instill their lessons. They learn how to think like a dog, to communicate in the verbal and non-verbal language of "dogspeak." If this is the pet care path you have chosen, you have made a lifetime commitment to learning, and your rewards will go way beyond the monetary.

As a society, we adore dogs. Madison Avenue knows that we can't resist their cute and comical faces peddling everything from automobiles to clothing to beer. Dogs are here to stay, and so dog trainers will always be in demand. The good news is that dogs love to learn. They thrive on the one-on-one attention they get when we work with them to teach manners, skills, and tricks, and they are very good pupils. Obedience training gives us a dog to be proud of, a companion who will be at our side in all situations. It opens up the lines of communication between human and canine, strengthening a bond that goes back 13,000 years.

# Tracking Your Training Career

Most professional dog trainers working in the field today are self-educated. They usually start by training their own dogs. They may take a pet through puppy kindergarten to learn the basics of happy coexistence within the home and to socialize it with puppy pals in the process. They may enroll in a basic obedience course where their dog learns to follow a prescribed set of commands—heel, sit, down, stay, come—and along the way they experience that lightbulb moment when they realize how rewarding it is to work with their "best friend." They may complete the AKC Good Citizen Program, winning a certificate for their dog's mastery of the skills necessary to be confident and well behaved in all situations within the community. Entering the world of obedience competition may whet their appetite further.

There are numerous titles in obedience offered by the AKC: Companion Dog (CD), Companion Dog Excellent (CDX), Utility Dog (UD), and Utility Dog Excellent (UDX), onward and upward through National Obedience Champion (NOC) or Obedience Trial Champion (OTCH). Depending on your dog's breed (and the function it was bred to perform) as well as its natural ability, you can compete in agility, water sports, field trials, herding, tracking, hunting, lure coursing, carting and earthdog events. Then there are the fun dog sports: Flyball, Frisbee, and Freestyle (dances with dogs!). The AKC offers a multitude of activities to enjoy and titles to achieve as you and your dog progress through the levels of your chosen field. As a trainer, you will open these doors to others, becoming their trusted guide to a whole new world.

Your best bet is to join a local dog club to help you train and compete in your sport. There are five kinds of dog clubs to explore: obedience clubs, tracking clubs, all-breed clubs, group clubs (devoted to a specific group like herding breeds or terriers), and specialty clubs (devoted to one specific breed). To locate such clubs in your area, contact the AKC on-line at www.AKC.org. Here you will find a plethora of information, books, videos, a monthly magazine (the *AKC Gazette*) as well as a wide variety of items you may need for your particular activity.

From your own involvement in training your pet and breed club membership, you can move on to attending training seminars, workshops, and conferences. These are generally inexpensive; most charge fees ranging from $30 to $50 a day. After you get a few of these under your belt, the next logical step is to enroll in a formal course or apprenticeship program. A listing of recommended training schools and apprenticeship programs is available on-line at the American Dog Trainers Network page called "How to Become a Professional Trainer" (www.inch.com/~dogs/protrainer.html). The programs listed here range from a four-month apprenticeship to behavioral studies at the university level. Some top trainers handpick their most promising students to work with them as apprentices and assistants, adding them to their staff. Although there is no formal apprenticeship system in dog training per se, such opportunities exist if you doggedly (pun intended!) pursue them.

Among the courses most highly recommended by fellow trainers are the Top Dog School and Training Camps offered by Jack and Wendy Volhard in Phoenix, New York. With graduates worldwide, the Volhards have trained more than 20,000 people since 1971 using their "Motivational Method," which emphasizes positive reinforcement. Their camps are held annually in April and July in New York, Connecticut, and Virginia. Tuition runs around $700, with on-site accommodations available at an additional cost. Phone them at (315) 593–6115, e-mail them at topdog@aiusa.com, or log on to their Web site at www.volhard.com.

Industry insiders also highly recommend the annual five-day instructor training course offered each September in Accord, New York, by Sue Sternberg, Donna Duford, and Dana Crevling. For information and registration for this course, which costs around $800, call (508) 529–3568 or 529–3564.

Before enrolling in a training school or program, you should do your homework. There is no nationally recognized certification for trainers, but many such schools will "certify" you upon completion; in other words, they will give you a diploma. The Association of Pet Dog Trainers (APDT) is currently working on its own program to offer certification. Despite claims of positive reinforcement and humane techniques, there are still programs out there that use harsh and abusive methods or controversial behavior modification such as electric shock and physical intimidation. Training should never break a dog's spirit or strip it of its natural instincts.

Enrolling in a training school involves a big commitment of your time and money. New schools open and close every year. A visit to the school is a must and you should pose many questions before making your decision:

- Will it provide a well-rounded course of instruction on all areas of obedience training, with the focus on training for real-life situations?
- Is the school approved by the State Board of Education?
- Does the Better Business Bureau know of any unresolved complaints against the school?

- Does the school have a proven record of success? Does it provide the names of graduates you can call for references?
- Do you feel comfortable with the faculty and other school representatives? Are they approachable and willing to provide any information you seek?
- Does the school offer courses in business management, computer programs, teaching techniques, and client relations to help you manage your business?
- Do instructors employ harsh physical handling, shock collars, or drugs in their training methods?

Some schools, such as the National K-9 School of Dog Trainers in Columbus, Ohio (www.NK9.com), provide comprehensive Web sites for you to explore. The K-9 School's site outlines its six-week course in all phases of training and related business skills. In business since 1975, it has been certified by the state of Ohio for the past twenty years and boasts a 98 percent graduate rate.

"Our philosophy differs from any other school in that we train each dog as an individual," says Director of Training Bob Jervis. "Each dog tells us how to train it, based on its personality. Even within one breed, you may find any number of personalities. We try to recognize the breeds for what they are and their original functions, but not to pigeonhole them." Tuition and student housing for the Master Trainer course is around $6,000. The school offers part-time courses and graduate workshops as well.

Graduate Nancy Bradley of Bradley's Canine Education in Norton, Massachusetts, had high praise for the school, although she noted that she had been involved in training for many years before she sought formal instruction. She liked the fact that it specialized in training for family pets, not for the show ring or obedience competition. "That's fine, but it's an artificial environment," Bradley observes. "I train the dog for the house, going in and out of the car, around the park. I teach the client how to lead the dog. My goal is to train so that the owner can take the dog anywhere."

Predictably, the need for obedience trainers and the marketing opportunity that goes with it have not gone unnoticed by the national pet supply chains. PETsMART is currently recruiting trainers, offering a 120-hour course of instruction. According to Tim Murray of the chain's recruitment department, students receive an hourly compensation while they learn, and PETsMART requires no employment agreement once their training has been completed.

Obedience Training

Petco contracts its training business to Animal Behavior and Training Associates of Los Angeles. ABTA President Steven Applebaum realized early on that the pet chains would carve out a sizable niche in the pet care industry. Trained in the Air Force as a patrol dog handler and trainer in the late seventies, Applebaum's career has been a classic case of a home-based business that mushroomed into a huge success story.

Once he completed his military service, Applebaum went into business in 1980 by posting flyers on supermarket bulletin boards. With a partner who has since left the company, he founded ABTA five years later, initially offering only private lessons in the home. Group classes were added in 1986, and in 1990 it began its affiliation with Petco in the Los Angeles area. By 1994, the company contracted all obedience training for Petco in California; the following year the chain appointed ABTA its exclusive provider of dog obedience classes nationwide.

Applebaum initiated a similar partnership with Canada's Petcetera Warehouse chain in 1998. Today ABTA runs some 400 classes a month in forty-one states and all Canadian provinces except Quebec. ABTA's Web site is www.good-dawg.com.

In 1998, Applebaum founded the Animal Behavior University (ABU). At that time, most trainers recommended waiting until a dog was at least six months old before beginning training, and then would use harsh compulsion-training methods. Although this is no longer the norm, according to the ABU Web site, "there are still no state or federally regulated standards for obedience trainers. This means that anyone can print up business cards and call himself or herself a dog trainer."

ABU trains instructors through its own unique combination of home study and hands-on experience. With the course designed according to the student's schedule, completion takes twenty-one to thirty-two weeks; expert trainers hold the group instruction phase at 400 locations. This home study approach works well for those who can't give up their day jobs to go to school, but it does require strong motivation and self-discipline to do it on your own. The $2,500 tuition and its own financing plan make it more affordable than most residential training facilities. Information is available at www.animalbehavioruniversity.com.

The ABU curriculum includes a foundation of academic and theoretical information as well as problem solving, safety, public speaking, client relations, business practices, and fourteen weeks of group class participation. Those who pass the exams to complete the course receive a certificate of graduation ("certification"). Many top students are offered jobs on the ABTA staff.

On the other hand, many self-educated trainers with impressive credentials and a long history in the field are highly skeptical about any schools that purport to turn out professional trainers within weeks or months. One of these is Donna Laconti, animal behavior therapist at Boston's Angell Memorial Hospital, program support director of the National Education for Assistance Dog Services (NEADS) service dog training program in West Boylston, Massachusetts, and faculty member at Becker College's Animal Care Program in Leicester, Massachusetts. She has some specific advice for those who choose the self-directed path to this career:

- First, take a general animal care course at the college level to learn all your can about dog health, anatomy, and animal behavior. Before you make a decision to enter this field, you need plenty of hands-on experience with dogs. "You may love training your cocker spaniel, but will you really like working with that Akita?" asks Laconti.
- Take courses on psychology, relating to both dogs and people. You need to learn how animals learn. Learning takes place in a certain environment, for both animals and people.
- Try to sample as many different trainers and their methods as you can. "Some trainers will be happy to let you come in to observe and help out with their classes," she notes.
- Join national training organizations and attend conferences. "You must keep up-to-date and not get stuck in a routine where you never learn anything new," Laconti cautions. "You need to change with the times and give your customers what they want."
- Take business courses. You need to know how to manage the financial aspect of your business. You also have to learn how to promote yourself and let people know what you have to offer.

"The dog training part is really simple," advises Laconti, who doesn't even like the term *trainer*. "This job is best suited to people who have the skills of a teacher."

## Professional Organizations

Laconti also recommends joining the APDT (www.apdt.com). Started by noted trainer Ian Dunbar in 1993, this organization is dedicated to education for trainers and pet owners alike, encouraging the use of positive reinforcement, and opposed to aversive techniques. Its annual conference and trade show in New York offers a comprehensive overview of the training world. The 2001 conference featured workshops on such practical topics as writing a business plan, legalese and insurance, people skills, and making the Internet work for you, as well as a wide variety of training methods and techniques. Find out more at www.apdt.com/Ellenville/conprog.html.

With the recent acquisition of *Off-Lead* magazine, Barkleigh Productions (www.barkleigh.com) now incorporates animal behavior and training programs into its huge Groom Expo show held each September in Hershey, Pennsylvania. Its sister show, Animal Behavior and Training Expo West, takes place in Southern California in February. For listings of other conferences and seminars, check magazines such as the *AKC Gazette, Off-Lead, Front and Finish, Fetch the Paper, Forward, Dog World,* and *Dog Fancy.*

The National Association of Dog Obedience Instructors (NADOI) is another highly respected industry organization. It serves as an agency to endorse qualified obedience instructors. Although "provisional" memberships are available, you will not be eligible to become a full member until you have at least five years of experience in obedience training and have taught at least 104 class hours. Membership also requires a written exam, interview, and evaluation.

Noting the lack of a licensing agency for dog obedience instructors today, NADOI purports to fill this gap. "A dog owner can rely upon NADOI's membership procedure to evaluate the instructor's ability for him," says the agency. According to NADOI, "A member instructor has had his qualifications reviewed by his peers and has been considered capable of providing competent instruction using humane methods of training. He is a person who enjoys learning as well as teaching and will be keeping abreast of the latest developments and newest knowledge in the field of dog obedience training." Find out more at www.nadoi.org.

## Beyond Education

The need for effective and humane obedience training methods continues as the debate on how to produce them rages on. It's up to you to plot your own course of action. But how do you know if you have what it takes to succeed? You need to be healthy, strong, positive, and courageous. You need to be passionate in your love for dogs and your fascination with the human-animal bond. You also need excellent people skills; you will be training the owner as well as the pet.

"Training the dog is one aspect of it, but that's only half the story," says trainer Nancy Bradley. "You've got to relate to an owner too. Part of the job is trying to convince an owner that dogs are not people. A lot of people are anthropomorphic about their dogs, but they don't think like people, they don't act like people, and you can't teach them like people."

## The Business End of Training

When it comes to organizing a home office, you need to be as dedicated to good record keeping as you are to training dogs! Beyond your desk, chair, telephone and answering machine, and basic clerical supplies, you will need business forms, including daily and monthly schedule forms, evaluation forms for clients, training contracts, and invoices.

If you plan to sell the basic equipment needed for obedience training—leather leads, training collars (also known by that ugly term "choke collars"), cotton web lunge leads in various lengths, muzzles in all sizes, retrieval dummies—you will need storage racks and shelving for these as well. You may want to add a few more retail items like training treats or grooming supplies for your captive audience. To sell any supplies, you will need to obtain a state tax number, and you will be required to file either monthly, quarterly, or annually, depending on your sales volume. Ask your accountant or visit the Small Business Administration's Web site, www.sba.org, to direct yourself to the specific agency in your home state.

If you plan to hold classes at your home location, of course you will need a permit from the zoning board. For more information on zoning issues, see Chapter 4. Most home training operations are limited in scope, both because of space requirements and to maintain good neighborhood relations. A large basement or garage will do. You will need waterproof flooring mats, available from training supply outfits. In good weather, it's also great to train outdoors. Wherever dogs gather, you need disinfectant and deodorizer, paper towels, and poop bags, as well as a large trash container.

Most trainers offer a variety of courses at different levels for their clients. Your contract will spell out what is covered in each course. Payment in part or in full should be made upon registration. Some trainers offer extra lessons for dogs that need them. Contract forms usually include a "release clause" including such wording as "The owner assumes all responsibility for the dog's health and safety and the

**DOWN, BOY!**
**Canine Education**
Training for Dog & Owner

1151 River Road
Plainfield, MA 02011
(508) 555–3824

# Training Contract

Date: _____  Owner's name: _____

Home phone: _____  Work phone: _____

Address: _____

Dog's name: _____  Breed: _____

Age: _____  Spay/neuter: _____

Veterinarian: _____  Vet's phone: _____

# Training Program

[  ] **Basic On-Leash Obedience** (includes owner handling instruction): heel, heel with automatic sit, down and sit in heel position, sit and down in motion, come, stand, square off 90, finish, come from heel and place.

[  ] **Advanced On/Off Leash Obedience** (from 50 feet, includes owner handling instruction): heel, heel with automatic sit, down and sit in heel position, sit and down from front, sit and down in motion, come, stand, square off 90, finish, come from heel and place.

[  ] **Agility**            [  ] **Tricks**

[  ] **Retrieval**          [  ] **Scent Tracking**

[  ] **Personal Protection**    [  ] **Special**

[  ] **Additional Commands** _____

**Sample training contract (page 1)**

## Training Agreement

Training will be done in accordance with what was shown in demonstration and specified in this contract. Included in training will be sessions with the owner. The owner understands and agrees to cooperate fully in completing requirements recommended by the trainer. If the owner cooperates fully to the satisfaction of the trainer, and the owner shows a need for additional lessons, Down, Boy! Canine Education will offer extra lessons at no extra cost to the owner.

Down, Boy! Canine Education agrees that, while the dog is on the owner's premises and under its control and training, Down, Boy! Canine Education will exercise the utmost diligence and care to protect the health and safety of the dog. However, as owner, you assume all responsibility for the dog's health and the safety of all who have contact with the dog during and after training. The owner also understands and agrees that as owner he/she is fully responsible for the dog's behavior during and after training.

If training is interrupted for any reason that is not the fault of Down, Boy! Canine Education, including illness of the dog, the owner must pay the balance of the contract price. Training will resume and the program will be completed at a future date agreed to by both the owner and trainer at no additional cost to the owner.

The owner acknowledges that to the best of his/her knowledge the dog has not been exposed to rabies, distemper, or parvovirus in the past thirty (30) days and is fully inoculated, and the owner has fully read and understands this agreement.

**Sample training contract (page 2)**

| Description | Price | Date | Recvd Pmt |
|---|---|---|---|
|  |  |  |  |
|  |  |  |  |
|  |  |  |  |
|  |  |  |  |
|  |  |  |  |
|  |  |  |  |
|  |  |  |  |
|  |  |  |  |
|  |  |  |  |
|  |  |  |  |
|  |  |  |  |

**Approximate completion date** _____

**Owner's signature** _____

**Down, Boy! Canine Education by** _____

**Sample training contract (page 3)**

health and safety of all who have contact with the dog during and after training." You should also spell out in writing the owners' responsibility to pay for your services whether or not they show up for instruction. For training that is interrupted for good reason, you may opt to resume lessons at a future date. It's wise to consult your lawyer as you create your own service contract.

## Playing It Safe and Being a Good Neighbor

At the present time, none of the training organizations offers liability insurance benefits to members, although the APDT is looking into this option. That means it's up to you to obtain a policy that will cover you and your clients whether you are on your property or theirs. The most commonly recommended coverage is for $1 million protection. Shop around to find the best policy tailored to your needs. If you are holding classes at home, be aware that your homeowner's policy will not cover this liability. You also need a rider to cover the equipment in your home office.

When it comes to neighborhood concerns, it is up to you to let your neighbors know that your training will not endanger them or interfere with their way of life. Neighborhood complaints can effectively shut you down. If you plan to hold exercises outdoors, of course your property should be fenced, preferably with a chain link system.

If dogs are coming to your house, you should make sure your grounds and the surrounding area are patrolled and picked up daily. Your indoor training area should be soundproofed to keep noise from becoming a nuisance. Clients should be instructed not to park where it will cause problems or block neighbors from their driveways. If your neighbors are "dog people," by all means offer them a special discount on your services. Hold obedience demos for local Boy Scout or Girl Scout troops or school groups. It's up to you to become your own goodwill ambassador.

It's up to you to represent this profession well, always conducting yourself in a professional manner. If you know your stuff and treat both your human and canine students with patience, kindness, and respect, obedience training will become far more than your job; it will be a whole way of life.

## Chapter Fourteen

# Marketing and Public Relations

You already know you love working with pets, but can you make a living at it? Will your income maintain and eventually improve your standard of living? Will it finance your retirement? Before you take this life-changing plunge, you will need to test the waters by familiarizing yourself with the economic climate of your community. You will also need to become your own personal Madison Avenue when it comes to announcing your arrival on the scene.

## Setting Your Prices

Before you set the prices on your services, you will need to do some market research in your community. Depending on which pet care area you are entering, you need to know the going rate for grooming, boarding, pet sitting, or obedience training. The cost of living varies widely in different areas of the country, and prices for all of the pet care services fluctuate accordingly. Hold on to this research information. It may be valuable data for future reference.

Although the government does not allow standardized prices within any industry, when groomers gather at seminars and trade shows, one of the most frequent questions they ask each other is, "How much do you charge for (fill in the breed)?" Comparing notes on prices is often the number one topic when they start chatting. Surprisingly, I never hear them talk about how they arrive at their prices.

In any business, the bottom line in figuring pricing is always based on your cost of operation combined with sufficient compensation to make a profit. To succeed in business, you need to know how to figure out the average cost of your services. Your profit margin depends on how much you spend as well as how much you take in.

One vital finding in the 2001 *Groom & Board* report on pet care professionals was that pet care providers with the highest profit margins did not necessarily charge the highest prices. They simply managed their businesses more efficiently, holding down their overhead costs for supplies, labor, and advertising. Some groomers who sold pet food took a lower markup on the food but used a higher markup on dry goods and boutique items. They used the food as a "leader" and a convenience for their customers, but were more pricey on impulse items and luxury goods than the big chains. In the same vein, some top boarding kennels charged lower-than-average daily rates for large and extra-large dogs but higher than average prices for small and medium-size pets. Top performers know their market and fine-tune their prices accordingly.

## Grooming

Groomers usually have a base price for each breed. According to the *Groom & Board* report, the average fees for the top six breeds were as follows: miniature poodles, $28.93; cocker spaniels, $31.23; shih tzus, $29.60; bichon frises, $34.61; golden retrievers, $35.68; and miniature schnauzers, $26.17. Extras are usually tacked on to the base price. Most groomers will allow fifteen minutes or so for dematting or extra brushing of a dog's coat, but after that, an additional hourly dematting rate (now $25 to $35 per hour) kicks in. Flea baths and dips, medicated baths, expelling anal glands, deskunking and deodorizing treatments, hot oil treatments, tooth brushing, and extra time allotted for a "tough strip" (shaving down a severely matted coat) are typical add-on items. Some attach a "handling charge" for dogs that have behavior problems.

Because time is money, your speed in grooming also plays a role (this will improve as you become more experienced). There are industry workshops like the one given by John Stazko to teach you "speed grooming" techniques and help maximize your profits. Videos of these programs are also available. To see a seminar schedule or obtain the videos, log on to www.stazko.com.

Another method of charging for grooming is to use an hourly rate no matter what breed of dog you are grooming or which additional services you provide. Some feel this is a more professional approach, and you won't be surprising clients with extra charges at pickup time. If you make a practice of evaluating each dog

# Sample Grooming Menu

**Dogs**

| | | | | |
|---|---|---|---|---|
| Poodles | | Collie (rough) | $55 |
| Toy | $35 | Old English Sheepdog | $65 |
| Mini | $40 | Afghan Hound | $65 |
| Standard | $65 | Golden Retriever | $40 |
| Terriers | | Labrador Retriever | $35 |
| Schnauzers | | Dachshund | |
| Mini | $38 | Smooth | $25 |
| Standard | $48 | Wirehair | $35 |
| Giant | $65 | Longhair | $35 |
| Yorkshire Terrier | $35 | Pug | $25 |
| Cairn Terrier | $38 | Beagle | $40 |
| West Highland Terrier | $38 | Bassett Hound | $35 |
| Scottish Terrier | $38 | Dalmation | $35 |
| Wirehaired Fox Terrier | $38 | Bulldog | $35 |
| Soft-coated Wheaten | $48 | Bullmastiff | $40 |
| Airedale | $38 | Great Dane | $45 |
| Lhasa Apso | $38 | Pomeranian | $35 |
| Shih Tzu | $38 | Keeshond | $45 |
| Maltese | $35 | Husky | $45 |
| Tibetan Terrier | $45 | Alaskan Malamute | $45 |
| Bearded Collie | $55 | Portuguese Water Dog | $50 |

**Cats, Longhair**

| | |
|---|---|
| Bath and brushout | $45 and up |
| Haircut | $55 and up |

**Handstripping**          $45 per hour

**Additional charges:**

| | |
|---|---|
| Flea baths | $5 to $15 depending on size |
| Medicated baths | $5 to $15 depending on size |
| Teeth brushing | $5 |
| Anal glands expelled | $5 |
| Dematting | $35 per hour |

Prices on mixed breed dogs and cats will vary according to size, coat condition, and temperament. All prices listed are base prices only. We do not quote exact prices until we examine the pet. We reserve the right to administer a flea treatment or a medicated shampoo if pet's condition warrants it. All pets must have proof of being up-to-date on vaccinations.

**Nail trims**

| | |
|---|---|
| Cats | $5 |
| Dogs | $7.50–$10 |

For your convenience and the health and beauty of your pet, rebooking at pickup time is highly recommended.

when it comes in for its appointment, you can give the client an idea of what that dog needs, alleviating the "sticker shock" effect when they return to pick up and pay.

Proponents of the hourly rate maintain that it's a fairer method because it allows for such factors as temperamental differences that add up to increased time on "problem" dogs. On two little poodles, for example, it takes a lot less time for the one who is well-behaved and cooperative than for the one who fights and bites the hand that grooms it!

## Pet Sitting

The amount that pet sitters charge per visit varies according to location. If yours is a predominantly affluent clientele, you can charge more than your colleague in a blue-collar or low-income area. Start your research on pricing by finding out what the local kennels charge for overnight visits. Then add two to four dollars for the personalized service you plan to provide.

Ken Clark, who operates Animal Works pet sitting service with his wife, Catherine Flynn, in East Walpole, Massachusetts, stresses the importance of keeping track of your mileage. "If you are ever audited," Ken cautions, "you will need this information." In business for seven years, he and Catherine average 50,000 to 60,000 miles per year. They currently charge $14 per visit with a "dollar discount" for daily calls. They allow fifteen minutes between visits and do not consider driving time part of their typical thirty- to forty-five-minute visit.

Pet sitters usually charge an additional dollar or two per visit for each extra pet in the home. Some charge more for dogs than for cats because dogs need to be walked and exercised. Some offer a 10 percent discount for senior citizens; others offer discounts for long-term contracts, typically if clients are away for a month or more. Like plumbers or electricians, many sitters charge an additional fee for visits made on legal holidays.

## Training

The prices charged for a trainer's services are affected by factors ranging from the affluence of the community to the numbers of dogs in a class. A trainer located on Park Avenue in Manhattan will command a heftier fee than his or her counterpart in a rural midwestern town. In general, private sessions range from $30 to $75 per hour, however, they can be as high as $150 per hour when the trainer has a degree in animal behavior or veterinary medicine.

Basic and advanced six-or eight-week courses taught in a group setting usually run from $100 to $500. Ostensibly, the more class participants a trainer can handle the less he or she would need to charge for the course. Professional experience and reputation, the demand for his or her services, and the facility where training takes place all have a bearing upon price structure. Stated simply, the trainer is free to charge what the market will bear.

## Other Considerations

For the pet sitter, mobile groomer, or trainer, the costs of operating your vehicle also need to be calculated. The going rate for mileage allowed for deduction by the IRS is 32.5 cents per mile. (Check with the IRS on-line at www.irs.gov to make sure this hasn't changed.) Pet sitters and mobile groomers usually average 7 to 10 miles per visit; with gas prices on the increase, you need to add three to five dollars per trip to cover transportation costs. You also need to consider wear and tear on your vehicle as well as the overhead involved in paying for it. Are you making payments on that vehicle? How about your auto insurance costs?

# Never Apologize for Quality!

Pricing is determined by the value of a product or service and the costs related to producing it. However, price is not the only factor considered by clients when it comes to choosing a pet care service. They also look for quality, expertise, dependability, dedication, professionalism, and a humane approach to animal care. Chances are that people who make a decision based on price alone will not become the mainstays of your business; they will probably jump ship the minute someone comes along to undercut you. You need to believe in yourself enough to command the prices that will allow you to grow and prosper in this business and provide the lifestyle you seek for yourself and your family. People do not dicker with the mechanic, the plumber, the dentist or the hairstylist about the cost of their services, and they shouldn't do it with you.

As a longtime veteran of the grooming profession, I know that many of us have difficulty asking the prices that we deserve. We are too self-effacing and we sell ourselves short. We literally work like dogs throughout our careers but often end up with precious little to show for it. Maybe it's because we chose the pet care field based on our love for animals.

Times have changed. We are now legitimate entrepreneurs who care for pets. According to the IRS, we are all in business to make a profit. We certainly pay our share of taxes to the government based on that profit. That's how it works, and it's nothing to be ashamed of! Some folks will always try to nickel and dime you, but when you believe in yourself and have the knowledge of what it takes to run a business, you will project that confidence when pricing your services. Keep in mind that pricing also has a lot to do with perceived value. Do you really want to be known as the cheapest groomer or trainer in town? Do you think of "bargain basement" as second-rate? The economics of your area come into play here, but in most cases, people will pay a little more for the best.

You should also reserve the right to refuse jobs that don't live up to your standards of animal care. "We don't do 'garage care' for pets," comments Ken Clark. "If it makes us uncomfortable, we don't do it."

Because it is your business, you will determine your prices, but bear in mind that it's easier to start out with fees that will make it worth your while. Price increases require notifying everyone in your clientele as well as changing some of your literature. So it's wise to put a great deal of thought into what you will charge for your services.

When I was rather new at the grooming game and someone questioned my fees—"I had Buster groomed in Florida for half what you charge!" or "Fifty dollars for giving my dog a haircut? You've got to be kidding!"—I would get defensive and feel I was obliged to explain that the cost of running a professional grooming salon includes such overhead as taxes, utilities, insurance, supplies, salaries, employee benefits, and so on. In other words, I tried to justify my prices by offering way too much information!

No matter which area of pet care you are involved in, you have overhead. It took lots of time and training for you to gain your knowledge. It's really not necessary to get into one of these tit-for-tat arguments. Instead, you may politely explain that these are the fees you charge for your services and that they are justified because of the quality you provide. You may remind outraged clients that all costs go up every year, including your overhead. They don't pay the same price to get a haircut, fill up the gas tank, or dine at a fine restaurant that they did five or ten years ago. You may even politely suggest that if the lower costs they are paying elsewhere are more in line with their budget, you would certainly understand.

You do not have to care for every dog in the universe. Your services are not for everyone, but that's OK. Do not get into giving price breaks; it will come back to haunt you. Most businesses increase their prices on a yearly basis. Haggling is for the flea market, not a business that is concerned with delivering the highest quality care it can provide.

## Should You Barter Your Services?

Bartering is one of the oldest ways of doing business. Throughout history, people and nations have traded goods for services. When cash currency became the worldwide standard, this system fell out of favor, but with the introduction of computer networks, instant communication, and modern record-keeping systems, it is reemerging in the business marketplace, growing by leaps and bounds every year.

As a pet care provider, you could barter your services for any number of goods and services from other merchants, both within your community and nationally as part of a barter service network. For a small transaction fee, members of these networks become eligible to swap services and goods through classified ads in newsletters or on-line. The barter exchange does the record keeping for you. It keeps track of your "trade credits" (the cash value of what you barter, usually one dollar per credit) in your account. These credits are used just like cash to make transactions. For example, you could spend those credits on landscaping services from the firm down the street or save them up to take a Caribbean cruise.

There are now more than 600 barter exchange clubs operating nationwide. As barter networks begin to flourish on-line, they are actually becoming more affordable. Like trading stocks, when you eliminate the middleman—the broker—you can save as much as 60 percent by making your own trades on-line. Look into www.Ubarter.com, where you can barter everything from a villa rental in Jamaica to NASCAR tickets or water filtration systems.

Before you join a barter exchange network, you should do your homework. Don't forget that once you affiliate with it, you will be putting the reputation of your business on the line as well as your trading credits. Some questions you should ask:

- How large is the network and how long has it been in business? If the exchange folds, you could be out a lot of hard work and money!
- What categories of goods and services are available? If you can't find something you want to spend those credits on, they won't be of much value!
- Does it offer references? Contact some current members to see if they are happy with its services.

You may also wish to visit www.i-barter.com, a good place to learn about the world of business bartering. Some topics covered here include how to negotiate trades; how to tell a good trade from a bad one—before it's done; barter as a complement to business networking; using barter to get profits from excess inventory; how to barter for advertising; barter resources, on-line and off-line; barter exchanges; and types of trade/barter.

At year's end, your barter exchange should provide you with a 1099 Form showing the value of any services or goods you received during the year. The IRS will also be sent a copy.

You need not join a barter exchange to engage in this method of doing business. If you choose to barter on your own, however, the IRS requires that you keep records and list the fair market value of all goods and services as income. You may deduct any costs you incurred to perform the work that was bartered. To find out more, log on to the IRS site at www.irs.org. You may request Publication 525, Taxable and Nontaxable Income, which can also be downloaded from this site.

# Gift Certificates

In the pet care field, selling gift certificates for your services is a great idea. More than ever, it seems, people struggle to come up with ideas on what to buy for "the person who has everything." Often, that person is a retired parent or busy career professional who gets harder to buy for every year when holidays, birthdays, or anniversaries roll around. You know their pets are dear to their hearts. What could be more thoughtful than a day of beauty for Buffy at the grooming salon, an obedience session with a trainer for Mom's new puppy, or an offer to cover pet sitting costs so that someone you love can get a well-deserved weekend getaway?

It's a lot more common for groomers to offer gift certificates than it is for other pet care providers. Blank certificates are available at stationery supply stores and are printed in duplicate. The purchaser gets the top copy; the seller keeps the carbon for verification when it is redeemed. You could also produce your own version on your computer with a program like Microsoft Publisher, embellishing it with some pet-related clip art.

The next thing you need to do is let people know about it. At a grooming salon, that's easy—just post a sign on the counter for all to see. For other pet services, you could note it in your brochure, business card, Web site, or print advertising. Your gift certificate may just provide the perfect answer for the harried shopper, and it won't even require wrapping paper or a fancy gift box!

# Advertisements for Yourself

The purpose of advertising is to sell products or services. Manufacturers use it to convince us we need their products. If we buy a certain brand of shampoo, we will become irresistible! Companies rely on advertising to create a favorable image. It plays a key role as businesses compete for the consumer's dollar. In this country, businesses spend more than $200 billion on advertising every year.

Advertising your services will be a critical factor in the success of your business, playing a big part in your marketing plan. You can be the best groomer, trainer, or pet sitter in the world, but if you keep it a secret, you won't be in business for long. Think of the service you wish to provide as a product. Who will be interested in buying it and why? How will you reach these folks to let them know you have arrived on the scene?

Packaging your product is also important. For the pet care provider, this means your image: the way you look, speak, and present yourself and your services. If people are coming to you for your services, this "packaging" is also reflected in your salon or training area. The knowledge and confidence you project and your winning attitude are every bit important as the way you look.

Many pet care starter-uppers are pinching every penny and they fail to realize the importance of getting the word out about their new venture. Before you decide where to spend your advertising dollars, you need to think about your target audience and how much you can afford to spend.

Advertising in mass media like metropolitan daily newspapers, TV, and radio is generally geared to businesses that have a broad target audience and a big advertising budget. Home-based service businesses usually have a more tightly targeted audience and limited resources. Where will you begin?

First of all, get those brochures and business cards out to your fellow pet care professionals. Once you are a known commodity in the pet care community, these referrals will be a lifeline for you. Next, consider the yellow pages. This is still the place people turn to when they are looking for a product or service. You don't have to go overboard with a quarter-page in color; a small ad will do. Once you become established, you can go smaller still.

You may need to place your ad in more than one yellow pages directory. We have a large ad in the one that serves our town and three adjacent communities and a smaller one in the editions of two nearby areas from which we also draw clients. There are now numerous privately owned single-town telephone directories popping up everywhere, with rates that are considerably lower than the official yellow

## Words That Sell

Include some pet-related artwork in your ad, and a slogan if you have one: "Expert Grooming with a Loving Touch," "Loving Care For Your Pampered Pet," "Humane Training for the Educated Canine." Consider the picture your words will paint and deliver your message in as few words as possible. "Warm and fuzzy" is good; it's reassuring to the pet owner.

One of our most successful newspaper ads informs people about "Baby's First Bath." The baby, in this case, is their new puppy. If it's less than four months of age and has had its second series of shots, the first visit for a bath and nail clipping is on the house. This "freebie" acquaints the pup with the grooming process and brings its owner into our establishment. It's a chance for everyone to bond, and those who take us up on the offer usually become our customers for grooming and pet supplies. But it's that little cartoon drawing of a pup in a tub with some bubbles floating around it and the word baby that catches a prospective client's eye.

We are giving owners permission to dote on their pets just as they would a human baby, telling them we are just as loving as they are and even a bit silly ourselves. Our words are tuned in to their sense of fun. Words also instill confidence: "Celebrating Ten Years of Caring for Pets." If you have achieved any form of certification or belong to a professional organization in your industry, your ad should include that information as well.

pages. These little books have a hometown feel and are more convenient for the busy consumer, so they are well worth considering. Try not to go overboard though. After all, how many pets will you need to care for to pay for all those ads?

Direct mail is another option. For a small fee you can get the list of all owners of licensed dogs in your town and neighboring communities from the town clerk's office. It's very effective when you are announcing your business opening because you know you are reaching your target market. The rising cost of postage, however, has turned this into a fairly expensive proposition.

It is not a good idea to hand deliver flyers advertising your business. Stuffing mailboxes without paying for postage is a crime and an intrusion upon the sanctuary of a person's home. Papering auto windshields at the shopping mall presents a nuisance to drivers. It's a lot of work, it can get you in trouble with mall security, and it does not create a favorable impression of your services.

# Media Choices

No matter how small your town, you should have an ad announcing your grand opening in your local weekly newspaper. For your business, this is your official birth announcement, and it's a matter of pride. The cost will depend on how large an ad you choose to run and how many times it will be published. Once your business is familiar to your hometown residents, placing an ad in a regional weekly that is delivered free to all residents is a better long-term vehicle for you. One factor affecting the price is size; to get noticed, consider at least a "2 by 2" or "2 by 3" ad. The paper's circulation and the length of the contract you agree to will also determine the cost. In the suburban Boston area, the usual charge for such an ad that size varies from $31 for a paper that goes to 6,000 homes to $85 for one with a readership of 30,000.

Ads in large metropolitan dailies are usually too costly and aimed at too wide an audience for a local pet care provider, but occasionally they offer deals for specific types of businesses. A special section is included in the newspaper (usually on a weekend) where your ad will be featured along with other pet-related firms at a reduced rate. If you enter into a contract agreeing to advertise in this type of promotion a few times a year, you can also get a sizable discount.

Big-city radio and television stations are also aimed at a mass audience and not really suitable to our needs, but local cable TV is becoming more popular among small businesses that want to publicize their services. While thirty seconds on network TV could cost a million dollars, thirty-second daily "spots" on local cable can go for as low as $25 per ad. In AT&T-Broadband's Cape Cod zone in Massachusetts, for instance, such advertising is offered on three tiers, the most popular of which airs your ad locally on CNN, ESPN, Lifetime, USA, Nickelodeon, A&E, Discovery, TNT, TNN, and HGTV.

Your contract can be customized to fit your needs. A few years ago, we ran a series of spots using some of our furry clients as models; they were a big hit. For such ads, a copywriter creates a script and storyboard outlining the various shots and action involved in your TV commercial. Creative touches like computer animation that makes it look like the dogs and cats are talking or singing can add a fun touch. (I now have a whole new appreciation for the hard work and long hours in the studio under hot lights that went into producing those ads.) Call your cable company and ask for the advertising division to find out how you and your furry friends can have a shot at stardom!

The Internet provides another venue for advertising today. If you have a company Web site, you can exchange links with area shelters and fellow pet care providers to offer as a resource for clients. If you are a member of your local chamber of commerce, you can purchase an ad on its Web site. Your community newspaper probably solicits ads for local businesses on its site as well. You may also help sponsor a youth organization or humane society by purchasing advertising on its site.

## One of the Locals

There are also some fairly inexpensive ways to make your presence known, such as having your logo, business name, and phone number on your vehicle as you drive around town. Magnetic signs are the best bet for pet sitters because they can be removed as a security measure for your clients when you make your home visits. Personalized license plates provide another way to publicize your services. Just don't get nervous when people follow you to ask about your vanity plate!

Have some T-shirts made up to turn yourself, your friends, and family members into walking billboards for your business. You could even sell them to your clients. Have a plastic badge made up with your name and business logo on it and wear it every day—at the supermarket, at the post office, and in line at the bank. People will notice and ask about what you do.

Purchase space in your church bulletin, local theater production program, high school sports schedule, Junior League newsletter, or kennel club publication. Hang flyers with tear-off strips at the supermarket, senior citizen center, skating rink, hospital, feed and grain store, bookstore, coffeehouse, or on any community bulletin board. You can turn these out on your computer, using any publishing program. Never leave home without a supply of business cards. It's amazing how many people you meet who love to talk about their pets! Join a "lead group" with other business professionals who hold social gatherings periodically to network and swap business leads.

Donate gift certificates to area church and civic groups or specific fund-raising drives. You will get free advertising, and the winner may become a regular customer. Do be cautious about donations to any charitable organizations though, especially those who solicit you over the phone. In our years of operation, we have had hundreds of people soliciting our contributions; an amazing number of them were scams, including some posing as support groups for law enforcement or the elderly.

Tell them you need to contact your local police department or the Better Business Bureau before you give any donations. Ask them to mail you their literature because you do not take such calls on your business phone. Or tell them your advertising budget has been depleted for the year. Wish them a pleasant day and hang up!

With all these options vying for your advertising dollar, the choice can be a tough one. Remember that every advertisement is a legitimate business deduction, but don't spread yourself too thin. You can't afford to overspend your precious startup capital. After you've made your advertising choices, find out which ones work best for you. When you meet a new client, always ask, "How did you find out about our services?" For my grooming and pet supply business, the results break down like this: referrals from existing customers, 50 percent; print ads and yellow pages, 30 percent; local veterinarians and other pet care professionals, 10 percent; Web site, 10 percent.

## Networking and Petworking: Referrals Mean Business!

In the pet care field, networking—or, in our field, petworking—is vital to your success. Referrals from other pet care professionals provide positive results for all concerned. The vet is happy that he or she can refer the matted little shih tzu's owner to professionals who know what they are doing and who run a clean, safe grooming shop; the groomer recommends a pet sitter to a client who must leave town on short notice and has no one to take care of little Fifi; the trainer will be pleased to work with that grumpy little cocker who thinks its groomer's arm is a chew toy.

Contacts like these don't come out of the blue. You need to nourish them and feed them. Your vet—and more importantly, his or her technicians—will not feel comfortable handing out your cards unless you are a known entity. Before you set up your business, you should always make the rounds of vets, trainers, pet shops, kennels, groomers, and shelters, in short, anyone who works with animals who could recommend your services.

This does not mean dumping a bunch of business cards on the counter and bolting for the door. You need to establish a personal relationship. When you first met with that local vet, unless you were already a client, you should have made an appointment—and paid for it. If you are a pet sitter or a trainer, when you drop by the grooming salon, don't go during early-morning intake time; the harried owner will not even have time to notice that you're there. Call ahead a little later in the morning and ask how she likes her coffee.

If you are a groomer, meet with shelter personnel and see if there is any way you can help out, possibly by offering a free grooming to unkempt potential adoptees. Place shelter canisters in prominent places in your shop to help collect donations. Donate out-of-code pet foods or damaged items to these needy pets. Send over a basket of cookies or catnip treats at holiday time or a box of chocolates to the hardworking volunteers on Valentine's Day.

You wouldn't dream of recommending someone to baby-sit for your neighbor's child unless you knew and trusted the person. When it comes to beloved family pets, it's the same situation. Trust is everything. Having a vet send us new clients tells us that they respect us and value our services. If I use pet sitters who I think are angels from heaven, I will be happy to share this precious resource with my clients. If I know a trainer would never "helicopter" an unruly dog by swinging it through the air but instead would use only humane techniques and positive reinforcement, you can be sure I will need a steady supply of business cards from that person. In all such cases, I am helping my clients by putting them in touch with these caring professionals.

Once you have become a success in your community, it is extremely gratifying to help another pet care provider get started. You have no idea of the power you wield once the public puts its trust in you. In this business, which is, after all, based on love for our pets, there really is room for us all.

## Word of Mouth: Still the Best

After all is said and done, word of mouth still works best when it comes to advertising pet care services. If you benefit from it, return the favor. When one of your loyal customers sends you a new client, reward the referral with a free or discounted grooming, pet sitting visit, or training session. Most important: Keep doing a great job so your clients will keep coming back and sending their friends as well!

## Public Relations: Tooting Your Own Horn

The squeaky wheel gets the grease. That's another one of those old sayings we've all heard so many times. But when it comes to promoting your pet care business, it expresses an important truth. In your small business, you wear all the hats, including that of Director of Public Relations. By now you've pretty much decided where you will spend your initial advertising dollars but when it comes to PR, guess what? Besides your time, imagination, and the cost of paper and ink, you can do it for nothing! Virtually everything you do can be turned into a PR opportunity. You just need to decide which venues you will use to get the word out about your services, your accomplishments, and what makes you unique.

## News Releases

A news release is nothing more than an advertisement you don't have to pay for. Every business has numerous opportunities to send out these image-enhancing messages. In the pet care business, we are more fortunate than most because all newspapers periodically feel the need to run appealing stories related to animals, especially if accompanied by an irresistible picture. It's like those typical summer shots you see every July: the bathing beauty at the beach or the kid eating an ice-cream cone. You've seen them countless times before, but you're still compelled to look!

Begin your foray into publicizing yourself by compiling a list of local and regional newspapers, noting the name, address, and editor of each. Add the phone number too; you may need to contact the editor if your release doesn't get into print in a timely manner. Always be courteous when you call to inquire about whether an editor plans to run your news release. This is strictly an editorial decision; you don't want to burn your bridges by acting as if it was an announcement from the White House! Newspapers are bombarded with news releases every day, and the volume of news they need to print also affects what they will use. News releases are considered "filler"; they can run them today or save them until next week. If you do make a follow-up call, ask the editor if more information is needed. You may even get lucky and have this contact lead to an interview and a feature story about you and your business!

Your first news release can be about your grand opening. You could send it out on your business letterhead, but be sure to include your name as the contact person in case a follow-up is needed for clarification or additional information. Designate it "For Immediate Release," and print the headline in capital letters. Include a candid black-and-white shot of yourself with a pet or pets, if you have one. The first paragraph should provide a brief summary, answering the standard

Contact:
Mary Jones
(508) 555–2240

For Immediate Release

## SISTERS DELIVER PURR-FECT PET CARE TO YOUR HOME

PLAINFIELD, MA—Sisters Mary Jones and Judy Black have turned their love for pets into a new business venture. Starting April 1, they will be making the rounds in Plainfield, East Greenville, and Johnstown, providing in-home care for all manner of creatures in the place pets love best: their own homes. Jones and Black describe their business as an alternative to kennels or having to ask friends or neighbors to baby-sit for Fido and Fluffy while pet owners travel for business or pleasure. Besides feeding, exercising, and playing with the pets, they will also water plants, take in mail and newspapers, and turn lights on and off to give the home a "lived-in" look while owners are away.

"Some pets do not adjust well to the kennel," says Jones. "They may get depressed or refuse to eat; others are traumatized by strange surroundings. We plan to provide loving care and individual attention in the familiar surroundings of the home, and our presence will offer added security to pet owners."

Both women are avid pet lovers. Black and her golden retriever, Mandy, are familiar faces at the Shady Hill Retirement Home as they make weekly pet therapy visits to senior citizens. Jones is a well-known breeder of Himalayan cats; her MoonMist Cattery has produced several champions. Because both women have growing families, their new business will allow them to make their own hours. "Our husbands think it's great," Jones says. "As long as we promise not to bring home any of our furry clients!"

The sisters are bonded and insured and are members of Pet Sitters International, an educational organization for professional pet sitters. To find out more, pet owners should call them at (508) 555–2240 or 555–4267. Before booking their services, they will make a home visit to discuss special needs and get acquainted with the pets.

END

reporter's questions: who, what, when, where, why, and how. This "lead" should be punchy enough to capture the readers' interest, compelling them to read the entire article. State the information as briefly as you can; most newspapers have tight requirements when it comes to space. Make sure it's typed, double-spaced, and dated for immediate release.

At the end of your release, type in "-30-" or "END," centered, after your last paragraph. Before you mail it off or hand-deliver it to the newspaper office, addressed to the editor by name, be sure to proofread it to check for spelling errors.

If you win an award, publicize it—PR opportunities just don't get any better than that! Here is a typical release based on a groomer's first grooming competition win. Ideally, it would be accompanied by a professional photo taken at the show.

---

Contact:                                      For Immediate Release
Jane Smith
(508) 555–2345

### LOCAL GROOMER WINS AWARD

PLAINFIELD, MA—Professional Pet Groomer Jane Smith of Fur Magnolias Grooming Salon brought home the glory last weekend with her first grooming competition win at the New England Pet Grooming Professionals Fall Festival held in Sturbridge, Massachusetts. She received first prize in the toy and miniature poodles division with Coquette, a black miniature poodle owned by client Arthur Rogers of Johnstown. As a novice, she competed in the "B" division against a field of twelve other groomers.

Smith was awarded $100 plus a trophy, ribbons, and assorted merchandise for her salon. "It was a great experience and a chance to sharpen my skills," she said. "I loved the challenge of competing. I learned a lot, and I will definitely return to the contest ring to compete again!"

### END

---

Other events worthy of a news release include hiring a new employee, expanding your business, adding a new service, volunteer activities (especially those related to pets), attendance at industry conventions, gaining certification or accreditation in your field, or completing a course in animal care, training, or behavior. If you are a trainer or groomer working with an unusual client—a dog who will play "Sandy" in the local production of *Annie,* for instance—or a pet sitter caring for a rare and exotic pet, this may be deemed worthy of public interest by your newspaper or local cable television station.

## All the World's a Stage: Special Events

Special events are also newsworthy. If you hold a Halloween costume party for dogs at your grooming shop or plan a photo shoot with Santa Claus, get the word out to the media beforehand to line up coverage. If proceeds from any such event, in part or in full, go to charity, that's frosting on the cake!

Any event you hold for charity should draw media interest. A bake sale—including cookies from the new doggie bakery—to benefit the shelter, a dog walk at a local park to raise funds for the humane society or a spay/neuter fund, a day of beauty for the shelter with grooming services donated to spruce up adoptable pets, a flea market for a pet-related charity, or a block party for people and their pets in your parking lot or in a local park (with official permission, of course), these are public relations stories waiting to happen!

Your outdoor event could feature an obedience training exercise or police dog demonstration, a "freestyle" exhibition of people dancing with their dogs, an agility demonstration, or a cart-pulling event. My daughter held such a block party to commemorate the birthday of her toy poodle, Mookie, our beloved shop mascot, complete with balloon animals, clowns, pony rides, refreshments and a "Moon Walk" for the kids. All proceeds from Mookie's party were donated to New England Poodle Rescue.

Fun events like these draw media coverage from newspapers and TV stations, making your presence known in the community. They offer a great chance for informal camaraderie with your clientele, and they raise funds for animal-related causes. Granted, planning and hosting them takes a good deal of effort, but the work you put into them will pay off in a public relations bonanza for you and your business.

Your news release can also announce your presence as you host a booth at someone else's fund-raiser. We manned a nail-trimming booth to collect donations for a pet walk hosted by a local shelter, and offered a table of pet-related items at another's fair and flea market on the town common. Such "petworking" opportunities strengthen your connections to your fellow pet care professionals. Refer people to them just as they refer people to you, keeping a ready supply of their business cards on hand for your clients.

If there is an indoor pet fair in your community or if your local chamber of commerce holds a trade show, consider renting a booth. You could cut the cost by splitting the rental with another pet care provider, each using half the space. Usually, event promoters provide table skirts and electricity for each booth. If you have a small TV/VCR, you could run educational information videos. If you have been a guest on a local cable show, the tape they normally give you would be perfect. Bring plenty of cards and brochures. Of course, having some cute pets in attendance is a natural draw!

Have a drawing for free services or a pet-related prize. Use a fishbowl to collect the names and addresses of all who take part in your drawing. Offer refreshments like candy or cookies for browsers. Have pictures of your furry clients on display. Your participation will identify you as a professional, and you'll have a good time in the process!

> **Thanks a Bunch!**
> Public relations also involves nurturing the connections to those who have helped you along the way. When the holidays roll around, don't forget those fellow pet care professionals who have fed your business. Besides candy, cookies, or a fruit basket at Christmas and Hanukkah, you could send a gift certificate for dinner at a nice restaurant, an Easter Basket of goodies, or a big box of the best chocolates your town has to offer on Valentine's Day. You could drop by during the busy season with some home-baked treats or a box of doughnuts and a big container of coffee. At my grooming salon, we view such remembrances as manna from heaven during the Christmas rush!

# For a Good Cause:
# How to Be Both Charitable and Wise

You will no doubt be astonished by all the requests that come your way for donations to civic groups, youth sports teams, school fairs, churches, and so on. One way to be generous and publicize your business in the process is by donating gift certificates for a free grooming, a weekend of pet sitting services, or an introductory obedience training session, with the dollar amount spelled out by you. Along with your donation, you will receive free advertising and the added goodwill of helping out in your community. We've gotten some wonderful grooming clients this way! In addition, your donation can be written off as a legitimate business expense. Do try not to go overboard and give away the store; if you have any questions about the legitimacy of a charitable request or organization, check it out with local law enforcement before you agree to donate any of your hard-earned money!

## Sharing Your Knowledge

When it comes to questions about pets and their care, you're a natural. You will be amazed at the number of times you will be asked how to crate-train a puppy, what kind of treats are safe to give a pet, which dog food to use, and how to correct a pet's annoying habits. It's wonderful to be thought of as a resource in your community, and you should make the most of it!

To polish up this image even further, contact your local cable TV or radio station to see if you could be a guest to talk about pets and their care. You could also prepare a resume of your credentials to introduce yourself to these media outlets for future reference. My daughter and I have done several shows about grooming and pet care careers on our local cable station. When summer rolls around, a reporter calls or shows up to interview us about hot-weather safety tips. At holiday time, we are called upon to discuss seasonal do's and don'ts for pets.

Your local newspaper may welcome a column about such pet-related topics. If you have a talent for self-expression, write one up and submit it to the editor. Whether or not you get paid for it is irrelevant; you will be getting your name out there as an expert in your field.

When folks are looking for a puppy or an older dog to adopt, they often come to us for the names of breeders or breed rescue groups. They ask about the traits of a particular breed and whether it would be a good choice for their lifestyle. They want to know who we recommend when their pet needs a veterinary specialist for orthopedic work or vision problems, or if we know of an inn on Cape Cod where dogs are welcome.

Making yourself into a community resource is incredibly rewarding. It's great to be able to tell people about your fellow professionals: the trainer who offers puppy kindergarten classes, the pet sitter who will make midday visits to give medication to a canine senior citizen. Helping people and their pets is one of the biggest perks of a pet care career.

You can also share your expertise and the joys of pet ownership with the children in your community. Volunteer to speak at career days, bringing along a kid-friendly pet or two (with the school's permission, of course). Sponsor an essay contest or a drawing contest during National Pet Week in May. At Christmastime, hold a "Make Your Pet a Stocking Day" for kids at your grooming salon. The possibilities for creating fun events that also publicize your business will be limited only by your imagination!

# Public Speaking

If you are like me, just the thought of getting up to speak in front of a group of people is enough to get those butterflies in the stomach ready for takeoff! In the category of stressful situations, I'm told it rates right up there with divorce or death! The good news is that almost everyone can master this skill. If you can overcome your fears, it can become a great public relations tool for you and your business.

There are various ways to hone your skills in this area. In many communities, courses are offered in evening adult education programs, which are inexpensive and fun. Organizations like Toastmasters International and the Dale Carnegie courses in leadership training exist nationwide to instruct people in this type of communicating and help build self-confidence. Check their Web sites (www.toast masters.org or www.dalecarnegietraining.com) for the chapter nearest you. There are also private businesses and coaches listed in the yellow pages under Public Speaking—Instructions.

In all such courses, everyone is in the same boat when it comes to being nervous but participants are usually kind and supportive as they help each other build confidence and skills.

Speaking engagements before community groups will bring you new customers. Organizations like the chamber of commerce, the Rotary, Kiwanis, the Lions Club, Jaycees, and local business and professional groups will provide you a venue for speaking about your services. Senior citizens and their pets share a very special life-enhancing bond; your presentation about pet care at a senior center would be welcomed and appreciated. Schools and youth organizations would enjoy your talk about pets, emphasizing education on responsible care in addition to highlighting the services you provide.

Don't forget to inject some humor into your speech. If you can bring a pet or two along, so much the better; they make great ice-breakers. Use visual aids if possible, an overhead projector and slides or a video related to your services. Remember to bring brochures and business cards. If your audience is made up of children, advertising items like pens, key chains, and business card magnets are always a big hit.

To increase your comfort level, practice with family and friends first and ask for an honest critique. When you speak in public, it helps if you visualize yourself telling your story to a friend. Learn to smile and make eye contact; nothing is more boring than a person who steps up to the podium and simply reads a prepared speech. Most folks in your audience will be very supportive and kind and will be genuinely interested in the information you are providing. Invite their questions when you are through. Don't forget, when they get up to speak, they probably get butterflies too!

## Your Personal Pipeline: Publishing a Newsletter

If you can use a computer, you can publish a newsletter. Programs like Microsoft Publisher or any desktop publishing software will walk you through the process, customizing your layout, fonts, clip art, and columns as well as answering any questions that might crop up in the process.

A newsletter is a great image-builder as well as an advertising tool. It adds a new level of professionalism to your business services. What will your newsletter have to say? My daughter Missi usually begins ours with a personal message to thank our clients and to outline any new services we have to offer. She may explain why we do things a certain way, answering questions like "Why does it take so long to groom my dog?" or "Should I get my pet shaved for the summer?" She may share personal reflections or remembrances from our thirty-one-year history. (She swears she learned to ring the register at age four!) Because we are now serving our third generation of pets for some families, these trips down memory lane are very popular.

Missi also includes a column on pet care, usually focusing on seasonal information, highlighting health care and safety tips. She spotlights new products and announces any changes in staff we may have had since the last issue. And of course, it's a great forum to "toot our own horn," publicizing any conventions we have attended, public speaking she has done, grooming contest awards, or even her mom's writing assignments!

Any previously published material you wish to use, including cartoons, may be used only with the permission of the publication from which they came. Plagiarism and copyright infringement are against the law and should be taken very seriously. Most trade journals, pet-related Web sites, and veterinary school publications will be happy to give you permission to use such information.

You can use your newsletter to announce special promotions or memorialize beloved pets or their owners who have passed on. You can share a humorous anecdote about one of your own pets or a four-legged customer, or write about a client, telling about a recent trip, job, or activity; everyone loves those "fifteen minutes of fame." You may include letters from clients or help-wanted ads. No matter what information you choose to impart, keep it light and avoid getting up on your soapbox unless the issue concerns the welfare of pets.

You can print your newsletters yourself or take the original to the local printer, where they will turn them out for pennies per copy. Mailing them is another matter. Depending on how many pieces and how often you plan to publish, a bulk mail permit from the post office will usually cost between $125 and $200, a fee that must be paid annually. The cost varies according to the number of pieces, and you can get a discount by sorting them according to zip code. To obtain such a permit, you must send at least 200 pieces or 50 pounds of mail.

Another alternative is to have a mailing company such as Mail Boxes Etc. handle the mailing for you. Not all franchisees do it, so call ahead to check. The ones that do will take your copy either on paper or on disk, then print, tabulate, address, and sort your newsletters according to zip code. (They actually add a bar code, which automates the mailing for the post office.) An average run of 1,000 pieces may cost you up to eight cents per piece, but you would save about five cents on postage, making the process much more affordable.

Some businesses offset the cost of their newsletters by offering advertising space to other businesses or organizations. With enough advertisers, you might even turn a profit! Pet food companies, vets, other animal-related businesses, pet supply stores—all would be good places to start looking for "patrons." They may even distribute the newsletters in their places of business. Only you can decide if the amount you will spend on a printed newsletter will generate enough business to make it worth your while.

There are alternatives to mailing a newsletter, the most modern of which is publishing yours on-line. Have your clients sign up by giving you their e-mail addresses. If you have a Web site, be sure to include a link to your newsletters. We have begun doing this, but we still offer copies to our customers on our counter-top as well. They disappear like hotcakes! How you distribute your particular newsletter will depend on your business and your costs, but it's a great way to communicate with your clients and polish your image in the process.

## Check Us Out on the Web!

In 1984, there were 300 Internet users. There are now more than 30 million in the United States and an estimated 60 million worldwide. Internet commerce has gone hand-in-hand with this unprecedented growth explosion in a whole new mode of communication. On-line shopping has arrived. Forty-two percent of Internet users now say they regularly or occasionally make purchases on-line, compared to 31 percent in a 1998 study. With Internet usage increasing every day, having a presence in cyberspace has become part of doing business.

So why should you have a Web site? Because everybody else does? Well, yes. If your competition has a Web site, you should have one too. It gives you a distinctive presence and identifies you as an up-to-the-minute member of the business community.

By logging on to your site, your clients can get information about your services from the comfort of their homes. You can explain everything you need to about your services, policies, background, and prices. In doing so, you will be reaching a highly desirable demographic market, the modern consumer who considers computer use a vital part of everyday life.

Depending on your pet care business, your site can offer strictly promotional and informational services or it can feature interactive capabilities, such as booking appointments or selling goods. Our site, www.villagegroomer.net, features biographical information, pictures of our canine and feline clients and family members, our mission statement, a menu of services, tribute pages for pets who have passed on, a guest book, and links to my daughter's "other career" as a musician and to articles we have written. It also provides links to the AKC, several humane shelters and rescue groups, a pet sitting service, the Pet Loss Grief Support Network, and some pet food companies whose products we feature in our retail store. We are considering adding on-line sales in the future.

To establish your presence in cyberspace, the first thing you need to do is secure a domain name and register it. Currently, this costs around $40 per year per name. It is recommended that your name be registered with the .com, .net, and

.org suffixes to protect it from infringement by others. Some Internet Service Providers offer free hosting; our ISP hosts the site for a fee of $20 per month.

Ours was the product of a local Web designer, with plenty of input from us. The most basic design packages usually start at around $100, with $300 being an average fee. If you have computer skills and the right software, you could design the site yourself.

OK, now you're up there on the Web, but how will people find you? For a small server fee, your host will register your Web site with several of the most popular search engines. You could also register it yourself with a company like SubmitIt!.com, which will list your site in up to 400 search engines and directories for $59 a year. There are community-based plans available, such as Shoplocal.net in southeastern Massachusetts, which will feature your Web site in regional business directories only, most offering community links and other useful information as well. With a site design package cost of $200 and a hosting fee of $120 per year, this can be a good way to establish an Internet presence for minimal costs.

There are usually additional costs attached to custom graphics, animated banners, digital photography, and Web site maintenance plans. It may sound like an expensive proposition, but compared to other forms of advertising, it offers a lot for your money. Take the plunge! One day, all businesses will consider being on the Internet as natural as being listed in the yellow pages.

# Advertising and Promotion Checklist

COMPLETED

1. Write your own bio story and announce the opening of your business as a news release for your local and regional newspapers. . . . . . . . . . . . . . . . . . . . . . . . . . . . . . . . ☐

2. Volunteer to give a talk on pet grooming at local schools as part of career day presentations. . . . . . . . . . . . . . . . . . . . . . . . ☐

3. Look for business organizations in order to meet new people and publicize your services in the community. . . . . . . . . ☐

4. Volunteer to do a grooming demonstration at your community's annual fair. . . . . . . . . . . . . . . . . . . . . . . . . . . . . . . . . ☐

5. Volunteer to host a nail cutting booth at the local humane society's annual fund-raising dog walk. . . . . . . . . . . . . . ☐

6. Volunteer to donate a free grooming to shelter pets who need it to make them more adoptable. . . . . . . . . . . . . . . . . ☐

7. Publish a shop newsletter giving seasonal pet health and safety tips and news items regarding yourself and your clients. . . . . . . . . . . . . . . . . . . . . . . . . . . . . . . . . . . . . . . ☐

8. Decide how to best set up your Web site. . . . . . . . . . . . . . . . . . . ☐

   Register your domain name. . . . . . . . . . . . . . . . . . . . . . . . . . . . . . ☐

   Call your current ISP and other hosts to compare Web hosting rates. . . . . . . . . . . . . . . . . . . . . . . . . . . . . . . . . . . . . . ☐

   Decide whether to use a fee-based or a no-fee hosting service. . . ☐

   Decide if you will hire a professional Web site designer, or research appropriate Internet software and Web design courses at the local community college or adult education courses at the local high school. . . . . . . . . . . . . . . . . . . . . . . . . ☐

Decide how you want your site to look—pictures, text, content—and the number of pages you will require. (Hint: Consider hiring a high school or college student to help design your site.) . . . . . . . . . . . . . . . . . . . . . . . . . . . . . . . . . ☐

9. Investigate the cost of installing a toll-free phone number. . . . . . . . . . . . . . . . . . . . . . . . . . . . . . . . . . . . . . . . ☐

10. Request catalogs from companies specializing in promotional products such as bumper stickers, pens, magnets, key chains, and calendars. Identify items you can use and afford to best promote your services. . . . . . . . . . . . ☐

## Chapter Fifteen
# The Personal Touch

Among the joys of a pet care career are the personal bonds you forge with clients and their beloved pets. In this line of work, you automatically gain admission to a private world where not many people are invited to visit. This happens because people trust you. Otherwise, they would not seek out your services to care for their "surrogate children." If this is your calling, then along with the grooming, pet sitting, or obedience training services you provide, you will also be delivering loving care and peace of mind.

My late husband, David, was a great animal lover. He had unlimited patience and found joy in even the shaggiest beast that came into our shop. The love he projected was one of the things that helped our business to succeed. In fact, I believe that in their heart of hearts, every pet-owning client harbored their own precious little secret: They were sure that of all the animals that came to The Village Groomer, Dave loved theirs the best!

## When Work and Play Are One

Does this sound like deception? It shouldn't. Caring for animals is not a cold and mechanical job. If you don't love them, you won't enjoy it. Eventually, they will get on your nerves and leave you wondering whatever made you decide to do this for a living. Opening up your heart to the love and appreciation of your furry clients will do wonders for you and your business. It will also keep your phone ringing and make you more successful.

Many midlifers and downsized nine-to-fivers enter the world of pet care because it offers something different, outside the mainstream of the buttoned-down corporate world. It's a way of living that allows us to have fun. It is said that people who can combine work and play are the happiest of all. They are doing something they love and getting paid for it! Some of us have learned along the way that even if we were making a lot of money, if we dreaded going to work every day, the paycheck was not enough. You can be rich and still be miserable. The pet care career path offers us loving interactions—and fun—each and every day.

Share this attitude of play with your coworkers and your clients too. Have a sense of playfulness, a special little nickname for each pet, an anecdote to share at the end of the day. When reminiscing about my husband, one prim and proper matron tearfully confided that it always tickled her funny bone when he called her chubby cocker spaniel "Chunky Chicken." My daughter Missi has this gift as well. When a baby bonnet ended up in our lost and found and went unclaimed, she started using it as a playful prop. If any of our employees are having a tough day or just feeling sorry for themselves, she gives them the "baby hat" to lighten things up. It brings a laugh because it is done with love. On several occasions, she's been known to wear it herself.

One of the reasons that people have pets is to relieve the stress of the workaday world. In your pet care business, your welcoming presence gives them permission to be silly, to let their tender feelings show. This business is all about personal interaction. Develop the skill of really listening to your clients. This will help you to take better care of their needs and the needs of their pets. You will get to know these folks well in the process. They are the ones who are paying your bills, putting the groceries on the table, and helping to pay for your son's braces. Developing a personal relationship will keep them coming back. Just like at Cheers, that homey Boston bar made famous on TV, those regulars kept coming back because it was a place "where everybody knows your name"—we even know their pets' names too!

Beyond doing a good job of caring for your clients' pets, there are other ways to enhance the personal touch. If a client is ill, send a get-well card (with animals on it, of course!). In times of loss, attend their services and send a sympathy card or spiritual bouquet. Make a memorial donation to the loved one's favorite charity. If they need to get the dog groomed or require pet sitting services at the time of bereavement, offering to take care of them without charging for your services is a caring touch that will always be remembered.

If you are a groomer and there's a wedding coming up, match the color of Buffy's bows to the bridesmaids' dresses. Give a little stuffed dog or cat when a client has a baby. If you sell retail products, take the time to show clients something that will interest them: "I was thinking of you when I picked up this item." Gestures like this cement the personal bond between you and your clients.

# Sweet Remembrance: Seasonal Gifts for Your Customers

The holidays offer a whole new opportunity to say thanks to your loyal customers. Some pet care people send out personalized holiday cards, featuring a picture of them with their pets and a hand-written message of goodwill and thanks. Every year, Village Groomer clients look forward to our calendars, which feature pictures of adorable pets, of course. As for their animals, we always give out little boxes of holiday cookies. If you sell pet treats, you may be able to get them in individual-size holiday gift packaging. Our gift-boxed cookies come from a local supplier and cost one dollar each. You could also go on-line and search for "dog bakeries" on the Internet. You'll come up with hundreds of businesses, many of them near you.

Don't forget the diversity of your client base when it comes to holiday gifts and items for sale. Not everyone celebrates Christmas. Get out your calendar and make yourself aware of the dates for Hanukkah and Kwaanza. Our "cookie man" provides us with brightly colored plastic dreidels filled with treats for our Jewish clients. Our gift cookie boxes bear the message "Happy Holidays" rather than "Merry Christmas."

Our groomers go into a bow-making frenzy using Christmas and Hanukkah ribbon, curling ribbon, and jingle bells as they adorn each and every pet with a holiday bow. Some pet care providers use bandannas instead. Most pet supply houses offer them for every holiday, along with a huge variety of ribbons. Contact our supplier, the Ribbon Warehouse in Cleveland, Ohio, at (800) 875–5204, or e-mail them at RIBBONWHSE@aol.com.

Instead of cookies, you can give each pet an inexpensive toy, bought in bulk and completely deductible, of course. For dogs, it might be a squeaky toy; for cats, a catnip pillow or furry mouse with a holiday ribbon. You can also make up your own little remembrances, a framed magnet picture of each pet, a homemade ornament, your own little bag of goodies, or some pet-related item you come across at an industry convention like Intergroom or GroomExpo.

You may also shop for such items at a regional gift center. Now that you are in business, you will need to obtain a tax number for resale from the state allowing you to purchase from these wholesalers or attend their gift shows. They are not open to the public. Conduct an on-line search for gift wholesalers and shows in your area. My daughter recommends The Gift Center in Bedford, Massachusetts, a 100,000-square-foot facility housing sixty showrooms that display thousands of gifts and decorative accessory product lines. It is open to retailers every Monday except holidays; some showrooms remain open during the week. Its seasonal shows draw merchants from all over New England. On its Web site, www.thegift center.com, you will find a comprehensive list of vendors whose products are on display there.

You can't actually buy items at these wholesale centers or gift shows, but you can get a look at the products and place orders. The time to start planning how you will make the holidays a special time for you and your customers is during the summer months. By the time you get into the busy holiday season, it will be too late.

# Dealing with Difficult Clients

The vast majority of your pet-owning customers will be pleasant and reasonable, but sooner or later you are bound to run across that difficult client who really tests your people skills and professionalism. It may be the woman who calls at the last minute and gets highly irate because you can't accommodate her. It may be someone who feels the need to haggle over your prices. It may come out of left field, a person who accuses you of being negligent or harming a pet in your care.

How will you handle these problem people? First and foremost, try to remain calm and professional. Every business on the planet gets complaints. Second, deal with the situation immediately. If you leave a complaint unanswered, it will only add to your stress level and the unhappy client's indignation. The person who comes at you all puffed-up and ready to do battle can usually be defused by a calm and understanding approach. Before you offer any remedy, listen to what the person has to say.

## Communicating Clearly

Most client problems revolve around the issue of communication. If you think the complaint has any merit, ask what the client thinks you could do to correct the situation. If it's a misunderstanding about a grooming style ("You clipped Muffy's head way too short and I told you not to trim her ears"), and if you want to keep that person as a client, offer the next visit at a reduced fee or free of charge. Compensating for a client's disappointment with a future free or discounted service is far superior to refunding the person's money. Whether they were pleased with the results or not, you performed the service in good faith. If it is something you can correct about the grooming job then and there, by all means do it while the client waits.

In a busy grooming shop, things can get hectic at intake time. The best way to avoid such miscommunication is to go over each dog or cat to see what kind of shape it's in before agreeing to do a certain style. You cannot imagine the repercussions of agreeing to "just give him a puppy cut" as the client bolts out the door before you have had a chance to examine the coat. In our salon, we will not shave a pet down without the owner's consent, and we take great pains to explain what we mean by "stripping" a pet's coat. At best, most clients retain about a third of what you tell them; honing your communication skills is the best way to avoid disappointing them with your work and causing an angry backlash directed at you.

In the client's eyes you are now a pet care expert, and an important part of your job involves client education. When a new customer comes in for an initial appointment, take the time to explain the grooming needs of the pet. Demonstrate proper brushing techniques for maintenance care between grooming appointments. A cautionary note: If you use groomer jargon and fail to explain your terminology, the person could be too embarrassed to ask what you mean and might completely misunderstand the information.

## Last-Minute Callers

Another area of frequent friction involves the last-minute caller. If you are a pet sitter, you can discourage these requests by adding a "last-minute surcharge" to your fees. If you are a groomer, you can politely but firmly tell the client that if you squeeze Spot in for grooming, you would be shortchanging all those clients who had previously booked your services. Tell the disappointed client that you are sorry you cannot accommodate him, but you would be happy to make a future booking and put his name on your cancellation list. You should not have to apologize for being booked up in advance. It tells people that you are doing a good job and your services are in demand. That should make you feel proud, not guilty!

## Aggressive Pets

Sometimes clients get offended if we do not want to care for their aggressive or dangerous dogs. A dog with its neck and back hair bristling, that cowers in fear, growls, snarls, or tries to bite you, is not a safe dog to handle. Trainers may exercise more leeway than other pet care pros when it comes to accepting these pets as clients. They are skilled at evaluating a dog's behavior, and most will go to the mat before deciding they cannot help an animal with a behavior problem. Correcting problem behavior is their calling. But like groomers and pet sitters, occasionally they also have to say no.

If a dog shows signs of vicious behavior as you take it from its owner, do yourself a favor and do not accept that dog as a customer. As you become more familiar with dog behavior and body language, you can usually tell the ones that will pose a real threat to you or your employees. When I have ignored my intuition and agreed to groom a dog that was dangerous, I have often regretted it. No matter how much I charged, the risk involved was not worth it. Some people think that just because we work with animals, we can handle anything. They get offended when you tell them that little Spunky spent his whole grooming session trying to chew on your arm. They look at you with suspicion and wonder what you did to provoke him! Contrary to the beliefs of owners like these, pet care providers are not immune to injury. When we get bitten, we bleed just like everybody else.

In most cases, we can read canine or feline body language. If the animal does not calm down enough to cooperate or shows serious aggression, we make that phone call to the owner explaining that we tried but we were unable to groom the pet. On the other hand, there have been many times when my staff and I have worked successfully with grumpy or fearful pets and have won them over with patience and time. This is a great ego-booster. All of a sudden, you feel you're on a par with Siegfried and Roy!

It's an individual call, but before you agree to groom a pet that wants to eat you for lunch, remind yourself that you cannot work if you are injured. If one of your employees gets bitten, it's even worse. Not only do you feel concern for the injured worker, you also feel responsible for taking that dog as a client. In addition to the stress level such a crisis brings, you are faced with the hassle of insurance claims, workers' compensation reporting, and notifying the animal control officer, the local health department, and the pet owner. Even if the animal is up-to-date on its vaccinations, it must be quarantined for ten days after a biting incident. Then there is the added strain of working understaffed while your injured employee recuperates. My advice? When in doubt, go with your intuition. If you do not feel comfortable grooming a pet, don't do it. The world is full of lovely pets that will not endanger you or your staff.

Pet sitters face similar dilemmas every day. If you feel at risk on your initial meeting with Mrs. Brown and her dog, Chopper, how much more uncomfortable will you feel when you must go into that house alone to care for him? Instead, offer the names of area kennels, where Chopper would not need to feel so protective of his territory. After all, if you are afraid of him, you cannot provide secure care.

As a pet sitter, one of the basic tenets of your business policy should be that you do not take care of pets that have a history of biting or acting aggressively. During your initial client interview, you should have covered the area of temperament problems, but people are not always truthful about their beloved but "misunderstood" pets. Thank these folks for considering your services, but tell them that you're sorry you cannot help them.

There may be times when you do not discover that a pet is aggressive until you are in the middle of a grooming session. If you begin the grooming procedure and the dog proves too dangerous or difficult, place it back in the crate or cubby and call the owner to explain why you cannot complete the job. Aggressive behavior can often be corrected by an obedience trainer, and there are some trainers who specialize in handling this particular problem. You might even refer the owner to a trainer who can help. But this is not a job for a groomer.

## Other Dangers

If someone requests your pet sitting, training, or mobile grooming services in a crime-ridden neighborhood or if a client's home is filthy or unsafe, you must find a way to tactfully decline the assignment. You may say that the area where they live is outside your territory, that you have a scheduling conflict and you are already overbooked. Offer your apologies and tell the person that other arrangements will need to be made.

## Nonpayment for Services

Once in a while you may run into the client who refuses to pay for your services. Grooming is usually a "cash and carry" business, and most of us are not set up to do credit billing. The client pays for our services when they are performed. I have run into only one client who just plain refused to pay my price, offering me only a small portion of what was due. The police were called and, once the situation was explained, she chose to ante up for the remaining amount. I was lucky in that case because it was my word against hers. Legally, I would not have been allowed to hold her pet until such time as she paid me—which was fine with me, as her "baby" was a 90-pound Samoyed!

Most unpaid bills are the results of bad checks for which you are not reimbursed. In my experience, this has happened rarely. Most such instances are the result of checking account mix-ups or people who are disorganized in handling their accounts. Be diplomatic when you call to inform a client that a check has been returned. You should have a policy requiring clients to pay any bank charges incurred by overdrafts. Most businesses also assess a fee for bounced checks, commonly ranging from $10 to $20.

If two calls from you do not result in the person coming in to make good on the check, send a letter bringing the matter to the client's attention and requesting payment within five days. Your tone should be friendly but firm, indicating the date your services were rendered, the number and date of the check that was returned, and the dates of the calls you made to the person. Your letter may state: "We enjoy grooming your pet and value you as a customer. We feel certain this matter is just an oversight on your part but we need you to take care of it immediately so we may clear it from our books. Therefore, we thank you in advance for remitting payment for these services to us within the next five (5) days."

For the pet sitter, the bill is usually left at the client's home when the final service visit has been completed. For lengthy assignments, it makes sense to require a deposit to cover any unforeseen expenses that may occur. The professional trainer's clients usually pay up-front, prior to the start of a training course, or per private session as they advance through their lessons. Some trainers request a deposit at the start of the course, with the balance due either halfway through or when it has been completed.

To protect against nonpaying clients, pet sitters' and trainers' service contracts should include a clause stating when payment is due and noting that a monthly interest rate will be charged on unpaid balances after thirty days. A statement concerning your company policy on returned checks should also be included in your service contract.

Pet sitters and obedience trainers need a filing system that records payments as they come in. Whether you enter this information in a ledger or use a computer program, your accounts receivable records should have a minimum of four columns: total due, payments, interest, and balance due. Most businesses operate on a 30/60/90-day schedule. Although payment for services is expected when the services have been provided, if the bill is paid within 30 days, it is considered acceptable. If payment has not been made within 60 days, it is considered past due; and after 90 days, it becomes delinquent. Sooner or later, any business that operates on a billing system will experience delinquent accounts.

You will need form letters to send out to clients whose accounts become past due or delinquent. The first letter, to be sent when the account is past due, should have a friendly tone, outlining the dates of the services you provided and the amount you are owed. Include such a statement as "We enjoyed caring for your pet and would like to do so again in the future," or "We value the relationship we have built with you. We enjoyed our training sessions and the role we have played in making pet ownership a more beneficial experience for you." Follow these statements with "We thank you in advance for remitting your payment to us within the next five (5) days."

The next letter, when the account has become delinquent, should be sent by registered mail. This "official" method, which requires the customer to sign for the letter, will usually be taken more seriously. The delinquent letter should be more matter-of-fact: "A review of our records shows that you still have an outstanding balance of $_____ for services rendered on (dates of visits or training sessions). We provided the services you requested in good faith and in a responsible and caring manner. Our business is not set up to extend credit. We hope that this is just an oversight on your part, but we must inform you that if your balance is not paid within 90 days, you will leave us no option but to take the matter to Small Claims Court."

A claim can be filed in Small Claims Court for unpaid bills or restitution involving $2,000 or less. (That's the current amount in Massachusetts; it may be different where you reside.) Small Claims sessions are somewhat less formal than other court proceedings, usually held at the District Court level. The filing fees are minimal. Although you may hire an attorney if you wish, you are entitled to represent yourself. By choosing to go the Small Claims route, as the plaintiff, you will give up your right to a jury trial. The case will be heard before a clerk magistrate. If the defendant, the party you are suing, loses the case, he or she may appeal and have a trial in front of a jury. As the plaintiff, you may appeal only in very limited circumstances, such as if the defendant has filed a counterclaim against you and you have lost that claim.

The overwhelming majority of such cases are settled without going to trial. If the judgment is decided in your favor, the court will order the defendant to pay. However, he or she will have ten days to file an appeal, posting $100 bond and paying a filing fee for the appeal ($29 in Massachusetts). If the defendant decides not to appeal the decision, he or she must pay you within a specified period of time.

When a judgment is made against a person in Small Claims Court, a lien is placed against that person until such time as the debt is settled. The guilty party must also pay court costs. If you do not receive the payment the defendant has been ordered to pay, you must notify the court so that the clerk magistrate may take further steps to enforce the order. For further information on Small Claims Court, call the District Court in your county or the office of your state attorney general.

Taking someone who owes you money to Small Claims Court is a fairly straightforward procedure, but for a small-business operation, it does present an inconvenience because you lose a day's income while you are at the courthouse waiting for your case to be heard. It's up to you to decide whether you should write off your loss as a "bad debt" instead. If so, you must provide documentation of the services and all communication you have made in trying to settle the matter to your accountant when you pay your taxes at the end of the year.

Sticking to your policies and safety practices is the best way to avoid problems in your pet care business. First and foremost, you must view yourself as a professional. We are all building a new industry, and our standards will add to its legitimacy and professionalism. It's natural to grow more confident as you build on your experience, but

## For the Record

In today's increasingly litigious society, you must document anything unusual you encounter in caring for your clients. For the groomer, this means recording any health problem discovered during the grooming process. If a pet is injured while in your care, you must notify the owner and take the pet to the vet for treatment. It is extremely unfortunate and stressful when such things happen, but if you feel you caused an injury, you must take responsibility for it. Your insurance should cover the medical costs.

Pet sitters should document any problems that crop up with the pets or in the home, such as urine stains on the carpet. Never bend your rules when it comes to security. Nobody but you or an authorized member of your staff may enter the client's home unless you have been given explicit permission by your client, or in the case of emergency personnel such as police or firefighters. If you observe evidence of a break-in, contact the police immediately. Never forget that your word is your bond. As pet care providers, our clients place their trust in us. Honesty is not just the best policy, it is the *only* policy.

it is not good to become complacent. Animals are unpredictable flesh-and-blood creatures. Letting down your guard for a few minutes can cause major problems. When you are asked to lower your standards or make exceptions to your policies, it's OK to say no. It will help lower your stress level and add to your longevity in the career you have chosen.

## Helping Clients Deal with Pet Illness and Bereavement

One of the most difficult aspects about working with pets has to do with illness and bereavement. Because their expected lifespans are so much shorter than our human life expectancy, loving a pet brings with it a built-in heartbreak down the road. As a pet care provider, you will find yourself sharing in the grieving process with your clients when a beloved pet dies or when they face that difficult decision about whether it's time for euthanasia. They will count on you for support, and it really is a privilege.

You can provide a safe and respectful place for grieving pet owners to process their loss. How heartbreaking and maddening it is to hear "It was only a dog" from somebody who just "doesn't get it." Some people have no idea what an emotional blow it can be to lose a four-legged family member. You are faced with the whole grieving process—anger, denial, acceptance, and healing—before you are able to move on. Like it or not, as a pet care provider you've been thrust into the role of bereavement counselor.

Beyond a few friends and family members, who else really grieves with people who lose a pet? Who acknowledges the impact such losses have upon our lives? You cared for their pet and you knew its little idiosyncrasies. It's perfectly normal to share a smile at that pet's antics and shed a few tears when you comfort your grieving client. We know from experience that the first person they call when the loss occurs is their groomer, pet sitter, or trainer.

Beyond your words of comfort, it's nice to acknowledge the loss with a card bearing a personalized message, a bouquet or plant, or a donation to a shelter or rescue organization in the pet's name. There are pet bereavement products available, such as the Pet Memorial Candle offered by Furry Angel of California. The candleholder has a moving poem inscribed on it; the process of lighting it can be a peaceful, calming ritual for the bereaved owner. (It is also a nice item to carry if you sell pet-related retail products.) You can find the company on-line at www.furryangel.com, where you will also find links to other pet loss sites.

At www.petloss.com you will find the Pet Loss Grief Support Web site, a wonderful resource for clients who have lost a pet. It includes a link to the Rainbow Bridge (www.rainbowbridge.com), a moving and beautiful poem about the journey of our departed pets. Whether or not the afterlife is part of your belief system, it is comforting to visit this site and read the story. Its final paragraph speaks of a meeting that may await you when your own life is over:

"You have been spotted, and when you and your special friend finally meet, you cling together in joyous reunion, never to be parted again. The happy kisses rain upon your face; your hands again caress the beloved head, and you look once more into the trusting eyes of your pet, so long gone from your life but never absent from your heart."

Those visiting the site are invited to take part in the worldwide Pet Loss Candle Ceremony, visit tribute pages, read inspirational poetry and articles, participate in on-line chat rooms and local support groups, or receive telephone support if needed. For those whose pets are ill, there is also a link for "Special Needs Pets."

At my business Web site, www.villagegroomer.net, my daughter Missi has created a link called Up In Heaven Barking, which includes links to the Rainbow Bridge and the Pet Loss site as well. We invite our clients to send in pictures of their pets to be featured on this page along with a few words of tribute. We also request that they include a small fee to be donated to one of the rescue organizations when we publish the picture. It has proven to be enormously popular. If you have a business Web site, this would be a wonderful resource for your clientele.

Sometimes our clients seek our advice when a pet is terminally ill or incapacitated. They are suffering with the decision of whether it's time to have the pet "put to sleep." It's an honor to be the trusted confidante they seek out at this difficult time, but the decision they will make is ultimately their own. No matter how compassionate your intention, if you are the one to advise they have the pet euthanized, you are overstepping your bounds. You could even incur their resentment or blame later on. Be there to offer your support as a listening ear for them as they wrestle with this painful decision, and extend your condolences if a client decides to let a beloved pet go to its rest.

It helps to remember your own experiences with pet loss, how necessary it was for you to take the time to be sad and grieve before you moved on. If you ever find yourself going through it again, your clients will be there for you too.

# Chapter Sixteen

# Watching Baby Grow

As the pet industry grows, so does the need for pet care services. You may have opted to start small, running your business alone or with a partner, but within a few years, you may find yourself "maxed out" in meeting the demand for grooming, pet sitting, or training. You're becoming overbooked and overworked. You may have come to a crossroads where you need to make a decision about your future growth.

This is the time to sit down with your accountant and go over your volume of business and income since you opened. Has it increased every year? Are there other factors that have impacted your business? Have any of your competitors retired or gone out of business? What about the economic health of your community? Are housing values and population figures on the rise? Now is the time to look at your pricing structure. If you are booked solid most of the time, it's time to consider raising your prices. The law of supply and demand applies to pet care workers too.

Reviewing your financial records will help you set goals. Refer to your business plan to see if you have achieved any of the milestones you set for yourself back in the planning and dreaming stages. Your records will reveal the busiest and slowest times for your business. These figures will help you make the decision on whether it's time to add staff.

Your accountant's input is key in making decisions regarding your growth. Together you will crunch the numbers, looking at such considerations as starting wages you could offer, the cost of benefits, and the tax implications. Once you have employees, you must pay workers' compensation tax and withhold state, federal, and social security taxes from their paychecks.

# Growth Opportunities

If you are a professional trainer, it may be time to add a full-time or part-time assistant. For the groomer, hiring a bather-brusher will allow you to spend more time on your grooming and increase your productivity. If you are working longer hours to care for your pet sitting clients and becoming exhausted or stressed out in the process, it may be time to grow by adding another sitter. Burnout is a recognized occupational hazard in this field. Too many of us are "people-pleasers" who regularly put our customers' needs ahead of our own.

Beyond their traditional duties of pet sitting and dog walking, many sitters aspire to open their own doggie day care centers, either at home if they are properly zoned or in a separate facility. Starting pet taxi or pet shipping services and offering delivery of premium pet foods are logical add-ons to a pet sitting business as well.

You started your venture as a home-based business, but in some cases, you may need to leave home to grow. For the trainer, this could range from renting a hall a few nights a week to building a training facility where you help pay the mortgage by renting out space to other businesses. For the groomer, a commercial location will allow you to build a larger clientele. Both home groomers and mobile groomers have a built-in ceiling on how many pets they can accommodate in their limited space. In planning for your future, including retirement, you should take into account that when you own or lease a commercial property, your business will be far more attractive and worth much more to a prospective buyer.

Selling a home-based business is another matter. Unless you are selling your house and business as one, the potential buyer is faced with moving the clientele and adapting his or her own residence to suit the business. Local and state regulations that apply to home businesses grow more stringent every year. Your costs to set up your home salon were considerably less than those of your colleagues who rented commercial space, but at retirement time you will be faced with self-imposed limitations when it comes to net worth and resale value.

# Adding to Your Staff

Right now you may envision your business as a one-person show, but it is quite likely that will change. As you build your clientele and your desire to work more efficiently, you will probably consider hiring employees. If you're a groomer, you

## Managing Your Financial Growth

Do you know your *average* grooming, pet sitting, or training fee? Do you know how much of that figure is the cost of grooming, training, or sitting? How much goes to overhead and how much of it is profit? These vital pieces of financial information will help you and your accountant make key decisions about your business and its growth.

For example, if you are a groomer you would total the number of pets groomed per day and by year's end. Now look at your gross revenues for the year for grooming. Divide that gross figure by the number of pet services you provided to arrive at your average fee. For example, if I grossed $52,500 for the year and groomed 1,500 pets, my average fee would be $35. But what was my *cost* to groom each pet? If I deduct what it cost me for my labor, supplies, and overhead (lights, water, heat, etc.) from that gross revenue, I would arrive at my profit, or in the case of a sole proprietor, my income. If that "bottom line" was $22,000, it cost me $30,500 to groom all those critters.

I would divide that cost figure by the number of groomings to find out my average cost to groom each pet. In this case, that figure is $20.33. Therefore, for every pet that brought in $35, I made $14.67 in profit. If I want to generate more income, there are two ways to achieve that goal: I could groom more pets or I could increase my prices.

To increase the volume of pets groomed, I may need to add full-time or part-time staff. This is a decision I will need to review with my accountant. It involves a host of variables—salary, taxes, benefits, etc. I could also raise my prices. So now you can see that the prices you set for your services need to be based on much more than what your competitor down the street is charging. A savvy businessperson does not pull that figure out of thin air! To even be able to have this discussion with my accountant, however, I need to know my gross revenues, average price of my services, costs incurred in providing those services, my overhead, and my profit. Knowing these figures will enable me to operate my business more effectively and plot my course for the future.

might start with a bather-brusher, perhaps initially just on Saturdays. Later, you may wish to add another groomer to accommodate your customers. Where in the world do you look for help?

The first thing you need to do is to check to make sure you can have employees. Some municipalities do not allow additional employees, other than family members, in a home-based business. Many small-business owners have their spouses or children pitch in as employees. If that is not an option for you and it is legal to proceed, then you need to get the word out that you are hiring.

Finding pet care personnel is not easy. It's not like working at the fast-food restaurant or the car wash. This field requires true animal lovers who have an abundance of kindness and compassion and are willing to work hard. They need to be dependable and trustworthy. If they will be dealing with the public, they need people skills because they will be representing you and your business. A rude or crude employee can do serious damage to the image you have worked so hard to build. If they will be pet sitters, they need reliable transportation to get to their assignments.

Begin your search by word of mouth. Tell your clients, business associates, and friends that you are looking. Tell the woman at the coffee shop and the stylist where you get your hair done. Post a sign where all can see it. Advertise in your newsletter; put flyers on bulletin boards at the vet's office, the kennel, the training facility, the pet supply store, and the humane shelter. Talk to your fellow merchants at the chamber of commerce.

Sometimes a friend or relative will step forward to offer their help. Although this can be a blessing, it's important to let them know that this will be a business relationship. You will not expect any less of them in handling their responsibilities because you have a personal relationship.

If you have exhausted your personal and business connections and still come up empty, it's time to place a help-wanted ad in the newspaper. Be upbeat and positive in your choice of words. "Have fun and earn money caring for pets! Must love animals, be dependable, and provide references." State the hours when you would like applicants to call to schedule an interview.

A word of warning: The folks who answer ads can be an interesting bunch. Weeding out prospects for a job in a pet care business can be tricky. Most people have no inkling of how hard the work actually is. They think we spend all day playing with the pups. You must be totally honest in describing the job to applicants. If they have starry-eyed notions of working with pets, it won't be worth going through the entire hiring and training process, because they won't last long on the job.

Hiring from among your clientele can sometimes be a sticky matter as well. If it doesn't work out, you might lose a customer. If you are a groomer, can you really envision that nice poodle-owning lady hefting big dogs in and out of the tub, cleaning up pet hair, and scrubbing that dirty dog who comes in from the farm once a year? Here's a hint: If the job candidate has an elaborate hairdo sprayed into place and long, perfectly polished nails, this might not be the job for her! Trainers and pet sitters also need to be cautious when hiring. No matter how adeptly she has trained her Pomeranian, the petite senior citizen who aspires to be your training apprentice will not be able to control those exuberant retrievers. The teenager with the twenty-year-old car that's always breaking down cannot be depended on to get those puppies out to potty when their owner is in Aruba.

Local grooming schools are a good source of employees. The best schools offer placement services for their groomer graduates. Vocational high schools are another possibility. Although the skills taught in their animal sciences program may not train full-fledged groomers, they do teach the basics, and their students are usually willing to work hard in animal-related careers. On-line classifieds for employers and prospective employees in grooming are also worth checking out. Visit www.groomers.com (The Pet Groomers Lounge) and www.petgroomer.com.

Another source of employees is your state employment agency. Operated under federal auspices, some 2,500 of these offices exist across the United States. Their services are provided free to both employers and employees and are paid for by payroll taxes. In many offices, computer job banks match jobs with applicants. Vocational and professional schools, high schools, and colleges may also be a good resource. Schools normally have placement counselors, and some maintain job bulletin boards. Again, referral services are free.

Most trainers find their prospective staff members from among their own clientele. You know them when you see them: that dedicated Sheltie owner who stays after class to help and can't wait to bring her dog to the next level, the enthusiastic Lab owner who has a gift for helping his fellow classmates.

For potential pet sitters, it's a bit more dicey because your employees will be entering clients' homes. Many sitters draw upon their family and friends. Local cat and dog breed clubs, humane shelters, and veterinarians are also an excellent place to find reliable candidates.

Because of the ever growing demand for trained groomers, some shop owners are now helping to underwrite the cost of grooming school for a bather or grooming assistant who demonstrates the potential to become a full groomer. If you consider this route, have your attorney draw up an employment agreement to work out terms of employment once the person finishes school.

# The Art of the Interview

When a potential employee shows up, have him or her complete an application form. Review the questionnaire and ask any relevant questions regarding previous employment. If the person looks like a serious prospect, check references thoroughly. Now is the time to set your hiring policy, determining how many references you will require and how much background checking you will do. Pet sitters who will be going into clients' homes will need to be bonded, so you should discuss your screening procedure with your insurance agent. Due to the risks and liabilities involved, you need to feel comfortable and secure about the character of people you bring on board in your pet sitting operation.

During the interviewing process, you will have the opportunity to assess the applicant's appearance and demeanor. Is the person clean and well groomed? Did he or she show up on time? Would you feel comfortable having this person represent your business? Ask questions about previous experience and the applicant's own relationships with animals. This will help break the ice and you will learn about the person's social skills, personality, and intelligence.

> **Digging Even Deeper**
>
> Some business owners use the services of a background screening company to check into the past of prospective employees. Look in the yellow pages under "Employee Background Checks" or enter the words "background checks" into your Internet browser. Such services usually range from $39 to $200, depending on how far you want to extend your search. Background checks are highly recommended for prospective pet sitters.

Your particular pet care job has its own requirements. If you need a pet sitter, for instance, a retiree might work out fine, but if you need a bather-brusher in your grooming shop, the same person may find the job too strenuous. A student might be great for your grooming support staff, but might not have the level of maturity needed for the pet sitting position. While such individual qualifications may be uppermost in your mind, you need to make yourself aware of the labor laws so that you do not open yourself up to a discrimination charge in your hiring practices.

As an employer, you are not legally entitled to ask questions regarding age, racial or ethnic background, religious affiliation (including what church an applicant attends or what religious holidays he or she observes), national origin, native language, marital status, number and/or ages of children, provisions for child care, pregnancy or child-bearing issues, general medical condition or state of health, or any non-job-related physical data.

Another subject in which care is required is in asking applicants if they are handicapped. The definition of handicapped under federal law is very broad. For example, people are handicapped if they have a mental or physical condition that substantially affects their ability to perform one or more major "life activities," if they have a record of such a problem, or if the employer thinks they have such a problem. In addition, courts have ruled that obesity, suicidal tendencies, post-traumatic stress syndrome, diabetes, and sensitivity to tobacco smoke are all handicaps protected by federal or state law.

Under federal law, alcoholics and drug addicts are also considered to be handicapped and protected by antidiscrimination laws unless their condition currently prevents them from performing a job adequately. More than thirty states have decided that AIDS is a physical handicap entitled to protection under antidiscrimination laws, just as are other communicable diseases. Asking applicants whether they carry the AIDS virus and screening them out of the work force is illegal in many jurisdictions. Although federal law does not in all cases prohibit asking job applicants if they have a particular handicap, some courts have ruled that such questions may be illegal. State laws vary as to what employers may or may not ask. You will be on safer legal ground if you follow the more stringent of the two laws, be it state or federal. You can learn more about such statutes by contacting your state and federal Department of Labor or checking with the SBA on-line at www.sba.gov. Its Women's Business Center at www.onlinewbc.gov offers easy-to-read guidelines on this subject.

In your eagerness to fill the position, don't rush through the interviewing process. You need to explain job duties and responsibilities fully, presenting a truthful description of your business and the job. This will help you avoid workers who become disillusioned after a few days, wasting your time and theirs. Don't dwell on the negatives, however. You could end up talking the person out of the job before giving it a chance.

You can use your help-wanted ad as a foundation and expand on it for interviewing purposes, using the criteria you stated that you are seeking as a starting point and moving on to the particulars. Listen to what the applicant has to say, offering plenty of time to talk. This will put the person at ease and help you gather information. Try to avoid phone calls and other interruptions during the interview.

Keep an open mind, and look for the applicant's positive attributes and strengths. The best employees are those who are motivated and enjoy what they do. Your task is to find people who want to do the job for which they are hired. Be up-front about salary and benefits, and let the person know the next step in the process.

Don't leave applicants hanging. Extend the kind of courtesy you would give to one of your clients. If someone has taken the time to come in and fill out an application, you should take the time to respond. As was the case in the interviewing process, to protect yourself against charges of discrimination, you need to be careful in telling applicants why you did not select them for the job if they request such information. You are on the safest footing when you offer a general response, basing your selection on experience, willingness to work, and a positive attitude, or simply stating that you are continuing the search process.

Make sure you provide the prospective employee with a complete job description so you won't have to hear "You never said I had to do that!" You should probably steer clear of the delicate soul who will balk at pooper-scooping the potty walk or cleaning up the mess that big dog just made in his crate. You'll need the employee to know his or her responsibilities regarding caring for equipment, safety rules, end-of-the-day cleanup, even the correct way to answer the phone when things get hectic.

## Training for Success

Because all pet care occupations involve safety issues for animals and their caretakers alike, intensive training is required for each and every employee. Most entry-level pet care workers have no idea how hard we work in this field; having them spend a day or two observing what the job entails is a good idea. Walking new hires through the process of their job requirements is the first step in the training process.

You should institute your own checkpoints during the training process. If you notice bad habits developing, take the first opportunity to nip them in the bud. Be tactful in your corrections, explaining the reason behind your methods. In the grooming shop, the biggest dangers in pet handling involve leaving pets unattended in the tub or on a grooming table, and the chance of pets escaping, a danger also faced in pet sitting. No dog or cat should ever be allowed to run free in the grooming shop. A dog that is taken out for a potty run must be leashed and wearing a training collar. Vigilant monitoring of pets under the dryer is also a must.

The safety and security requirements involved in training dogs are every bit as detailed and involved. As the experienced instructor, it is up to you to bring your apprentice trainers along gradually, evaluating their skills as you give more responsibility. If you are training pet sitters, their orientation should cover every aspect of pet safety and security as well as issues regarding their own safety as they go in and out of clients' homes. A cell phone is a must, programmed directly to the police and fire department. They should carry mace and know how to use it. The security of client keys must be controlled by your strict regimen of checks and crosschecks.

## Shop Policies

As you grow and hire new people, review your mission statement with them. You need to make sure everyone who works in your business knows your philosophy and agrees to carry it out. If your statement speaks about "beautiful grooming performed with kindness and respect," the last thing you want is someone yelling and swearing at a dog in your establishment. That kind of behavior is decidedly not what you're about!

Your mission statement spells out your personal ideals, and you should never lose sight of that vision. As far as the day-to-day operation goes, you also need to institute shop policies to help the place run smoothly. Those need to be spelled out and understood by employees as well.

Your shop policies may look like this:

1. No smoking. Secondhand smoke is harmful to pets as well as people. If you need a cigarette, have one when you take your break outside and clean up butts.
2. Lunch breaks are limited to 30 minutes. A morning and an afternoon break are each 15 minutes long.
3. Quiet music is allowed on the radio—classical, New Age, smooth jazz. No rock or rap, please!
4. End-of-the-day cleanup duties are to be shared equally by all employees.
5. Employees are required to wear smocks or similar uniforms. No off-color logos on shirts, no tube tops or beachwear. Shoes must be worn at all times.
6. The telephone is for business use only. No personal calls are allowed without the permission of the owner.

7. Wages are based on ability, attitude, and improvement and will be reviewed on a six-month basis.

8. Because we are booked weeks in advance, employees must provide ample notice for days off and vacation schedules.

9. Physical and verbal abuse of the pets in our care is strictly forbidden and is grounds for immediate dismissal. If a dog is aggressive or unruly, ask for help. In this shop, there is never an acceptable reason to hit a dog.

It's your business and you have the final say over how it is run. Your leadership and management skills will be called into play as your business grows and you grow as a person right along with it.

## Learning to Be the Boss

In your new role as the employer, it is up to you to train your personnel in proper handling techniques, teaching them when to ask for help and how to read animal body language that warns us of aggression and fear. It is up to you to set policies on all aspects of your business and make sure that employees adhere to them. Becoming complacent about these issues is the biggest threat to the safety of any pet care operation. All workers should have a copy of your policy handbook and should be required to familiarize themselves with it as soon as they join your staff.

For many of us, adapting to the role of "the boss" is not easy. It seems a lot more comfortable to relate to our employees as friends. As the owner of the business, however, the sole responsibility of every decision and every business policy rests with you. You do not need to run your company like a dictator, but it is necessary for your employees to recognize your authority. To gain their respect, you need to conduct yourself as a professional. You can start by not dumping your own personal baggage on your employees. Your business can provide a warm and friendly atmosphere without turning it into a group therapy session.

Small home-run businesses usually mimic the family model, but try to avoid getting too personally involved in your employees' lives. This can be a slippery slope. Someone has to be the boss; in this case, it's you. Everything that goes on in your shop is your responsibility. If mistakes are made, the buck stops with you. It's important to be a warm and caring boss and to keep the lines of communication open. The feedback we get from our employees can be highly beneficial to the way we operate. But steer clear of giving advice on relationships and other personal matters. You are not Dear Abby, and personal problems are best left at home.

If you get too enmeshed in an employee's problems, you can end up bending over backward to accommodate that person's agenda. Such issues as transportation, child care, and punctuality are the employee's responsibilities. Acting as a surrogate mom can quickly turn you into a doormat. Always listen to your employees' concerns, but let them know you are running a business and you expect them to be professional in carrying out their duties.

Having a trusted employee who can take the reins in your absence can be a great blessing. Illness, family problems, or just the need for a well-deserved vacation requires that you either close down the business or have a well-trained second-in-command in place. Sometimes it is difficult for a shop owner to delegate responsibility. We tend to think of ourselves as indispensable. It takes time and patience to train someone else to walk in your shoes. It goes without saying that the person you select needs to be totally trustworthy and have good people skills with clients and other employees. Although the acting manager can make on-the-spot decisions in your absence, all policy decisions are still up to you. With such a key employee in place, you might find that you can actually own a business and have a life!

> ### Hiring Young People
> When hiring young people, remember they do not share the same priorities as you do. Their first concern is usually, "What's in it for me?" That may sound harsh, but it's part of being young. Once they are properly trained, try not to micromanage their every move. Listen to their ideas; they are members of a new generation and they look at the world in a whole new way. Let them know you appreciate their efforts, thanking them and praising them for a job well done. To find and keep good employees today, you need to be flexible and treat people the way you would like to be treated.

## How to Pay Employees

In the grooming industry, it seems that there are as many ways of paying employees as there are breeds of dogs! Salary, commission, a combination of both, hourly, even a certain amount per dog—I've heard them all. In addition, some groomers are independent contractors, responsible for filing their own state and federal withholding taxes.

Commission rates vary depending on the skill of the groomer and how much income he or she brings into the shop. The most common rates are 40/60, 50/50, and 60/40, the first figure representing the groomer's share, the second the owner's share. Because the owner usually provides all grooming products and equipment (except clippers, scissors, and blades), and sometimes provides a bather as well, this type of pay seems weighted in favor of the commissioned groomer. If bathers were paid on commission, the typical rate would be 20/80, or 30/70 if the employee provides other support services.

Such varied forms of compensation are not the case in the pet sitting and training industry where employees are customarily paid an hourly rate, which may increase as their job skills and value to their employer improve.

The way you pay your employees is totally up to you. I prefer to compensate groomers and bather-brushers with an hourly pay rate. We start a little above minimum wage for entry-level workers and gradually increase the rate as they grow in skill, speed, and responsibilities. In multigroomer shops where pay is based on commission, there can sometimes be intense competition among groomers vying to get the higher-priced jobs. If you are paid by the hour, it doesn't matter which dogs you groom; you will be assured a day's pay. The employer handles withholding taxes, and salaried employees usually get additional perks like paid vacations, fully or partially paid health and dental insurance and even paid holidays and retirement plans.

Gone are the days when groomers worked as second-class citizens with virtually no benefits. In today's economy, if you want qualified people, you need to be competitive with other employers who offer benefit packages, including the big chain stores.

## State and Federal Withholding Taxes

If you have employees, you are required by law to withhold federal and state income taxes as well as FICA (Social Security) Insurance. Depending on the size of your payroll, these taxes are due weekly, monthly, or quarterly. If you pay monthly, as I do, federal taxes must be paid by the 15th of the next month at a bank that is authorized to handle such deposits, while state withholding taxes are mailed in to meet that same deadline. (The monthly amounts you pay for both state and federal withholding taxes will be deducted from your amount due when you file quarterly returns as required for both these categories.)

If you have employees, you will also need to file quarterly forms and pay taxes for each of the following items.

- Social Security and Medicare taxes (Form 941)
- Federal income tax withholding (Form 8109) to be deposited at an authorized bank or by using the Electronic Federal Tax Payment System (EFTPS)
- State income tax withholding
- Federal unemployment (FUTA) tax (Form 940)
- State unemployment compensation tax

(Note: If your state has a mandated health insurance system, you will also be required to make quarterly payments for this fund.)

## Employees vs. Independent Contractors

When it comes time to add employees, you should be aware that there is more than one way to reimburse them. You should not even consider paying them "under the table." That method is fraught with potential problems and is not worth the risk to you or your business. Besides, it's illegal, and Uncle Sam does not take it lightly when he does not get his due. Failure to withhold, collect, and pay required taxes results in back tax assessments along with interest and penalties. Even if the person you are tempted to pay this way is a good friend or relative, things can change in your relationship or other people could become aware of your practices, giving them the opportunity to get you in big trouble.

That leaves us with two legitimate ways to pay staff, either as an employee or as an independent contractor. For an employee, you must withhold state and federal income taxes as well as Social Security (FICA) and Medicare, for which you match your employee's contribution. A newly hired employee must fill out a W-4 Form, telling you and the IRS how many deductions he or she will be claiming. The lower the number, the more taxes will be withheld.

As far as benefits go—vacation, health insurance, sick days, retirement plans—that is up to you, the employer. Customarily, such perks have not been the norm in the pet care field, but as we compete for good workers in today's competitive work environment, this is changing. In any case, the level of benefits you can afford should be discussed with your accountant before you make any promises.

The independent contractor is just what the name implies. Think freelancer. This person may work for more than one employer and is not considered a permanent staff member. It is up to the independent contractor to pay his or her own income taxes and Social Security, making it easier on you when it comes to expenses and paperwork. However, the IRS has stringent rules about workers who fit this classification.

Your accountant can help you in determining whether a worker is an employee or an independent contractor. It is extremely important that you know the legal requirements for classifying your workers. If you incorrectly classify an employee as an independent contractor and are challenged on the matter by the IRS, you can be held liable for employment taxes and have penalties levied against you.

For clarification on how to classify your workers, see IRS Publication 15, Circular E, Employer's Tax Guide, which will fully explain your tax responsibilities as an employer. It is available through the IRS Web site (www.irs.gov) or by calling the agency at (800) 829–1040.

According to IRS rules, certain workers are considered employees by law for purposes of the Federal Insurance Contributions Act (FICA), the Federal Unemployment Tax Act (FUTA), and for federal income tax withholding from wages. Unfortunately, pet care workers fall into a "gray area" when it comes to these classifications—we are out here on the fringe again! A worker's status is determined by applying the common law test, certain facts that fall into three main categories: behavioral control, financial control, and relationship of the parties. The IRS defines these terms in the following way.

**Behavioral Control:** A worker is an employee when the business has the right to direct and control that worker. The business does not have to actually direct or control the way the work is done, as long as the employer has the right to direct and control the work. For example:

- Instructions—if you receive extensive instructions on how work is to be done, this suggests that you may be an employee. Instructions can cover a wide range of topics, for example: how, when, or where to do the work; what tools or equipment to use; what assistants to hire to help with the work; and where to purchase supplies and services. If you receive less extensive instructions about what should be done, but not how it should be done, you may be an independent contractor. For instance, instructions about time and place may be less important than directions on how the work is performed.

- Training—if the business provides you with training about required procedures and methods, this suggests that the business wants the work done in a certain way, and you may be an employee.

**Financial Control:** These facts show whether there is a right to direct or control the business part of the work. For example:

- Significant Investment—if you have a significant investment in your work, you may be an independent contractor. While there is no precise dollar test, the investment must have substance. However, a significant investment is not necessary to be an independent contractor.
- Expenses—if you are not reimbursed for some or all business expenses, then you may be an independent contractor, especially if your unreimbursed business expenses are high.
- Opportunity for Profit or Loss—if you can realize a profit or incur a loss, this suggests that you are in business for yourself and that you may be an independent contractor.

**Relationship of the Parties:** These are facts that illustrate how the business and the worker perceive their relationship. For example:

- Employee Benefits—if you receive benefits, this is an indication that you are an employee. If you do not receive benefits, however, you could be either an employee or an independent contractor.
- Written Contracts—a written contract may show what both you and the business intend. This may be very significant if it is difficult, if not impossible, to determine status based on other facts.

Confused? Let me simplify a bit. In general, you are classified as an employee if the employer tells you when, where, and how to work, trains you to perform a service, and sets your work hours. If you have an ongoing relationship with the business, your services are important to its success, you are required to be available full-time, and either you work on the premises or the business provides tools, materials, and other equipment for you to carry out your job, chances are you are an employee.

As you can see by these complex distinctions, the difference between an independent contractor and an employee is not always clear-cut, nor is it something to be taken lightly by either the person doing the hiring or the one being hired. For the sake of the financial security of your business, do your homework. This is one area in which expert advice from your legal and financial support team is vital!

If you do employ someone as an independent contractor, you need to file a Form 1099 instead of the usual W-2 form provided to regular employees. This form is also used to report payments of $600 or more for services performed for your business by people not treated as your employees, such as fees to subcontractors, attorneys, accountants, or directors; and rent payments of $600 or more, other than rents paid to real estate agents.

For employees, you must file Form W-2, Wage and Tax Statement, to report payments such as wages, tips, and other compensation, withheld income, and Social Security and Medicare taxes, as well as advance earned income credit payments. By law, W-2 forms must be provided to each employee by January 31 for wages paid the preceding year.

Your accountant will walk you through this maze of tax requirements. I know it can be intimidating, but take heart and look around you—every other business owner has gone through the same thing. Your trek through this tangle of red tape may test your mettle, but you are not alone as you make your way to that little spot on the horizon you have carved out for yourself: your business.

## The Importance of Staff Meetings

Holding staff meetings on a regular basis is another good tool for employee motivation. These meetings allow you to interact with your employees on a personal level, away from the demands of the busy workplace. Schedule them as an early morning coffee klatch or an after-hours pizza party, a potluck supper at your home, or a dinner meeting at a restaurant—after all, it is a legitimate business expense! As your staff grows, you may even consider having a guest speaker come in to make a presentation on any number of topics, from animal care to employee benefits to self-protection techniques. In this way you will be offering in-service education as well as camaraderie.

Your staff meeting is the place to address any ongoing problems you have been experiencing and to provide a forum for employee input. It gives you the opportunity to welcome new staff members and bid a fond farewell to those who leave.

It offers a great venue for recognizing employee accomplishments and publicly praising a job well done. To keep your meeting running smoothly, always print up an agenda beforehand and make sure everybody gets a copy.

## Motivated to Succeed: Praising a Job Well Done

Keeping employees motivated is not as difficult as you might think. It's all about positive reinforcement. Employees' behavior is influenced by the results or consequences of their actions. Those consequences can be either positive or negative. When it comes to motivating your employees, positive works best.

The opposite approach, involving harsh criticism and reprimands, may change people's behavior in the short run, but it doesn't motivate them to maintain the desired behavior for any length of time. Moreover, there is a "punishment effect" involved in making a person feel inferior or ashamed. When the punishment mode is used to control behavior, people perform at a level just sufficient to avoid punishment. They are really not motivated to change.

On the other hand, there are many ways to positively reinforce desired behavior. Recognize your employees' contributions by thanking them, either in public or with a handwritten note. Honor them with awards, from simple certificates you make up on your computer to company T-shirts or jackets, movie tickets, or gift certificates from a nice restaurant. Pitch in to offer your help when they seem overwhelmed; show your concern when they have been working hard; put their pictures on the wall or on your Web site when they have won an award; give a promotion or a bonus—all of these make an employee feel proud and appreciated, like a valued member of your team.

Surveys have shown that praise and recognition boost an employee's performance more than any other measure, including a raise! Communication is critical. Let your employees know how the business is doing and how their efforts are helping you to achieve your goals. Involve them in your decision-making process. Solicit their opinions and encourage them to help shape ideas that will improve the business.

Avoid micromanaging your employees. If you have done your job right, once they have moved beyond the training period, you shouldn't need to be breathing down their necks. Step back and let them do their jobs. Be sensitive to their individual differences. Some people require more positive strokes from you than others. Be fair and consistent. Whether you know it or not, word gets around like wildfire when someone gets a raise. Make sure that you review everyone according to the same timetable. No one likes to feel taken for granted or overlooked. Your role as the boss is akin to that of a parent. All the members of your business "family" must feel that they are valued and appreciated equally in your eyes.

## Correcting Employee Problems

Bringing personal problems to work, job burnout, personality clashes, the poisoning effect of one negative person—all of these can cause poor morale in your growing business. Behaving like an ostrich with your head in the sand will only make things worse. Employees need to know that you will listen to their problems and concerns and do your best to address them. If a worker is bored within the limits of the job, think about broadening his or her duties and responsibilities. If you get a complaint from a client, always listen to the employee's side of the story. The key to motivating and retaining good employees is to be a good manager. You are the boss and you set the tone.

## Health Insurance and Benefits

One of the primary methods of holding on to good employees is an effective benefits program. I'm sorry to say the pet care field has lagged behind most other occupations as far as benefits go. According to the 2001 *Groom & Board* industry report, only 19 percent of grooming businesses offered health insurance to their workers; only 27 percent offered paid vacations. Now that PETsMART and Petco have entered the world of grooming and training, offering attractive benefits packages to their staffs, the bar will be raised for everyone else. That is one favorable aspect of the arrival of the corporate chains on the pet care service scene.

You need to be aware of the health of your employees. If you notice a good worker undergoing a personality change and the quality of his or her job performance is suffering, it's time to take a closer look. Ignoring psychological problems and substance abuse can be a costly mistake because they can have a direct impact on the atmosphere of your workplace and your productivity. When you select a health care provider, choose one that offers personal counseling for mental health along with provisions for physical illnesses and injuries.

Your policy handbook should plainly state that drug and alcohol use on the job is forbidden and that violation of this policy is grounds for disciplinary action, including dismissal. If your insurance package does not offer counseling, you may want to consider an outside Employee Assistance Program (EAP). These programs provide trained counselors who can offer short-term help and referrals to specialists, if needed. The cost is not prohibitive, usually about $2.00 to $3.50 per month per employee.

Today's most successful business owners and managers are creative and sensitive to their employees' needs. They realize there's more to motivating employees than putting money in their pockets. They are leaders who create a climate in which employees willingly and enthusiastically do their best work. As your business grows, you can move beyond just being the boss to becoming a leader who brings out the best in yourself and your staff.

# Closing Thoughts

My career in pet care has provided me with many rewards, including a lifetime of loving interaction with pets and their owners and the chance to watch my family business grow as it continues into another generation. Pet grooming was in its infancy when my husband and I began our business thirty-one years ago. It has been exciting to watch it come of age with state-of-the-art equipment, computerization, and the realization that even though we were drawn to it because of our love for animals, it is now part of the $28.5 billion pet industry, a legitimate business that has come of age.

In purchasing this book, you have taken a small step toward becoming a part of the pet care business. The need is there for your services; I hope I have provided you with some useful knowledge as you begin your career. I hope you will not only uphold the standards of those who have gone before you but build and improve upon them as you take pet care to the next level. You will work hard, but you will be rewarded with success, joy, and personal growth as you work toward achieving your own dream.

# Index

credit
  managing, 135
  obtaining, 132–33
credit cards, 48, 91–95
credit checks, 30
credit profile, 30
customer base, 31–32

## D

dangerous pets, 223–25
debit cards, 92–93
demand for pet services
  general, 3–10
  grooming, 3–4
  obedience trainers, 7–10, 177–78
  pet sitters, 5–7
demographics, 31–32
difficult clients, 222–29
diseases, transmittable, 156–58
dishonesty bonding, 173–74
distributors, 130, 132, 136–37
dog bites, 149
dog walking, 6
dryers, 121–23
Dun & Bradstreet, 133–34

## E

electricity, 120
emergency backup plan,
  pet sitters, 174–75
employees
  benefits, 248–49
  correcting problems, 248
  health, 248
  hiring, 234

interviewing, 236–38
managing, 240–41
motivating, 247–48
paying, 241–42, 246
training of, 238–39
equipment
  cages and crates, 118–19
  grooming, 48–50, 116–21,
    123–28
  pet sitters, 174
  purchasing, 131–33
  registration, business, 50
  training, 185
expansion, 51, 231–36

## F

family
  as employees, 233–34
  support, 26–28
  working with, 27–28
financing, 129–31
flea control in shop, 145
Furry Angel, 229–30

## G

gift certificates, 198, 202, 209
gifts, seasonal, 221
Groom Team USA, 163–64
GroomExpo, 162, 221
growth and expansion, 232–49

## H

health
  groomer, 154–58
  pet, 146–52

home office, 62, 65–66, 97–98

hours of operation, 152–53

housekeeping, 143–44

## I

image, 126

income statement, 76, 77

independent contractors, 243–46

injuries to pets, 151

in-service training, 159

insurance

    automobile, 84

    business interruption, 86

    employee health insurance, 248

    liability, 84–85

    pet sitters, 172–73

    property and casualty, 83–84

    workers' compensation, 86–88

Intergroom, 161, 221

Internet

    advertising, 202

    presence, 214–15

inventory, 138–39

IRS, 80, 195, 198, 243–46

## L

library, 125–26

licenses, 63–64

licensing

    groomer, 160–61

    grooming schools, 20

    trainers, 184

## M

mailings, 200

marketing, 191–92

    plan, 43–44

    research, 31–32

mileage, 195

mission statement, 39–40

mobile grooming, 139–41

Moran, Patti, 173

motivation, 28–29

## N

naming business, 32–38

National Association of Dog Obedience Instructors, 184

National Association of Professional Pet Sitters, 173

National Dog Groomers Association of America, 85, 159–60

neighbors, 64–65, 189

networking, 203–4

newsletters, 212–14

newspaper, 201

## O

obedience training, 187–89

office hours, 108–9

office setup

    general, 97–107

    obedience training, 185

    pet sitting, 166

organizations, professional

    grooming, 85

    pet sitting, 85

    training 85, 183–84

OSHA, 55

# About the Author

Kathy Salzberg is a freelance writer and a National Certified Master Groomer who has been in the pet industry since she joined her late husband, David, at The Village Groomer in Walpole, Massachussetts, in 1976. Since David's death in 1996, Kathy has run the grooming salon and retail pet supply store in partnership with her daughter, well-known industry writer and speaker, Missi Salzberg. Kathy is also the mother of David, Jr. and Peter Salzberg and grandmother of Allison and Cara Salzberg.

Born in Boston, Massachussetts, Kathy writes about grooming and pet care issues for such publications as *Cat Fancy, Popular Dogs, Puppies USA, Dogs USA, Kittens USA, Cats USA,* and *Pet Age.* From 1993 to 2001, she wrote a humor column for *Groom & Board* magazine, for which she was awarded The Cardinal Crystal Achievement Award as Grooming Journalist of the Year in 1995 and 1999. She shares her home in Walpole, Massachussetts, with Himalayan cats Woobie and Maxamillion, Silver Persian Ling-Ling, Domestic Shorthair Spike, and Roland, a French Bulldog.